Profiting
from Chaos

Profiting from Chaos

Using Chaos Theory for Market Timing, Stock Selection, and Option Valuation

Tonis Vaga

McGraw-Hill, Inc.

New York   San Francisco   Washington, D.C.   Auckland   Bogotá
Caracas   Lisbon   London   Madrid   Mexico City   Milan
Montreal   New Delhi   San Juan   Singapore
Sydney   Tokyo   Toronto

Library of Congress Cataloging-in-Publication Data

Vaga, Tonis.
  Profiting from chaos / using chaos theory for market timing, stock
selection, and option valuation / Tonis Vaga.
    p.   cm.
  Includes bibliographical references and index.
  ISBN 0-07-066786-1
  1. Investment analysis. 2. Speculation. 3. Chaotic behavior in
systems. 4. Stocks. 5. Options (Finance) 6. Hedging (Finance)
I. Title: Market timing.
  HG4529.V34   1994
  332.63'22–dc20   94-16325
                                                             CIP

1 2 3 4 5 6 7 8 9 0   DOC/DOC   9 0 9 8 7 6 5 4

ISBN 0-07-066786-1

*The sponsoring editor for this book was David Conti, the editing
supervisor was Fred Dahl, and the production supervisor was Suzanne
W. Babeuf. It was set in Baskerville by Inkwell Publishing Services.*

Printed and bound by R. R. Donnelley & Sons Company.

For Nancy and our daughters,
Alexandra and Maie

Contents

Preface

Trend is not destiny.
Uncertainty is not chaos.

So read two of the many lapel buttons handed out to the attendees of the Fraser Contrary Opinion Forum each fall on the shores of Lake Champlain. The Basin Harbor Club in Vergennes, Vermont, far from the noise of Wall Street, has been the setting for an annual gathering of a loose knit group of contrarian investors. Contrarians seek to separate themselves from the fads and fashions popular among the broader community of investors, preferring instead to search for values neglected by the crowd.

The speakers tend to be a diverse group of economists, politicians, journalists, and, of course, professionals from the investment business. Jim Fraser, a money manager from Burlington, Vermont, is the host of this event. His top hat and brass horn have become trademarks, while his jokes often draw more groans than applause.

Contrary opinion has a certain mystique. It is often portrayed as something the "smart money" is doing quietly while the masses hurtle recklessly from one disaster to the next. Fraser's interpretation is a little different. Fraser describes contrary thinking as the effort to think clearly amidst the noise and turbulence generated by the financial media and the markets. It is the effort to find simple truths that can be relied upon regardless of the latest crisis in the headlines and the latest uncertainty affecting the markets.

Contrarians don't necessarily look for a sure thing. They certainly don't look for a mechanical investment formula that guarantees results. Rather, they seek to evaluate each opportunity with an open mind, being skeptical of truths simply because they are accepted by everyone else. Many have reinforced this attitude through occasional treks to the quiet shores of Lake Champlain as the Vermont maples begin to turn bright crimson. This attitude can also be helpful in the course of reading this book.

My goal is not to offer a mechanical formula for predicting the path of the market; I haven't found one and don't know of anyone that has. Rather it is to offer a framework in which to think and evaluate opportunities as they come along, whether they be investment decisions, business decisions, or even social and political situations. In all of these environments we run across consensus thinking and action. It may be comfortable to conform with the consensus, but it may be more profitable to maintain a healthy skepticism.

Here my specific goal is to show how a simple nonlinear model offers practical insights on the behavior of financial markets. My interest in nonlinear models was triggered by the January 1975 issue of *Reviews of Modern Physics*. It contained an article entitled "Cooperative Phenomena in Systems Far from Thermal Equilibrium and in Nonphysical Systems" by Hermann Haken, a German laser physicist from the University of Stuttgart, Institute for Theoretical Physics. While the title lacked immediate appeal, a quick scan revealed a remarkable diversity of content.

Haken described problems from a diverse set of disciplines: lasers, semiconductors, fluid flows, biological problems, and even the behavior of people in social groups. He offered a new way of looking at all of these complex problems, introducing terms such as *order parameters* to describe systems at a macroscopic level, as opposed to detailed microscopic behavior. And he showed that regardless of the details of the subsystems, simple nonlinear models could be used to analyze macroscopic behavior.

One of Haken's examples was the behavior of people in social groups. I had seen Callen and Shapero's "A Theory of Social Imitation" in *Physics Today* (July 1974) and was familiar with the statistical model on which it was based. It turned out that formation opinions in large groups shared many of the statistical properties of systems from the disciplines of physics, chemistry, and biology. All of these systems involve random as well as deterministic forces, and Haken showed how the random walk model was a special case within a more general nonlinear framework.

Back in 1975, the widely accepted view of stock market behavior was the random walk model. Yet here was a more sophisticated nonlinear model in which random walk was the first step and also explained imitative behavior in social groups. I felt intuitively that Haken's approach could also be useful for understanding collective thinking and action (i.e., crowd behavior) on Wall Street and other financial markets.

My conviction was based on the correspondence principle of physics. Any new theory in physics must correspond to established theory where the latter has proven successful. For example, Einstein's Theory of Special Relativity corresponds to classical Newtonian mechanics as a special limiting case when relative velocities are much less than the speed of light. Likewise quantum mechanics merges smoothly into classical mechanics when the dimensions of the problem become large compared with the atomic scale. Since the random walk model is a special case of Haken's nonlinear model, correspondence is a key feature of this new theory.

In November 1978, an article in *Physics Today* by Rolf Landauer suggested that systems far from equilibrium, such as those described by Haken, are more susceptible to random shocks than systems at equilibrium. Landauer's article appeared shortly after the October Massacre of 1978. I suggested in a letter to the editor *(Physics Today,* February 1979) that the market could be viewed as an open system, far from equilibrium, in which state transitions can have a large effect on prevailing risk-reward characteristics.

In 1981, Marty Zweig published an article in *Barron's* on trading signals based on extremes in the New York Stock Exchange up volume to down volume ratio. His signals fit nicely with the nonlinear theory, and in March 1983 I set up an index fund money market switching experiment, based largely on this simple indicator and some additional ones he published later. Over the first five years of the experiment, the switching strategy beat passive indexing and cut risk as well. This was largely due to avoiding the Crash of 1987.

Over 11 years, both accounts have more than tripled. The index has regained the lead over the switching strategy by about 12 percent, with about 40 percent more risk. Therefore, the switching strategy has beaten the market on a risk-adjusted basis, a goal that has eluded many professional money managers. The first lesson learned from this experience is that indexing is a tough benchmark to beat. However, it can be done. Many active managers have achieved this elusive goal both on a risk-adjusted basis and in absolute terms.

Over the years I've become familiar with a variety of investment styles and strategies that appear to improve returns without simply taking a corresponding increase in portfolio risks. Part of this exposure has come from becoming a regular at the Fraser Contrary Opinion Forum. For example, on one occasion Arnold Wood of Martingale Asset Management spoke on the psychology of investing. I asked him afterwards if he had seen any of the work published by physicists on social limitation. He was quite interested and suggested that a group in New York called the Society of Quantitative Analysts (SQA) might want to hear about such new ideas.

I proposed an abstract for a luncheon talk for the SQA. They accepted and on September 19, 1989, I presented the "Coherent Market Hypothesis" to about 40 Wall Street "quants." It was well received. Then president Michelle Clayman suggested I publish the concept, and the "Coherent Market Hypothesis" appeared subsequently in *Financial Analysts Journal* (November/December 1990).

Practitioners have generally responded favorably to the Coherent Market Hypothesis. It seems to resonate with what they already know about the market. For example, James W. Ware, a portfolio manager at Allstate Insurance Company, summarized the Coherent Market Hypothesis in "Quantum Investing" (*Financial Analysts Journal*) as follows:

> In Vaga's view, the stock market can exist in different states—random and efficient or concentrated and "momentum-like." The former is the conventional efficient market described in textbooks. It prices securities accurately on the basis of all known information. The risk-reward tradeoff for efficient markets is described by Sharpe's Capital Asset Pricing Model (i.e., more return for more risk). The latter state—called *coherent* by Vaga—is seen in bull and bear markets, where the market averages move powerfully in a given direction, disregarding conventional valuation measures. In this state, the traditional risk-return trade-off is inverted and investors can earn above-average returns with below-average risk—a heretical idea to efficient market proponents. Vaga postulates a third state as well—"chaotic" which represents the worst of all worlds—low return for above-average risk.

The Coherent Market Hypothesis was included in Edgar Peters' *Chaos and Order in the Capital Markets* (Wiley, 1991) as one of two new approaches. Peters suggested that, "The CMH offers a rich theoretical framework for assessing market risk, and how it changes over time in response to technical and fundamental factors."

In this book I expand on how the nonlinear model corresponds to the established linear analysis of modern portfolio theory as well as to other work that has been done related to fractals and chaos in the capital markets. My emphasis is on practical applications. The efficient market school believes that those who have beaten the market have just been lucky. However, some practitioners have developed methods that make sense within the framework of the nonlinear theory. In turn, nonlinear theory suggests their results may well be more than a matter of luck.

The book explains the market states and associated risk-reward profiles that are predicted by the nonlinear model. For example, it is intuitively obvious that chaotic markets can present great risks (i.e., the manias, panics, and crashes that have plagued financial markets over the years). Less obvious is the prediction of nonlinear theory that the most profitable opportunities are not necessarily accompanied by correspondingly high risk. This offers hope for practitioners.

Recent findings of academic work support the Coherent Market Hypothesis, as do the track records of successful investors. Some examples are provided of methods used by successful practitioners for market timing, stock selection, and option valuation. While the examples do not prove the hypothesis, they suggest that active management can add value.

Ongoing research is proceeding at a rapid pace, and the development of new technology for investment purposes is in its infancy. The rocket scientists of Wall Street are busily harnessing technology to support global trading. However, even without sophisticated computers and software, a simple nonlinear model can be useful in a qualitative sense and support practical investment decisions. Nonlinear theory offers a new framework in which to think and evaluate the risk-reward potential for a given market or investment opportunity.

Acknowledgments

This book would not have been possible without the encouragement of past officers and current members of the Society of Quantitative Analysts in New York. I have also benefited from helpful discussions with some of the key researchers affiliated with the Santa Fe Institute including Blake LeBaron and Per Bak. J. Doyne Farmer of the Prediction Company has been helpful in explaining some of the more esoteric aspects of nonlinear theory. Jerry Bernas, a former Booz-Allen colleague, now retired, was of particular assistance over the years as a steady source of insights and encouragement.

Tonis Vaga

Profiting from Chaos

1

Chaotic Markets: Opportunities and Dangers

It was obvious that Wharton professors who believed in quantum analysis and random walk weren't doing nearly as well as my new colleagues at Fidelity, so between theory and practice, I cast my lot with the practitioners. It's hard to support the popular academic theory that the market is irrational when you know someone who just made a twenty fold profit in Kentucky Fried Chicken.

PETER LYNCH, 1989

Peter Lynch: Stalking the "Tenbaggers"

Peter Lynch is a hunter. His quarry is big game: "tenbaggers." He knows they are out there. When he was young he saw his elders at Fidelity relentlessly pursue this elusive prize. He learned the skills needed to join the hunt and became one of the best. Now he is a legend among his fellow hunters with enough skins on the wall to have retired in his mid-forties.

Lynch, the former manager of the Fidelity Magellan fund, compiled a long-term record of beating the market, which he attributes neither to luck, nor to the academic theory he learned at the prestigious Wharton school.

He credits success to a firm belief that at any point in time there will be numerous sound companies whose stock will climb 1000 percent or more over the subsequent five- to ten-year period. These "tenbaggers" as he calls them, are stocks in long-term uptrends. Even one or two can turn an otherwise mediocre portfolio into a real winner.

Lynch's success at Fidelity is eclipsed only by the legendary investor, Warren Buffet. Neither of these long-term investors have any interest in short-term market forecasts. Buffet's favorite holding period is "forever." Lynch claims that he usually doesn't make money until three to five years after purchasing an issue. Both of these practitioners have a keen eye for long-term megatrends and avoid the manias that can lead to short-term valuation extremes. Neither claims use of any secret formulas. Both believe in the inherent value of common sense, doing homework, and having the strength of conviction to stay with a position as long as the fundamental story remains valid.

But are the long-term track records of Lynch and Buffet reproducible? Or are they just the lucky ones; the inevitable success stories among the otherwise lackluster performance of professional money managers taken as a group. Passive indexing has beaten most pros and captured a large share of the market away from active managers. Will this trend continue, or will active managers be able to add real value and regain market share?

We will examine these questions within the framework of an emerging new science. *Complexity theory* deals with the emergence of structure, order, and chaos in systems that involve numerous interacting or adaptive component parts or subsystems. *Chaos theory* forms a part of the general theoretical fabric needed to explain the behavior of complex systems. But it is only one facet of the problem. In general, complex systems undergo transitions from disordered, unstructured states to more ordered states. At times they may behave in a chaotic fashion and at other times in a more coherent or predictable fashion. At times they may be at the edge of chaos, a precarious state in which large, long-lasting fluctuations may occur, across a wide spectrum of time scales and magnitudes, following the power law distributions that govern earthquakes of different magnitudes on the Richter scale and the fluctuations of cotton prices. They may be affected by random forces, or simple, deterministic interactions may lead to random-like behavior.

Financial markets clearly fall within the definition of complex systems. Here the traditional random walk model is under siege by proponents of the chaos theory. Deterministic chaos theory and, more generally, the theory of nonlinear dynamic systems have been the subject of growing interest among investment researchers and practitioners, particularly in the aftermath of the Crash of 1987. However, critics point out that little of practical value has been achieved. For example, Jonathan Laing notes in

Barron's (July 29, 1991) that "the value of science lies in its ability to predict. So far the chaos theorists have little to show on that score."

Science serves to explain even when prediction is impossible. Chaos, by definition, characterizes systems which become unpredictable at an exponential rate. One promise of chaos theory is to offer simple, deterministic models to predict the path of financial markets for short periods into the future. This would be analogous to weather forecasts which, though often criticized for mistakes, are normally taken seriously enough at least over a time frame of a day or two. A similar capability in predicting financial markets, even with errors, would be extremely important for short-term traders and market makers. However, even though economic and financial time series do show substantial nonlinearity, there is little empirical evidence of the type of "low-dimensional" chaos that would enable deterministic short-term forecasting.

While short-term forecasting remains an elusive goal of the proponents of deterministic chaos theory, nonlinear dynamics offers another approach more suitable for the investor with a longer time horizon. Stochastic or probabilistic forecasts can be based on the state transitions that occur in nonlinear systems. The information contained in state transitions can provide the basis for practical investment decisions. This may not sound like anything new to the market "technician," long given to the pursuit of indicators of transitions between up trending "bull" markets, and down trending "bear" markets. It may not seem new to the value investors who routinely screen out "high flyer" stocks (i.e., those with high price-to-earnings and price-to-book value multiples). However, until recently, the idea of any type of market forecasting has been ridiculed by the academic proponents of the *efficient market hypothesis,* who suggest that all such efforts are a waste of time.

The traditional academic view of technical market analysis is clearly expressed by Professor Burton Malkiel in *A Random Walk Down Wall Street:*

> Obviously, I am biased against the chartist. This is not only a personal predilection, but a professional one as well. Technical analysis is anathema to the academic world. We love to pick on it. Our bullying tactics are prompted by two considerations: 1) the method is patently false; and 2) it's easy to pick on. And while it may seem a bit unfair to pick on such as sorry target, just remember: it is your money we are trying to save.

The *efficient market hypothesis* (EMH) and associated *capital asset pricing model* (CAPM) represent the established academic view of how market prices behave. These tenets of *modern portfolio theory* (MPT), dating back to the 1960s, maintain that above average returns can only be attained by taking proportionately above average risks. However, even as these concepts were being proposed, discrepancies between the simple bell-shaped normal distribution underlying MPT and empirical distributions were observed.

Benoit Mandelbrot was among the first to offer an alternative model to account for the characteristic "fat tails" on empirical market return data. Fat-tailed distributions mean simply that there are substantially more large price changes than expected from a Gaussian noise process or normal, bell-shaped probability distribution. While most academic research focuses on short-term price changes (hours, days, weeks, and months), these distributions scale in self-similar fashion in time. Hence returns over longer time frames such as those of interest to Peter Lynch (three to five years or longer) will also show more big winners and losers than produced by a simple random walk.

Unfortunately, the nonlinear model proposed by Mandelbrot was difficult to handle mathematically and implied that risk was far more difficult to quantify than the simple linear relationship between risk and returns predicted by the CAPM. As discussed in the Appendix, Mandelbrot's "stable Paretian" distributions are a generalization of the normal or Gaussian probability distribution. Mandelbrot offered no explanation of the dynamics underlying the fat-tailed distributions, only a new description of them and their mathematical properties.

More recently, researchers affiliated with the Santa Fe Institute have been developing simple nonlinear models that provide more insight into the dynamics underlying fat-tailed distributions. For example, physicist Per Bak at the Brookhaven National Laboratory in Stony Brook, New York has been a proponent of "self-organized criticality," arguing that a wide variety of natural processes evolve into critical or unstable states where fluctuations follow a power law distribution. One example of this is earthquakes of various magnitudes on the Richter scale: there are more large earthquakes than would be expected from the Gaussian noise process. Bak is currently collaborating with economists Jose Sheinkman and Michael Woodford in the development of simple, nonlinear models of self-organized criticality in economic and financial fluctuations. Their work shows that nonlinear processes can lead to the fat-tailed or "power-law" distributions described by Mandelbrot.

Other researchers have continued to scrutinize empirical data. For example, Brock, Lakonishok, and LeBaron recently confirmed the statistical significance of technical trading rules: *simple moving averages can improve returns* and *reduce risk*. This finding implies that the random walk model and related efficient market hypothesis (EMH) are inadequate explanations of the behavior of capital markets, confirming what practitioners had long suspected, and offering the hope that nonlinear models can provide better explanations of why some practitioners have attained above average returns without proportionately higher risks over long periods of time.

It's fair to say that chaos theory hasn't produced any "get rich quick forecasting systems." However, to say that there are no practical results overlooks some important recent developments in the broader theory of complex systems which goes beyond deterministic chaos. The vindication of technical analysis is just the beginning. Our goal is to show how even a simple, yet quite general theoretical model of complex, nonlinear dynamic systems can explain why practitioners such as Lynch, Buffet, and others have been extraordinarily successful and why their results aren't just a matter of luck.

We will use our nonlinear model to explain why technical and fundamental analysis, long scorned by the efficient market proponents, are both necessary in evaluating the conditions under which the most profitable megatrends may emerge, and the conditions that spawn dangerous market manias, panics, and crashes. Our nonlinear model specifically predicts that, under some conditions, the classical risk-reward ratio will be turned upside down. Intuitively we expect that crowd psychology in the capital markets can lead to the most dangerous manias, panics, and crashes. Less obvious is the prediction of our nonlinear model that high returns are attainable without proportionately high risk. We call this prediction the *coherent market hypothesis* (CMH). However, coherent markets are only one state, and at other times chaotic markets, periods of instability, and periods of true random walk will produce more risk than return.

Hence nonlinear forces in the capital markets can produce both the most rewarding, as well as the most dangerous, investment situations. The investor's problem is to recognize the prevailing risk-reward characteristics of different market states and adopt an appropriate strategy. Different investors may prefer different strategies. This is not unlike the situation in golf where two different professionals on the same course may use quite different strategies and achieve entirely satisfactory outcomes. Professionals carefully evaluate the risk profiles presented by the course relative to their own strengths and weaknesses and make appropriate decisions that maximize their probability of acceptable performance. In contrast, a novice golfer will usually flail away, hoping for a big hit, oblivious to the risks and subtleties of the game.

Golf and Investing:
Learning from the Masters

Peter Lynch observed that "I'm not the only caddy who learned that the quickest route to the boardroom was through the locker room of a club like Brae Burn." As a caddy at this exclusive club outside of Boston, Lynch got his first education in stocks from the presidents and CEOs of major corporations. According to Lynch, "Especially after they sliced or hooked a drive, club members enthusiastically described their latest triumphant investment. In a single round of play I might give out five golf tips and get back five stock tips in return."

It was on the golf course that Lynch discovered that the stock market wasn't as bad as he had been taught to believe. Many of his parents generation had lived through the Great Depression, an experience that had soured them on investing for the rest of their lives. The prevailing belief among many was that the stock market is a place to lose all your money. In contrast, many of Lynch's golf course clients had actually made money in the market!

Golf is a complex game. As with investing, it can be highly frustrating for the unskilled novice and highly rewarding for the more patient player who has learned and applied a few simple principles. Learning some fundamental principles can likewise help even the novice investor develop a style that he or she is quite comfortable with and make investing both more enjoyable and rewarding than might otherwise seem possible. And for the professional, these principles can make the difference between a satisfying and successful long-term career versus a chaotic string of unpredictable successes and failures.

Nonlinear forces can dramatically affect your performance in a round of golf. Golf is both a game of skill and chance. For the novice player, a slight swing error on that big drive off the first tee can rapidly transform into a dramatic hook to the left or slice to the right. The ball seems determined to avoid the middle of the fairway toward which it was diligently aimed in the first place. It behaves as though it has a mind of its own, one that opposes your best intentions.

Let's take a closer look at both the random and deterministic forces that affect the flight path of the ball and, therefore, the probability that the ball will travel where it is aimed. On a soft stroke, such as when putting on the green, the sources of aiming error and ball path deviation are fairly simple. For example, the ball may not be perfectly balanced or there may be imperfections in the green such as a footprint that causes the ball to be deflected slightly one way or another. The grain of the grass may cause a persistent bias, or the green itself may be sloped. Even the putter may be less than perfectly aligned with the target line on which the ball is aimed, though normally this is the last possible source of error to which the true golfer will admit.

In Fig. 1.1, the probability governing the ball's actual path relative to the desired target line is shown as the familiar bell-shaped distribution, centered around the target line on a flat green. The skilled player will enjoy a more sharply peaked probability distribution around the target line than the

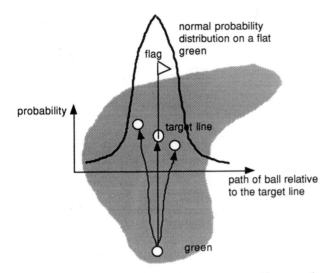

Figure 1.1. Soft shots in golf such as the putt are governed by a normal "bell-shaped" probability of the ball's path deviating from the target line; the width of the distribution will be narrower for experienced golfers than for the novice.

unskilled player. If the green slopes, then the ball will break in the direction of the slope and the peak of the probability curve will deviate from the target line. The curve may also broaden because of the greater aiming uncertainty in the putter's reading of how much the ball will break over a certain distance for a given putt speed.

On a drive, the probability distribution governing a successful shot is quite different. When the ball is hit hard, some important new effects occur that you don't have to worry about with putting. At high velocity, the sharp impact by the club head will cause the ball to temporarily deform slightly and spin. If the novice player attempts to drive straight down the fairway, the direction of spin will depend on slight random club face alignment errors and cause the ball to curve one way or the other away from the target line, except in the unlikely event that it happened to be struck perfectly. The latter is quite unlikely, whether the player is a professional or novice.

The deformation of the ball can be thought of as a slight nonlinear effect that has transformed some of the forward motion of the club into a spin that ensures the ball will move significantly away from the direction in which it was aimed. The harder the ball is hit, the greater the spin and the probability of the ball following the target line now changes dramatically to a bimodal distribution as shown in Fig. 1.2. Slight aiming errors will get magnified and the ball is more likely to wind up substantially to the left (hook) or the right (slice) than down the middle. Some players naturally

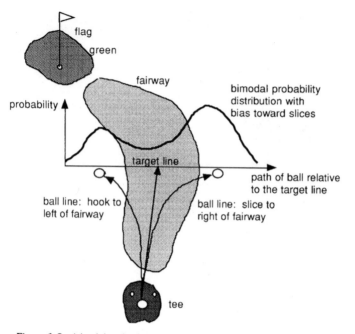

Figure 1.2. A hard drive by the novice golfer will tend to unpredictably hook to the left or slice to the right of the intended target line as a result of the spin imparted to the ball by small random aiming errors; this outcome is governed by a "bimodal" probability distribution.

tend to hit more slices than hooks or vice versa; in this case, the bimodal probability distribution becomes unsymmetrical, favoring outcomes either to the right or left of the target line.

Should the novice golfer notice that he or she is hitting more slices than hooks, a stance aiming to the left of center would help more often than not. Unfortunately, this will further aggravate a hook shot when it occurs. Hence, the novice will often find it extremely frustrating to master the game, until he or she learns to control the hook and slice. Not even the pros can eliminate the element of chance from the game of golf; however, the experienced player will adjust the club face angle to produce a deliberate spin and deliberately aim the ball away from the center of the fairway, letting the spin curve the ball predictably back toward the desired position in the fairway.

For example, Jack Nicklaus says that his bread and butter shot in golf is the "fade." A fade is played by "opening" the clubface angle and taking a stance aiming slightly toward the left of the desired target line, perhaps toward the left side of the fairway rather than down the middle. Then the spin will cause the ball to slice toward the right and compensate for the original adjustment in swing direction. By deliberately adjusting the club face angle, the experienced player ensures that small random aiming errors will only cause uncertainty in the degree to which the ball fades to the right. By controlling the clubface angle, the probability of a hook virtually disappears.

Even the professional can't control a fade perfectly, but by tuning his or her shot so that the peak of the probability curve is down the center of the fairway, the net result is a coherent or more orderly outcome since the risk of a hook has virtually been eliminated. This situation is shown in Fig. 1.3. Many experienced players favor a "draw" shot which is roughly the mirror image of the fade but flies lower and travels further. The club face is "closed" to produce a deliberate hook to the left and the swing stance is deliberately oriented toward the right of the desired ball path. There is still uncertainty as to how far the ball will curve to the left, but that is easier to live with than the chaos that can result from sometimes hooking and sometimes slicing unpredictably.

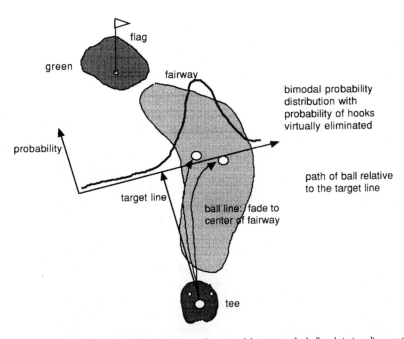

Figure 1.3. The experienced golfer has learned to control the spin on the ball and aiming alignment to achieve great distance on the drive without great aiming errors; likewise, experienced investors can attain high returns without proportionately high risks by learning to identify the risk-reward profiles of different market states.

By tuning a shot as either a fade or a draw, the experienced golfer is controlling the odds of a favorable outcome. The player understands how a few simple variables control the probability of placing the ball down the middle of the fairway: 1) speed of clubhead; 2) angle of club face at impact; and 3) stance and target line at impact with the ball. In contrast, the high handicap player may have hit it perfectly once or twice in the past and hopes for a repeat performance, only to be frustrated more often than not by ending up in the rough or losing the ball entirely.

Novice investors likewise learn quickly that investing is a game of chance in which individual positions seem to hook or slice unpredictably. In contrast, experienced investors have discovered that a few simple variables control the odds of making money. The probability distributions governing investment returns in our nonlinear market model are quite similar to those in golf. When a market is near equilibrium and there isn't much money flowing, investment returns are likely to follow a simple bell-shaped distribution, much as the path of putts around the target line. However, when the market is far from equilibrium and there's a lot of money flowing, nonlinear forces can cause persistent trends and bimodal distributions in investment returns. Therefore, in the money game, as in golf, our goal is to learn what predictable factors control investment returns in order to maximize the probability of success over the long run and avoid chaotic investment results.

Experienced golfers can swing hard and drive long distances with only moderate risks. Likewise, heavy hitters in the investment business have attained superior long-term performance with moderate levels of risk. There are more than a few success stories among professional money managers and private investors. Have they just been lucky? We can ask the same question in the game of golf. Was Arnold Palmer just lucky? Was Jack Nicklaus just lucky? Are the hundreds of thousands of highly skilled golfers who have mastered the game just lucky? Of course not. They may have enjoyed their share of luck along the way but their long-term success is based on repeatable factors. They have taken the time to learn the theory behind the game and successfully put it into practice.

Can the same be done with investing? That's a source of great controversy. The academics say no. The only factor that controls market returns is the level of risk. One is linearly related to the other: the only way to attain above average returns is to assume above average risks.

Here we will examine this issue within the framework of our nonlinear market model. In our golfing analogy we have seen that successful professionals have developed strategies that maximize their expected performance. The pros can hit the ball far without taking proportionately greater risks. They have not eliminated risk but learned to manage it. Our goal is to learn how successful investors have achieved the same result in the capital markets. Although the established academic theory suggests that large returns can only be attained by taking proportionately greater risks, practitioners such as Lynch, Buffet, and others have attained well above average, long-term results without simply assuming great risks.

The most important contribution of our nonlinear market model is its prediction that above average returns are theoretically possible without taking proportionately higher risks. We have seen how golfers have evolved strategies that achieve this goal. In this book, we will look at the simple strategies employed by successful investors. Our nonlinear market model helps explain the market's underlying dynamics. In turn the successful styles of master practitioners can help us implement investment strategies that effectively manage risk and attain above average performance without assuming proportionately higher risk.

Before presenting our nonlinear market model, we begin with an overview of some fundamental concepts that are used to characterize the behavior of a wide range of complex systems. A new interdisciplinary field of science has emerged over the past two decades. It provides insights into the nonlinear dynamics underlying a wide variety of complex systems.

Chaos and Complexity: Emergence of Nonlinear Science

During the past two decades, a dramatic growth of interest in the behavior of complex systems has produced a number of centers of research around the world dedicated to the study of the dynamics of complex physical, chemical, biological, and social systems. The scope of research extends to the origin and evolution of life, ecosystems, and the global economy. One of the leading research centers is the Santa Fe Institute (SFI) in New Mexico. A recent book by Michael Waldrop describes the ongoing research activities at the SFI, dedicated to the interdisciplinary pursuit of nonlinear science and its applications. Another book by Roger Lewin also addresses research on complex systems being performed by key scientists at the SFI. One area of focus from the beginning of the SFI program has been economic and financial systems.

The formation of the Santa Fe Institute is *de facto* recognition of the importance of nonlinear science. Its founders brought together highly capable academics from a diverse set of research disciplines such as physics, biology, medicine, and economics to explore new methods and techniques for analyzing complex systems. One early workshop focused on the global economy as a complex, adaptive system. Another brought together researchers in the field of "artificial life," an emerging new discipline seeking to use the computer to simulate the processes underlying the evolution of complexity in biological and ecological systems.

The emergence of nonlinear science in multiple disciplines marks an important watershed. Many have likened it to a new revolution in the sciences. And unlike the more esoteric revolutions created by Einstein's relativity theory and Schröedinger's quantum mechanics, the field of complexity deals with a wide spectrum of problems including many in our daily lives and experience. Examples range from the fields of physics and chemistry to biology and social systems. In financial markets, the new science of complexity offers the hope of more complete explanation of complex market dynamics, improved investment performance and better management of investment risk.

The game of golf provides a good example of the subtle interaction between the elements of chance and necessity, linear and nonlinear forces. It is a familiar example of a complex system. The probability distributions governing the path of the ball also apply to the behavior of a wide range of complex systems. All we need to do is imagine that the golf ball becomes a mathematical measure of some aspect of the system rather than a physical object. For example, the ball could represent a political opinion poll within a voter group. This is not a physical object, but is something that can be measured and quantified. Politics can have far reaching implications for investors, so this is of more than incidental relevance.

Politics is clearly a complex social process. Any population is made up of a diverse set of ethnic, racial, and economic special interest groups. A politicians goal is to maximize his or her popularity and avoid the risk of alienating major groups of voters. This is a complex, nonlinear problem.

On many issues, voters will not feel strongly one way or the other about the politicians views or performance. A normal or bell-shaped probability curve may best describe the likelihood of approval ratings among different voter segments. However, for some emotionally charged issues such as right to life versus freedom of choice, opinions may be more apt to cluster at one extreme or the other depending on which group is polled and whether the politician's position is perceived as in agreement or opposition to their own. In other situations, such as when the President puts American troops in harms way, there is normally a strong consensus (i.e., coherent support) that runs across nearly all population segments. For example, President Bush enjoyed his greatest popularity ratings during the war in the Gulf.

Physicists have developed quantitative models of polarization of opinions in social groups. For example, the German physicist Wolfgang Weidlich published "The Statistical Description of Polarization Phenomena in Society," in 1971. American physicists Earl Callen and Don Shapero published "A Theory of Social Imitation" in 1974, suggesting that the simple nonlinear model proposed by Weidlich could shed light on the tendency of fish to align in schools, birds to fly in flocks, and people to conform with fads and fashions. Each of these complex social groups may at times be either in a disordered state, or, under the right conditions, may exhibit collective, ordered behavior.

State transitions from disorder to order are a fundamental aspect of nonlinear dynamics in complex systems. A state transition involves some important macroscopic change in the system. For example, water freezing to ice is one type of state transition. A bar of iron may be in a nonmagnetic state with its molecules randomly oriented, or in a state in which the molecules are aligned, producing a macroscopic external field. Public opinion regarding the suitability of stocks as investments may switch from a negative bias in the post-Great Depression environment (when stocks were cheap) to widespread acceptance in the current global bull market (when stocks are at historical valuation extremes).

The behavior of a complex system can be represented by some parameter that measures the degree of macroscopic or large-scale order within the system. The key question in complex systems is how the order parameter behaves (i.e., what are the stable states, how do the dynamics evolve in time, and what types of fluctuations will occur in the system). In the capital markets, the return from a market index or individual stock may be regarded as the order parameter of interest, and the goal is to develop a model that explains how the returns from a given market will behave. Our simple model of market stabilities, dynamics, and fluctuations retains the random walk model and its normal (bell-shaped) probability distribution, but extends it into the nonlinear domain where bimodal distributions become important.

In general, there are numerous possible models that can be constructed to explain market fluctuations. The academic baseline is the simple, linear random walk model. More recently, there has been growing interest in making forecasts based on deterministic chaos theory. Our approach combines these two classes of models, with a nonlinear market model involving a simple underlying chaotic attractor, and also a high degree of random noise.

The concept of a chaotic attractor can be illustrated by the game of golf. When the novice strikes the ball toward the center of the fairway, invariably he or she hooks or slices the ball toward the trees or rough on either side of the fairway. The shot behaves as though there is some mysterious force field attracting the ball away from the desired target line. In golf, the nature of the attractor governing our drive is determined by the few simple factors described previously. In the capital markets, our nonlinear model involves a few control parameters that can be related to investor sentiment and economic fundamentals. These factors control the probability distribution that governs the uncertainty in market returns.

Figure 1.4 illustrates how the random walk model, deterministic chaos theory, and our nonlinear market model are related. In complex systems (i.e., those with many component parts or subsystems), each part may act independently or may be influenced by the behavior of other components. The horizontal or "x axis" represents increasing feedback or coupling among the components of a complex system. The vertical or "y axis" represents increasing randomness or influence of the element of chance. The four boxes represent different regimes with respect to the importance of nonlinear feedback and random forces on the macroscopic behavior of the system and the approaches that are required to model the system's stabilities and dynamics.

In the first box, there is little interaction between component parts and no element of chance at work. Under these conditions, the behavior of the system can be modeled as a simple, linear, deterministic dynamic system. For example, without random forces at work, the motion of a small physical particle or ball in a well or attractor with a single low point can be predicted far into the future if the shape of the well is known. If the position of the ball in the well shown in Fig. 1.4 corresponds to the return from a market index we could predict market returns. However, we know that there is little hope of accurately predicting the market's path because unexpected new developments (i.e., random forces) always affect the market's future direction.

As the degree of randomness increases, the behavior of the system can best be described as a random walk. For example, if the ball in the well is battered by random forces, its path becomes unpredictable. However, if the shape of the well containing the ball is known along with the average characteristics of the random forces, then the probability of finding the ball at any point in the well can be described by means of a probability distribution function. In fact, the scaling of the distribution in time, t, will follow the well-known $t^{1/2}$ rule. This is the widely accepted *random walk model*—the baseline academic theory of stock market behavior.

If the degree of positive feedback or coupling of opinions among investors increases, but random forces can be neglected, nonlinear dynamics becomes important. This is the realm of chaos theory. In Fig. 1.4, we use a simple chaotic attractor, the double well potential, to illustrate this case. Under these conditions the behavior of the system may look random, but in fact may be governed by relatively simple, deterministic nonlinear models. This situation was referred to as *type A chaos* by Allan Wolf at Fuzzy Day 1992, a chaos symposium for sponsored by the Society of Quantitative Analysts. With low-dimensional, type A chaos, simple nonlinear models can be used for short-term forecasting. By definition, chaotic systems tend to lose predictability at an exponential rate; however, short-term forecasts based on nonlinear models may be far more reliable than forecasts based on linear models. This is an area of active research.

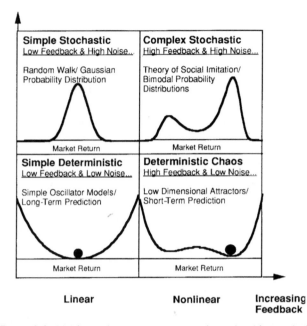

Figure 1.4. (a) A linear, deterministic process can be predicted far into the future; (b) a simple random process such as the random walk can be described by a normal "bell-shaped" probability distribution which widens in proportion to the square root of time; (c) a nonlinear, deterministic process has sensitive dependence on initial conditions enabling only short-term prediction; and (d) a nonlinear stochastic process, the most complex case, involves a "bimodal" probability distribution and a biased random walk.

Finally, our nonlinear market model is based on the case where both feedback between subsystems and random forces are important. This is the most general situation where the term complexity is particularly apt. Under these conditions, which Wolf referred to as *type B chaos*, the element of chance may prevent even short-term deterministic forecasting. However, nonlinear effects may be substantial and affect the probability distribution governing the system. *When applied to the stock market, nonlinear stochastic models offer the hope of making forecasts of major changes in the probabilities (i.e., the risk-reward outlook for the market).*

We will cover analytical methods applicable to each of the domains shown in Fig. 1.4. Our nonlinear stochastic market model of type B chaos in the financial markets includes both the simple random walk model and type A deterministic chaos as special limiting situations. We will also show how many existing methods developed by the most successful practitioners can be related to our nonlinear model, implying that their results may well be more than a matter of luck.

Nonlinear Market Model:
High Returns/Moderate Risks

Our nonlinear model presumes that the capital markets, like other non-linear systems may transition between states of disorder to more ordered states. Under the right conditions, a market will become more ordered and predictable, producing above average returns with below average risk. This prediction for the capital markets is the most important consequence of our nonlinear model applied to the capital markets. We refer to this as the *coherent market hypothesis.*

The coherent market hypothesis maintains that there are periods of time in the capital markets when the historical risk-reward ratio is turned upside down. For example, stocks have historically provided about a 10 percent total return with a 20 percent risk (standard deviation) or volatility. During coherent bull markets, the return from stocks is about 25 percent while risk drops to about 10 percent. This is the investment equivalent of the golf pro hitting a long drive without a corresponding increase in the risk of a hook or slice.

One can visualize the returns from a market index as a ball trapped in a "potential" well or "attractor." The well can undergo a state transition and change shape as shown in Fig. 1.5. In a random walk market, the shape of the well keeps the ball from bouncing too far in either direction from the center of the well as random forces (news affecting the stock market) buffet the ball (returns from the index). Large returns are unlikely, and the annualized return from a market index is governed by a "normal" or "bell-shaped" probability distribution.

The *theory of social imitation* predicts transitions or changes in market states as a function of changes in two key control parameters related to nonlinear technical forces (crowd behavior among market participants) and a fundamental bias. The transition state itself is unstable. This can be thought of as the potential well flattening out. The ball in this well (representing the return from a market index) is free to swing widely from one extreme to another. The probability of a particular annualized return is now governed by a nearly uniform or flat distribution. Here large, long-lasting fluctuations of returns may occur, following a power law as with earthquakes. Since market fluctuations are not "damped" out quickly (i.e., random news is not discounted quickly), these periods of instability can best be described as inefficient markets.

In a coherent bull market (crowd behavior with a strong positive bias in fundamentals), the lowest point of the well is deep in positive territory. Random news would still cause the ball to fluctuate. However, the fluctuations are most likely to center around a high annualized rate of return (in the neighborhood of +25 percent for the S&P 500 market index). Notice,

$$f(q) = c\,Q^{-1}(q)\,\exp\left[2\int_{-1/2}^{q}[K(y)/Q(y)]dy\right]$$

where:

$f(q)$ = probability of annualized return, q
$K(q)$ = sinh $(kq + h) - 2q$ cosh $(kq + h)$
$Q(q)$ = $1/n[\cosh(kq + h) - 2q \sinh(kq + h)]$

and:

n = number of degrees of freedom
k = degree of crowd behavior
h = fundamental bias

$$c^{-1} = \int_{-1/2}^{+1/2} Q^{-1}(q)\,\exp\left[2\int_{-1/2}^{q}[K(y)/Q(y)]\,dy\right]dq$$

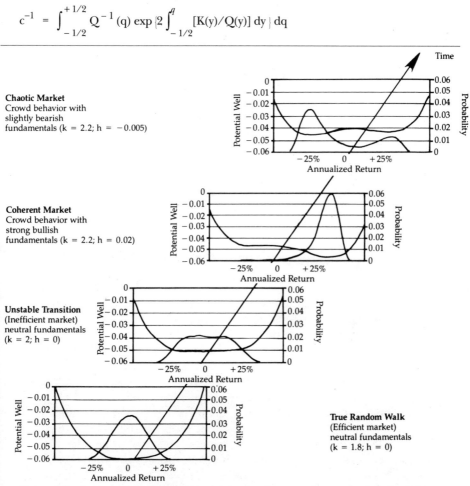

Chaotic Market
Crowd behavior with
slightly bearish
fundamentals ($k = 2.2$; $h = -0.005$)

Coherent Market
Crowd behavior with
strong bullish
fundamentals ($k = 2.2$; $h = 0.02$)

Unstable Transition
(Inefficient market)
neutral fundamentals
($k = 2$; $h = 0$)

True Random Walk
(Efficient market)
neutral fundamentals
($k = 1.8$; $h = 0$)

Figure 1.5. The returns from a market index may be viewed in terms of potential wells and probability distributions which can change substantially over time depending on the prevailing investor sentiment and bias in economic fundamentals. (*Reprinted with permission from* Financial Analysts Journal, *November/December 1990. Copyright 1990 Association for Investment Management and Research, Charlottesville, VA. All rights reserved.*)

however, that there is something of a ledge in the potential well in negative territory, and that there is a long tail on the probability distribution. The theory of social imitation predicts that even under the best of conditions, there is still a small but greater than zero chance of the market dropping substantially when conditions are extremely bullish. Even the pros will occasionally slice or hook the ball unintentionally.

If crowd behavior prevails and fundamentals are close to neutral, conditions are right for a chaotic market. Now the potential well has degenerated into two wells, separated by a barrier. This is a widely studied chaotic attractor, known as a *Duffing oscillator*. Under these conditions, the probability distribution has split or bifurcated into two parts. The extremes are more likely than the center for market returns. That's just the opposite of a random walk market. Under these circumstances it pays to be a trend follower. However, risk is high and sentiment may reverse abruptly and unexpectedly as it did in the Crash of 1987.

A chaotic market can be described as "quasi-efficient." Random news is discounted quickly but with a bias. The market may react to good news and ignore bad news or vice versa. Investor Marty Schwarz is quoted by Jack Schwager in *Market Wizards* as having said that "when the market gets good news and goes down, it means the market is weak; when it gets bad news and goes up, it means the market is healthy."

Evidence in support of the coherent market hypothesis has been developed independently by practitioners and researchers. While most successful practitioners may not be involved in research related to nonlinear dynamics, we find that their methods and strategies fit nicely within the framework of our nonlinear model. Some practitioners have been finding ways of actively managing money that have produced above average returns without correspondingly high risks. They have advanced the state of the art beyond the classical capital market theories developed by the academic community; now our simple nonlinear model suggests that their results may well be more than a matter of luck. Nonlinear theory may also offer new insights that can help practitioners refine their techniques.

While our nonlinear model offers important new insights, it does not discard the random walk baseline. The random walk model is an important first step. First it is a special case that occurs when market psychology is "rational" rather than prone to crowd behavior. Under these conditions, price fluctuations are likely to be relatively small and changes to the upside are likely to be nearly as large and frequent as steps to the downside. This is analogous to the soft golf shots such as putts on the green which are governed by the simple bell-shaped normal probability distribution.

When a market is far from equilibrium and investor psychology is prone to crowd behavior, market fluctuations will normally still follow essentially a random walk on a short-term basis. Likewise the golfer hitting a hook or slice will also have a normal distribution of ball path angles relative to aiming angle for a short time before the spin has a chance to take hold and systematically curve the ball. In the capital markets, when nonlinear feedback forces are important, the random walk will as a matter of necessity include a drift or price trend that compounds with time into a substantial gain or loss. This drift may be stable or unstable, depending on the prevailing bias in fundamentals, but is always small compared to short-term random fluctuations.

Hence the random walk is the first step within the framework of the coherent market hypothesis. Transitions from random walk to crowd behavior on Wall Street can lead to large changes in the risk, reward outlook for the stock market. Coherent bull markets are the safest, most rewarding opportunities (e.g., such as the periods following January 1975 and August 1982). Missing these markets would lead to under performance. Crowd behavior can also lead to the most dangerous, chaotic bear markets (e.g., October 1987). In coherent bull markets it is theoretically possible to achieve superior investment results (i.e., above average returns with below average risk). The rest of the time, the market may also include periods of sharply rising prices; however, the average of moves higher and lower in chaotic markets and periods of true random walk is typically well below average.

Likewise those who are fully invested regardless of overall market risk can still benefit by stock selection strategies that provide more issues with coherent returns and fewer issues with chaotic performance. Like the golfer who learns to control the factors underlying the fade and draw, the serious investor needs to focus on stocks that have the right blend of growth potential and fundamental value to ensure solid, long-term results. The risk-reward characteristics of the market and individual stocks theoretically depend on a relatively small number of variables known as *control parameters*. In the markets, the these parameter are typically related to technical and fundamental factors or, more simply, measures of growth potential and fundamental value.

Most investors fall into either of two investment styles: those that seek growth and those that seek fundamental value. This is akin to golfers who tend to hook or to slice. Sometimes one approach does better than the other; however it is difficult to predict in advance which approach will be best. While some professionals may prefer to draw the ball and others prefers the fade, and can be quite successful with either style, the superstars such as Jack Nicklaus use both techniques, depending on the particular characteristics of the hole being played. Likewise the superstar investors such as Peter Lynch use a blend of growth and value investing that has proven more effective than either approach alone.

The value investor often buys stocks that are out of favor and in a performance slump on a short-term basis: he or she is aiming away from the target, hoping that in time the fundamental value, like a predictable spin, will guide the performance back to the desired target. A value investor accepts poor short-term performance, knowing that a reversal for the better will occur at some unpredictable point in the future and provide a substantial net return. In contrast, the growth stock investor looks for high relative strength and earnings momentum: he or she knows that the rapid earnings growth and market performance will not last forever. A growth investor seeks to capture high short-term gains, knowing that some of these paper profits may be lost at unpredictable points in the future if there is a negative earnings surprise.

Control Parameters: Technical and Fundamental Factors

Technical and fundamental analysis are both important within the context of our nonlinear market model. Unlike the efficient market hypothesis which suggests that technical and fundamental analysis are a waste of time, these factors play a crucial role in describing the most likely state that the market will be in. While short-term random price fluctuations are always present in the capital markets, the deterministic part of the market's dynamics will be governed by the control parameters of the model (i.e., the technical and fundamental factors operative at any point in time or applicable to a particular market segment). We will see that the most successful practitioners on Wall Street have all recognized the importance of both of these factors in their investment decision process. However, the specific factors that they rely on may vary widely.

Applied to the stock market, the theory of social imitation has two key input variables. One is a *technical measure* of market psychology or investor sentiment, k. This is a measure of the degree of "group-think" or crowd behavior among participants in a particular market. It ranges typically from a high of 2.2, when crowd psychology dominates investor thinking, to 1.8, when cool heads prevail and rational thinking is more prevalent among investors. This control parameter is also related to the amount of money flowing in the market or how far it is from equilibrium. To return to the golf analogy it is a measure of whether we are putting the ball softly ($k = 1.8$) or driving with full force ($k = 2.2$). This is the factor that determines if we should expect a simple bell-shaped probability distribution or a bimodal distribution.

The second control parameter is a *measure of the external fundamental bias*, h. The selection of k and h as names for the inputs or control parameters for the theory of social imitation is based on historical factors (i.e., the scientists who originally came up with the theory used this notation). Economic fundamentals can be rated by assigning values that are typically in the range of +2 percent if there is a strong positive bias in fundamentals, to −2 percent if there is a strong negative bias. This is analogous to the slope of the green when putting or a natural tendency to slice versus hook or vice versa when driving. It is the factor that causes a shift in the bell-shaped probability distribution or one lobe to be larger than the other in the bimodal distribution.

Figure 1.6 shows how the most important market states are determined by investor sentiment and fundamentals in control parameter space. A true random walk market occurs when there is an absence of crowd behavior, at $k < 2$. Usually this occurs when the fundamental bias is also negative and there isn't enough money flowing into the market to stimulate a transition to crowd behavior among market participants. Under these conditions prices often drift lower. However, a true random walk with a positive bias can also occur.

At the other extreme on the sentiment scale, crowd behavior with a strong bullish bias in fundamentals can lead to a coherent bull market. These are the low risk–high reward opportunities where returns are high without the corresponding high risks. However, if fundamentals change during a period

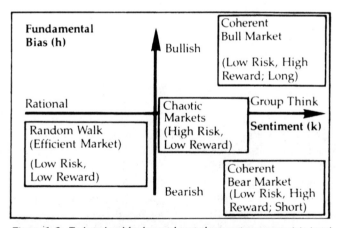

Figure 1.6. Technical and fundamental control parameters govern state transitions in our nonlinear market model. When investor sentiment is below a critical threshold, a true random walk market state will prevail in which fundamentals will have a weak impact on market returns. At the critical threshold, even small shifts in fundamentals can have a large, long-lasting impact on market returns. Above the critical threshold, a strong bias in fundamentals can create stable market trends. (*Reprinted with permission from* Financial Analysts Journal, *November/December 1990. Copyright 1990 Association for Investment Management and Research, Charlottesville, VA. All rights reserved.*)

of crowd behavior and become even slightly negative, a chaotic market is likely, where big moves could go either way and abrupt trend changes may produce abnormal volatility (e.g., the Crash of 1987). Crowd behavior with a strong bearish bias is rare but could be a suitable model of the Crash of 1929 and the 1973 to 1974 bear market.

Each of these market states has a distinctly different risk-reward outlook. To the degree that one can assess sentiment and fundamentals, the probability of a given return and the risk or volatility of the market is determined for each of these states. Hence much as the professional golfer controls the factors needed to fade or draw the ball toward the center of the fairway, the professional money manager or serious individual investor needs to control the contents of a portfolio of stocks to improve the odds of capturing more big winners (i.e., tenbaggers in Peter Lynch's jargon) without inordinate risks.

Summary

Nonlinear market dynamics revolve around transitions between states with widely divergent risk-reward profiles. These range from the simple bell-shaped distribution in a true random walk market to the bimodal distribution in a chaotic market. The unstable transition region itself tends to generate a power law distribution of returns over the long term. Fundamentals tend to bias these distributions. The value investor buys stocks that are out of favor but with sound fundamentals, and waits for future developments to trigger renewed interest in the stock. The growth investor looks for short-term performance to persist long enough to offset any potential future reversal the other way.

However, if growth and value styles alone were enough to beat the market, why do most active managers tend to underperform passive indexing? We propose that the reason active managers tend to under perform is not that the market is efficient, but rather that it is a system far from equilibrium. The stocks furthest from equilibrium may well be the least palatable to the prudent active manager. In contrast, the passive index fund is forced to maintain a complete portfolio, including value stocks that teeter on the edge of bankruptcy, and growth stocks at the extremes of valuation norms.

Buying stocks that are fairly priced and in equilibrium is the investment equivalent of driving with a putter. The results are predictable, but the ball doesn't go very far. Most blue chips and large capitalization stocks probably fall into this category. Growth and value players may miss the mark at times because many of the big winners may be in the market segments that they tend to avoid. The master golf pro such as Jack Nicklaus uses both a fade and draw depending on the shape and hazards of a particular fairway. The master investor such as Peter Lynch seeks out both growth and value stocks as they may occur in a particular market environment.

Passive indexing is a style that ensures capturing all the tenbaggers within the universe covered by the index. This may well explain under performance of professional managers as a group. Peter Lynch is said to have been a manager who never met a stock he didn't like. While Lynch wasn't an indexer, he did cast a wide net and typically maintained a portfolio of more than a thousand issues. This incubator clearly produced a substantial number of winners, enough to rank him first in the long-term performance ratings.

Can active management do better consistently than passive indexing? Warren Buffet's results suggest this may be possible by identifying stocks that have both growth and value characteristics. He has been known to buy whole companies in growing industries (i.e., sectors of the economy that are in long-term megatrends) and avoids the chaotic fluctuations associated with short-term investment fads (i.e., manias where the herd instinct is not backed up by sound fundamentals). However, what about environments in which the market is at historically high valuation extremes?

Active managers are aware of bubbles of various shapes and sizes in stock prices, sectors, and the overall market, and the risks that are posed when a bubble breaks. However, it is less obvious that collective thinking and action accompany the safest, most rewarding investment opportunities as well. In fact, fear of getting caught in a bubble may keep managers out of some of the most important trends and megatrends that occur in the economy and various sectors. Some of the major social and economic trends of the decade ahead, discussed by John Naisbitt and Patricia Aburdene in *Megatrends 2000*, present potential profitable investment themes. Our nonlinear model suggests that fundamentals are the single biggest difference between the most rewarding megatrends and the most dangerous manias.

2

Complexity: The Origins of Life and Bull Markets

There have been only 10 prior double-barrel buys since 1926. A month later the S&P 500 had risen another 7.5 percent even though prices were up substantially prior to the signal. Three months later the S&P was up 12.5 percent; six months later, plus 19 percent; a year later, up 26 percent; and 18 months after the signal, the S&P had gained 38.3 percent. By contrast, in the past 65 years the S&P index (without dividends) has appreciated at an annualized rate of only 5.1 percent.   MARTIN ZWEIG,
Barron's, February 11, 1991

Marty Zweig: The Worrier

Marty Zweig is a worrier. Growing up in the 1940s, he was close enough to the Great Depression era to have been left a lasting impression. Dinner conversations often turned to the depression of the prior decade. According to Zweig, "that dreadful period and its great bear markets are always on my mind whenever I deal with stocks."

Yet Zweig has compiled one of the best long-term track records among the advisors tracked in the *Hulbert Financial Digest,* a rating service of advisory letter recommendations. He has beaten the market over an extended period and done so with substantially below average risk. His methods and performance lend support to the coherent market hypothesis; in turn our nonlinear market model suggests that Zweig's results are more than a matter of luck.

Zweig's computers have back tested a wide range of technical and fundamental market indicators. He has distilled the results of this research down to two "sacred rules." The first is not to fight fundamentals (i.e., the interest rate trend or Federal Reserve policy). The second rule is not to fight market momentum. A trend set in motion can be a powerful force and strategies that are inconsistent with the market's direction can be devastated. Zweig's rules correspond directly to the technical and fundamental control parameters of our nonlinear market model. Rather than predicting the path of the market into the future, Zweig deals in risk and probabilities which are determined by his technical and fundamental indicators.

In spite of a thorough grounding in finance from leading academic institutions, Zweig repudiated the academic model of market fluctuations. He had gone to Wharton to learn about finance and, in particular, the stock market. Unfortunately, when he got there he found that the first year curriculum didn't include any stock market courses. Economic laws of supply and demand and accounting principles consumed his early years. Investment theory and stock market applications had to wait for his upper-class years.

Between semesters, Zweig gravitated toward the stock market. He sought work as a "chalk boy" recording price trends from quotations that came across the ticker tape. Before computers became prevalent, the most important stocks would have their prices listed periodically so that active traders could read the tape and make decisions. Unfortunately, no jobs were available, so Zweig's summers were spent studying *The Wall Street Journal.* During these periods he discovered the relationships between earnings, stock prices, and the ratio of prices to earnings as a benchmark for valuing stocks.

In his final two years at Wharton, Zweig took every stock market and investment course he could find. This included classical securities analysis based on the methods of Benjamin Graham, David L. Dodd, and Sidney Cottle. While the value-oriented analysis of these traditional investors was useful, Zweig felt that his education "was far from complete." The program at Wharton offered nothing related to market dynamics or the factors that control market action, including investor psychology and the role of economic fundamentals.

After graduating from Wharton, and a brief stint at New York University, Zweig moved back to Miami where he completed his masters program and traded stocks for his own account. At Miami he was influenced by Professor Wade Young, who had a strong technical orientation. Young was a proponent of relative strength: "buy on strength and sell on weakness." In Miami, Zweig also studied the methods of great traders of the past such as Jesse Livermore who exhorted readers to "cut losses and let profits run."

Zweig's exposure to technical analysis was complemented by a thorough grounding in economics and fundamental analysis of stocks as part of his PhD program in finance at the University of Michigan. At Michigan, Zweig also studied the random walk and efficient market theories which maintain that no amount of technical or fundamental analysis can add value to investment decisions. According to Zweig, "I rebelled at these ideas. In fact, one of my professors, Alden Olsen, didn't agree either. Professor Olsen had been successfully managing money for himself and others and generally proceeded on the basis of value and contrary opinion. That is, he bought stocks that were out of favor and that were undervalued."

Zweig's doctoral dissertation focused on trading systems for options. After studying over 50 different trading strategies, Zweig concluded that it wasn't worth playing the options market, primarily due to the high transaction costs. While he was disappointed in not finding a way to beat the market, he discovered that when option buyers became too aggressive, it was a pretty good indication that a market reversal was near at hand. Options traders tended to be a good contrary market indicator. Based on this observation, Zweig invented the put/call ratio which has become a popular tool among market forecasters.

The put/call ratio was to become just one of a large number of technical and fundamental indicators that Zweig researched and developed into a set of tools for market prediction. After graduating with his PhD, he went to work on Wall Street, writing a letter for institutional investors. At the same time, Zweig published the first of a series of articles for *Barron's*, including one which was based on his put/call research as a PhD candidate. The timing of the article was perfect. It called for a big rally based on the pessimism of call option buyers, and the market exploded to the upside just as *Barron's* hit the street. As luck would have it, the Wall Street firm for whom he wrote his letter went out of business, so Zweig solicited the inquiries that followed from his article and started *The Zweig Forecast*.

With the credibility of a PhD and a gift for clear thinking and writing, Zweig's letter grew into a successful business. In time he added a closed-end mutual fund, underwritten by Drexel Burnham Lambert. A second fund was launched a few years later. Today, Zweig runs a multi-billion dollar mutual fund family. He attributes his success to a strong desire to understand the markets and play them successfully. His advice: "In playing the market, remember you must deal with probabilities, employ sensible strategies to limit risk, and get aggressive only when conditions warrant."

Complex Systems

The stock market is a complex system. Most people throw up their hands in the belief that it is simply too complex to understand. However, Zweig's search for order underlying this complexity has been rewarded by the discovery that there are simple principles that can be used to practical advantage in making investment decisions. Other investment practitioners have reached similar conclusions. Researchers of complex systems in other disciplines have also come to the same conclusion, whether they be physicists searching for order in the fundamental laws of nature or biologists seeking to understand the evolution of complexity in organic molecules, cells, and the variety of species of life on the planet.

The stock market is just one example of a complex system. It has a lot in common with other complex systems, not just by way of casual analogy, but in the underlying statistical processes that govern such systems. By learning the basic characteristics of complex systems we can see how Zweig's simple indicators and strategies make sense within the framework of nonlinear dynamics. In turn, the theory can also help us better interpret empirical indicators, thereby helping us invest more profitably.

Complexity surrounds us. A trip to the neighborhood shopping mall has become a ritual most of us take for granted. Malls have been around for decades and have become the hangouts for a new generation. Gap, Limited, and other familiar names are outlets of choice for fashionable clothes. Many of these new chains are growing at the expense of older more traditional stores in urban settings. In the jargon of nonlinear dynamics, we might say that major shopping malls are "attractors" for major chains. Sharp money managers such as Peter Lynch, now retired, have taken advantage of these trends. A store that proves its business concept in one mall, successfully expands into a second mall, and on to a third, fourth, and so on, by induction, will be able to expand successfully into hundreds of malls with similar demographics.

While malls have been around for decades, this is an exceedingly short period compared to the time scales over which life has evolved or even within the context of the industrial revolution. Clearly the pace of social evolution has been accelerating. We are living in an increasingly complex society in which there continues to be a higher degree of specialization with new types of jobs being created as old jobs disappear. An entire new industry has been based on the invention of the microchip. New jobs are being rapidly created in the computer software, local area networking, laser technology, biotechnology and telecommunications areas. Our society is far from equilibrium; it is evolving and this presents investment opportunities.

Science is also evolving. Even as the face of retailing is changing and computer technology is proliferating, a growing number of scientists have become fascinated with the dynamics of complex systems. The science of complexity is an interdisciplinary search for the deeper knowledge that underlies the structures and ordered patterns that arise in physics, chemistry, biology, and social systems. Under the right conditions, disordered, random behavior may evolve into more structured ordered states on a macroscopic level. And unlike other revolutionary developments in physics, such as quantum physics and relativity which are far from our everyday experience, the science of complexity applies to the familiar world in which we live.

One of the pioneers of research on complex systems, Hermann Haken, a laser physicist at the University of Stuttgart, Germany, observed:

> We often analyze the properties of a system by decomposing it into its subsystems. In many cases, we discover that these properties cannot be explained as mere random superimpositions of the effects of the subsystems. Quite to the contrary, the subsystems seem to cooperate with each other in a well-regulated manner. Furthermore, the behavior of the total system may show characteristic changes which can be described as a transition from disorder to order, or as a transition from one state of order to a different one.

Haken coined the term "synergetics" to describe these types of phenomena and over the past two decades has edited the Springer-Verlag series of more than 50 scientific and technical books in this area.

Other researchers having established early reputations in this field include Nicolis and Prigogine from the University of Brussels. Prigogine's work on self-organization and spontaneous entropy reversal in chemical reactions far from equilibrium was recognized by a Nobel Prize in 1977. In effect, Prigogine's work showed that a flow process can result in spontaneous increase in the order of a system, in violation of the second law of thermodynamics which maintains that a closed system always tends to a state of maximum disorder. Disorder is related to probability theory. A system that becomes more orderly under the right conditions is also one where the odds of finding structure change. In the stock market, this means that sometimes the odds may be in your favor and sometimes they may not. Knowing that there are simple factors that control these odds is very important for investors regardless of their specific investment methods.

The potential applications of complexity theory are far reaching. Among the hotbeds of current research, scientists at the Santa Fe Institute are exploring applications of complexity theory in economic systems, biology, evolution, and the origins of life. Recent workshops on "artificial life" have explored how simple algorithms and rules of interaction among "adaptive agents" can lead to evolution. The economics projects have sought to add the elements of nonlinear science to traditional economic theory.

Specific examples of complex systems are not hard to find. The ones we will look at here include:

1. Fluid dynamics;
2. Sand piles and earthquakes;
3. Light and lasers;
4. Evolution and the origins of life;
5. Economies as complex adaptive systems; and
6. Capital markets and the origins of bull markets.

All of these complex systems are made up of numerous subsystems or components; all exhibit remarkable transitions from states of macroscopic disorder to more ordered or structured states. In the financial markets, such state transitions are from random walk markets to periods of collective behavior and profitable, trending markets; state transitions can also lead to the most dangerous manias, panics, and crashes.

Deterministic chaos theory so far has failed to provide any evidence that the path of capital markets is predictable. However there is evidence that stochastic forecasts of returns and volatility are possible. Nonlinear techniques may help us better understand the types of behavior that should be expected. While science's goal is to predict where possible, its broader goal is to offer explanations even if prediction is impossible. With that in mind, we examine various complex systems and associated models as we proceed on our search for the origins of bull markets.

Fluids Far from Equilibrium: Emergence of Structure

A simple example of complexity emerges in the behavior of a fluid between two plates at different temperatures. When the plates are at the same temperature, the fluid is said to be in *equilibrium*. A fluid in equilibrium has no macroscopic structure. However, as energy is pumped through the system in the form of heat, the state of the fluid moves further and further away from equilibrium. At a critical level of energy flow, structured convection cells emerge. The convection cells take on a regular pattern and represent a more ordered state within the fluid.

Figure 2.1a illustrates the case of the fluid near equilibrium. For very small temperature differences between the plates, the state of the fluid will be essentially homogeneous. The fluid sits there and does nothing apart from random thermal fluctuations.

a. The fluid is in equilibrium when T1 =T2

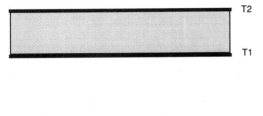

b. The fluid develops convection cells when T2 <T1

Figure 2.1. (a) A fluid between two parallel plates shows no structure when the plates are at the same temperature and the system is in equilibrium. (b) Far from equilibrium, the same fluid exhibits structured convection cells when the temperature difference between the two plates exceeds a critical threshold.

If the bottom plate is heated, and the temperature difference between the two plates becomes significant, heat energy flows from the lower to the upper plate. The density and pressure of the fluid will no longer be uniform or homogeneous. These state variables of the fluid will vary in linear fashion as one measures between the warmer and cooler layers.

As the temperature difference between the plates is increased, the system moves further from equilibrium. At a critical temperature difference, a new, more structured state emerges, characterized by a series of convection cells as shown in Fig. 2.1b. This behavior is known as the *Benard instability*.

Below the critical temperature difference the system is in equilibrium and a state of macroscopic disorder. Thermal forces cause each molecule of the system to move at random, and on a macroscopic level there is no structure. Above the critical threshold, far from equilibrium, there is a remarkable transition from the disordered state to a more structured, ordered or coherent state. Each convection cell involves the collective behavior of a huge number of individual molecules and the cells arrange themselves in an orderly pattern or structure across the plates.

The Belgian chemist Ilya Prigogine observed that:

Nonequilibrium has enabled the system to avoid thermal disorder and to transform part of the energy communicated from the environment into an ordered behavior of a new type, the dissipative structure: a regime characterized by symmetry breaking, multiple choices, and correlations of a macroscopic range. We can therefore say that we have witnessed the birth of complexity.

Prigogine admits that in this example "the type of complexity achieved is rather modest." However the Benard instability exhibits the characteristics of state transitions in a wide range of complex systems.

The term *symmetry breaking* is associated with the notion of distance in space. The spatial dimensions of each cell define a characteristic length. In contrast, the disordered state has no structure or any length scale of special interest. On the golf course, symmetry breaking is simply the familiar tendency of hooking or slicing drives. It doesn't occur on putts. In the market, symmetry breaking occurs when there is a transition from the disordered random walk state to cooperative or crowd behavior. Random walk has a single stable point for the probability distribution function. In contrast, a market dominated by crowd behavior has two stable points, far removed from each other: one stable state is a positive, bullish trend; the other stable state is a negative, bearish trend. Even if both states are equally likely, the market must end up in one state or the other and break symmetry. It will trend higher or lower but is unlikely to just go sideways.

The rotation of fluid in Benard cells could be in either of two directions—clockwise or counter-clockwise. The specific direction is a matter of chance. On one occasion, the rotation may be one way, on another occasion it could be in the opposite direction. The specific direction in any instance would be triggered by spontaneous initial fluctuations of clusters of molecules at the onset of the convection process. Hence macroscopic structure may depend on random microscopic forces. Likewise in the market, a trend one way or the other may be caused by minor random events, but once set in motion, would tend to persist long beyond the events that triggered the move.

Beyond the critical threshold, each convection cell's motion is "correlated" with the motion of distant cells. Unlike the random or disordered state in which the motion of each molecule is essentially independent of its neighbors, the convection cells behave as though molecules in each cell knew what its counterparts in remote cells were doing. The behavior of the system is predictable, given knowledge of part of it.

Similar state transition phenomena occur in other systems as well. For example, superconductors exhibit a state change as the temperature falls below a critical threshold. Even a small external electrical potential can then trigger a macroscopic, coherent electrical current in which the motion of electrons is correlated over a wide physical area and persists for a long period of time.

The Benard instability illustrates the concept of a phase or state transition. The transition is controlled by the rate at which energy flows into the system and the geometry of the experiment. Our model of nonlinear market dynamics in Chap. 1 also involves a state transition. Practitioners often talk of sector rotation within bull markets as some groups or industries heat up even as others fall out of favor. While the analogies are not important, the underlying state transitions are important because they contain information. The only information in a random walk market is the low point of the potential well; everything else is noise. However, in a bimodal well, there are two bits of information. The market could be in an uptrend or a downtrend; everything else is noise.

Our interpretation is akin to the way information is defined in a computer memory element. Each memory element contains either a bit or no bit. Everything else is noise—the aggregate result of random thermal fluctuations. Random events are always bombarding the market, but unless there is change the structure of the potential well governing market fluctuations, or a state transition, between a bull or bear state, there is no new information.

Sand Piles and Earthquakes: Self-Organized Criticality

One of the general characteristics of transitions from disorder to order in complex systems is an inherent instability at transition. At this critical point, even small forces are apt to trigger large fluctuations across a wide range of magnitudes and time scales. Per Bak, a physicist at the Brookhaven National Laboratory, has studied the critical nature of avalanches in a sand pile. He and his colleagues have also shed light on the nature of earthquakes and economic fluctuations.

A sand pile evolves to a critical state. If we incrementally drop grains of sand, a sand pile builds up from a flat layer to a cone shaped structure. The slope of the pile eventually approaches a critical point, where a new grain of sand dropped on the pile can trigger a landslide. Sometimes a large landslide will occur. More frequently, there will be small landslides. At the critical state, the size of the landslide doesn't depend on the size or number of sand particles dropped on the pile. A single grain of sand can cause landslides of all sizes because every grain of sand on the critical slope is coupled to its neighbors; the motion of one grain of sand or a small group interacting with its nearest neighbors on the critical slope can cascade until the whole side of the pile collapses.

Theoretically there is no way to predict what the impact of any incremental grain of sand will be. However, the theory of critical states developed by Per Bak suggests that the size of fluctuations is related to their relative frequency according to a power law as shown in Fig. 2.2. This is analogous to the relative number of earthquakes of various magnitudes on the Richter scale. Large earthquakes occur far less often than small ones; however they

Probability of Event

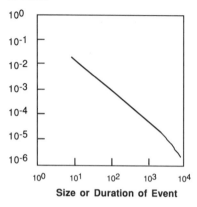

Size or Duration of Event

Figure 2.2. The size of avalanches down the side of a sandpile at a critical slope follows a power law distribution, where there are many small avalanches and progressively few very large avalanches. The same principle appears to govern the frequency of earthquakes of a given size on the Richter scale. Benoit Mandelbrot showed that financial fluctuations can also follow a power law distribution.

occur far more often than would be expected if they required catastrophic shocks to trigger them.

Bak and Tong have constructed a simple computer model of the earth's crust which illustrates some of the features of earthquakes. The earth's crust is modeled as an array of plates which are coupled to their neighbors and begin to slide when the pressure from neighbors exceeds a critical threshold, thereby simulating a small earthquake. However, motion of one element in the array can trigger motion of any number of other elements ranging from a few to a large percentage of the plates.

Large earthquakes, therefore, aren't necessarily produced by large shocks to the earth's crust. The same simple underlying mechanism produces large as well as small simulated earthquakes, just as the same basic mechanism (dropping a single grain of sand) causes avalanches of all sizes in the sand pile, once it has evolved to the critical state. Likewise the frequency of high energy earthquakes in the simulated environment is related by a power law to the frequency of smaller earthquakes.

Both sand pile avalanches and earthquake models evolve to a critical state at which point the power law characterizes the relative frequency of events of a particular magnitude. Other examples in which the distribution of objects (or events) of a given magnitude include the size of mountains, clouds, and stock market fluctuations. When the number of objects of a given size, r, follows a power law, r^D, where D is a constant, the distribution is called a *fractal*, a term originally coined by the French mathematician Benoit Mandelbrot.

Bak and Chen suggest that the widespread appearance of fractal structures throughout nature "can be viewed as snapshots of self-organized critical processes. Fractal structures and flicker noise are the spatial and temporal fingerprints, respectively, of self-organized criticality."

One of the characteristics of the critical state is that small changes in initial conditions increase far more slowly than the uncertainty associated with fully chaotic conditions. The uncertainty increases as a power law rather than an exponential. Therefore, systems at the critical state are not truly chaotic which in turn raises the possibility of long-term forecasting.

More recently, Bak and Chen have been working with economists Jose Scheinkman and Michael Woodford suggesting that economic activity also evolves to a critical state. At the critical point, the frequency of large economic fluctuations follows the same power law as avalanches in a sand pile and earthquakes. Therefore, severe recessions or depressions are not necessarily the result of large shocks to the system. Rather, even small triggering events can on occasion lead to a large disruption. Fortunately, as with large earthquakes, the frequency of large economic avalanches is far smaller than the frequency of smaller recessions.

Bak and his colleagues devised a simple model of economic activity which does lead to a power law governing the size of economic fluctuations. This is consistent with the earlier finding by Mandelbrot who suggested that the random walk model fails to capture the relatively high frequency of large fluctuations in financial and commodity markets. Mandelbrot's proposed stable Paretian distribution model conforms well to empirical evidence for some markets. Hence these markets may in fact be viewed as complex systems that have self-organized into a critical state.

The concept of a power law distribution has important consequences in the capital markets. Our model of nonlinear market dynamics in Chap. 1 suggests that a critical transition lies between the quiescent random walk markets and turbulent chaotic markets. If markets evolve to the critical state, then the power law distribution should also apply to investment returns (i.e., a financial "Richter scale" would have gargantuan returns at one extreme and smaller returns at the other end of the scale). At the critical point the number of gargantuan returns (i.e., the tenbaggers that Peter Lynch describes) are more frequent than would be expected from a normal distribution.

We cannot yet predict where the next earthquake will hit; likewise we can't predict which stock will be the next tenbagger. However, we can now see how a strategy such as indexing is guaranteed to include all the tenbaggers in a given universe of stocks. Hence passive indexing is far from a boring way to invest. It is simply the surest way of finding all the winners and holding them throughout their period of appreciation. These may be emerging growth stocks such as Microsoft and Cisco Systems, or turn-arounds such as General Public Utilities or Chrysler. These stocks may not look like prudent investments, either teetering on the verge of bankruptcy or highly priced with valuations that defy the norms established by the more numerous issues that are destined to appreciate very little.

As Lynch observes, even a few big winners will turn an otherwise lackluster portfolio into a star performer. As long as the economy is evolving and growing, big winners in the stock market will occur as a matter of necessity with significant frequency according to the principle of self-organized criticality. Indexing is the guaranteed method of capturing this effect and hence is a tough benchmark for active managers to beat.

But can we be sure that all financial markets will evolve to a critical state? The answer, in general, is no. We have seen that in open systems far from equilibrium, a flow is required to produce a state transition. In financial markets, this amounts to a flow of investment capital. If this flow dries up the associated market will languish in a quiet random walk around some equilibrium level; if the flow is large enough, and guided by a positive fundamental bias, a coherent market will produce even greater numbers of large winners than a power law distribution would suggest. If fundamentals turn negative, there will be chaotic fluctuations in the number of tenbaggers over a given period of time.

The critical state is the unique situation where the power law holds. However it is surrounded by coherent, chaotic, and random walk states, each with their own unique characteristics. In the markets, Federal Reserve activity is one of the key factors controlling which state the market will be in. Over the long term, given adequate economic growth, the power law distribution of stock market returns appears to be a reasonable "average" expectation and indexing is an elegant strategy for taking advantage of this characteristic. However, not all financial markets will necessarily organize into a critical state.

The question remains as to whether it is possible to do even better than indexing. Theoretically the answer appears to be yes. With the right combination of control parameters, coherent behavior should occur in the capital markets with returns well above average and risk below average. Practitioners have also demonstrated some ability to identify coherent stocks. In addition to Peter Lynch's long-term approach and Zweig's short-term strategies, advisors Louis Navellier and James Collins screen stocks on the basis of the ratio of excess return divided by risk or volatility. They have achieved top rated rankings in recent Hulbert performance sweepstakes.

However, any trading strategy involves costs which may be substantial. Strategies that work well in coherent market states may not be able to recover trading costs in periods of true random walk where trades may become more frequent and profits more scarce. Hence the prevailing market state is an important consideration in selecting an appropriate investment strategy. The goal is to identify coherent states which may arise with the overall market, sectors or individual securities.

The property of coherence is a special type of behavior that occurs in nonlinear systems. The conditions under which coherence occurs in physical systems are well known as are the properties of coherent systems. We will also see that simple technical and fundamental indicators can help us identify coherent bull market periods and coherent stocks. These are the periods of time or individual market segments in which above average returns are available without proportionate increase in risk.

Light and Lasers:
Characteristics of Coherence

Perhaps no other complex system has attracted as much attention as the laser. The laser is an example of a system far from thermal equilibrium. It also exhibits a remarkable state transition from macroscopic disorder to order. This transition is dependent on a critical threshold in the amount of power pumped through the system. Below the critical threshold, the laser emits ordinary random light. Above the threshold, the light from each molecule is coupled or emitted in phase with that generated by its neighbors. The light becomes orderly or coherent on a macroscopic level. At the critical transition the laser field undergoes large, long-lasting fluctuations which are analogous to the avalanches in a sand pile. Such *critical fluctuations* are a characteristic common to state transitions in a wide variety of complex systems.

The discovery of the laser was a major impetus in the rebirth of interest in complex systems and phase transitions from states of disorder to order. The laser transition has become a paradigm of an "open" system, far from equilibrium in which there is a state of macroscopic order. The coherent beam of light put out by a laser has many practical applications, not the least of which is its growing role in the telecommunications industry where it has tremendously increased the amount of information that can be transmitted over fiber optic media. The information "superhighway" is currently a key element of the nation's political agenda and an investment theme underlying more than one fund manager's portfolio.

A laser consists of a collection of energized atoms or molecules confined in an optical cavity as shown in Fig. 2.3. Energy flows into the cavity from an external pump. The pump serves to energize the electrons associated with the atoms in the cavity. Electrons tend to give up this energy in the form of light which is emitted into the optical cavity.

If the power pumped into the cavity is below a critical level, the laser will emit normal or random light. In this state, the electrons emit light independently and the waves from adjacent atoms or molecules are not in phase with each other.

However, under the right physical conditions (e.g., mixture of gas, pressure, alignment of mirrors), if enough power is pumped into the laser

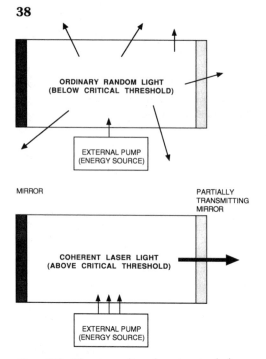

ORDINARY RANDOM LIGHT
(BELOW CRITICAL THRESHOLD)

EXTERNAL PUMP
(ENERGY SOURCE)

MIRROR

PARTIALLY
TRANSMITTING
MIRROR

COHERENT LASER LIGHT
(ABOVE CRITICAL THRESHOLD)

EXTERNAL PUMP
(ENERGY SOURCE)

Figure 2.3. A laser is a nonlinear dynamic system far from equilibrium with transitions between disordered and coherent states. It is an "open" system in which the flow of energy must exceed a critical threshold to cause the laser to transition from emitting ordinary "random" light to coherent "laser" light.

cavity, there is a critical threshold above which the atoms in the optical cavity begin to emit light in phase with that of their neighbors. A coherent or orderly beam of light emerges within the optical cavity even though the transfer of energy from the external pump to the atoms is a random process. Therefore, the laser may be viewed as a complex system in which its component parts act independently in disordered fashion below a critical pump threshold and in coherent fashion above the threshold.

The laser is a system far from thermal equilibrium. A state of order can only be created and maintained by pumping energy through the system. What is particularly remarkable about the laser is that its behavior during the critical transition is quite similar to state transitions in other systems such as a ferromagnet in thermal equilibrium, or the Benard instability in a fluid.

The laser can be viewed as a nonlinear, positive feedback system. The macroscopic electric field produced by the cooperative emission of light by individual electrons serves to regulate and control the emission process. In fact, the light field tends to stimulate emission from electrons that have been pumped into higher energy states and are "waiting" or poised to emit light. Parallel mirrors at each end of the optical cavity keep the laser intensity high within the cavity, though one of the mirrors is only partially reflective to allow part of the laser energy to be transmitted out of the cavity to do useful work.

The macroscopic state of the laser can be represented by the strength or amplitude of the electric field. This is the "order parameter" characterizing the macroscopic behavior of the system, as opposed to the details of the interactions among atoms, electrons, the external pump, and the laser field. We can draw analogies between the laser field and returns in the capital markets as the flow of money exceeds a critical threshold. The distribution of returns in a market is analogous to the distribution of field intensity in a laser or the probability of hitting hooks and slices in a round of golf. In all cases, when there is a sufficient flow through the system to take it far from equilibrium, symmetry breaking occurs and a bimodal probability distribution rather than the simple bell-shaped normal distribution governs the behavior of the system.

Representing the laser field amplitude by $E(t)$, the dynamics of the laser can be expressed on a macroscopic level, in terms of a laser potential function, defined as:

$$V(E) = -[(g_0 - L)/2]E^2 + (\beta/4)E^4 \qquad (2.1)$$

where L represents the losses, and g_0 and β are proportional to the electronic population inversion, s, the number of electrons pumped up into high energy states (ready to emit light) less the number in low energy states (unable to emit light). The condition $g_0 = L$ represents the critical threshold in population inversion, s_t, at which the pump energy is enough to initiate laser action. This laser potential function is illustrated in Fig. 2.4.

The well represents a force field acting on the laser and tends to confine the fluctuations of the laser field around values which correspond to the lowest points of the potential well. If the gains g_0 are less than losses, L, the low point of the well will be centered near zero. Under this condition, the only stable solution for the macroscopic laser field strength is $E = 0$. Any random fluctuations of the field, E, will die out in time. However, if gains exceed losses (i.e., $g_0 > L$) the stable solution becomes

$$E = A[(s - s_t)/s]^{1/2} \qquad (2.2)$$

where A is a proportionality constant. This represents a stable laser field with a large amplitude.

Using the idea of a potential function it becomes particularly easy to visualize the stabilities and dynamics of the laser on a macroscopic level.

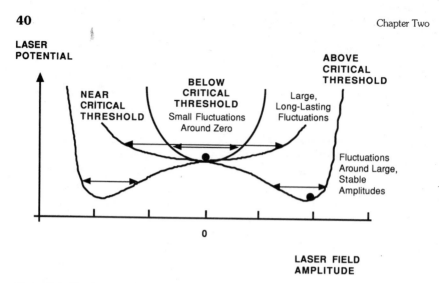

**LASER
POTENTIAL**

NEAR
CRITICAL
THRESHOLD

BELOW
CRITICAL
THRESHOLD
Small Fluctuations
Around Zero

ABOVE
CRITICAL
THRESHOLD

Large,
Long-Lasting
Fluctuations

Fluctuations
Around Large,
Stable
Amplitudes

0

LASER FIELD
AMPLITUDE

Figure 2.4. The dynamics of the laser light intensity can be though of as a ball which stabilizes at the lowest point of the laser potential well. Below the critical threshold for the onset of lasing, the ball (light intensity) is stable near zero. Above the critical threshold, the ball is moved by any slight fluctuation away from zero to a new stable point which is far from zero and corresponds to a large intensity for the laser field.

The electric field can now be thought of as ball trapped in the potential well or attractor. Below the laser transition threshold, the lowest point of the well is at zero. Any random fluctuations of the ball are met with resistance which tends to push the ball back to zero, following a normal distribution.

However, above the transition threshold, the well splits or bifurcates into two low regions separated by a barrier in the center of the well. Now the center of the well, corresponding to a macroscopic field strength of zero is no longer a stable state of the system. Any slight fluctuation would tend to be reinforced, pushing the ball down the well away from zero toward the new stable points far from zero.

The potential functions in Fig. 2.4 can also be thought of as attractors. They represent force fields that control the behavior of the system which in this case is described by the electric field strength. Below the laser transition threshold, the field strength is stable near zero (i.e., there is no coherent, macroscopic laser electric field). Above the threshold, the double bottom well attracts the laser field away from zero and it takes on a large value, corresponding to the strength of the coherent laser field.

Finally, the element of chance can be added to the picture. Rather than evaluate the behavior of the laser field as a deterministic problem, the element of chance or "noise" can be added. In this case the probability of finding a particular value of the electric field amplitude $p(E)$ can be expressed as a probability distribution

$$p(E) = \exp[-V(E)/ks] \qquad (2.3)$$

where k is proportional to the spontaneous emission rate per atom. Now the potential function determines the shape of the probability distribution rather than the deterministic path of the ball in the well.

Below the critical threshold, $p(E)$ is a normal distribution with a peak at $E = 0$. In this limiting case, the higher order term in the potential $V(E)$ can be ignored. However, above the critical threshold, this nonlinear feedback term creates a new stable stationary state at $E = E_0$.

As the laser undergoes a transition from ordinary (random) light to coherent laser light, it undergoes *critical fluctuations*. This is the same critical state that Bak and Chen describe. However, with a laser, the system can be controlled by tuning the system simply by adjusting the pump power or alignment of the mirrors. Many natural systems evolve to a critical state on their own rather than under the control of some external force.

The laser potential function illustrates how the system's fluctuations depend on whether the system is below, at, or above the critical transition threshold. Below threshold, fluctuations are strongly damped; likewise, above threshold, nonlinear forces tend to confine fluctuations to a small region around the new stationary stable point at $E = E_0$. However, near the threshold, the laser field fluctuation intensity is inversely proportional to how close the system is to the unstable point, according to $[s - s_t]^{-1}$.

Likewise the typical duration or "relaxation time" of amplitude fluctuations is inversely proportional to the curvature of the laser potential function at its minimum and is also proportional to $[s - s_t]^{-1}$. The reciprocal of the relaxation time is the correlation time of field fluctuations. While the critical fluctuation amplitude and correlation time become infinite at the threshold (and the reciprocal of the correlation time approaches zero), in practice the laser is limited by finite volume and energy and follow the power law distribution which characterizes the scaling of fluctuations in this critical state. The abundance of large, long-lasting fluctuations during transition is experimentally confirmed for the laser and this is a fundamental characteristic of state transitions in a wide variety of complex systems.

Our model in Chap. 1 suggests that the stock market is a nonlinear dynamic system which undergoes state transitions from disorder (random walk) to more ordered or structured states. Assuming that market returns are the state variable of interest, they will behave in a manner analogous to the laser field. Figure 2.6 illustrates the transient behavior of the laser field intensity as it transitions from a random to coherent state. In the capital markets, the prediction of coherence (i.e., above average returns with below average risk) is the most dramatic forecast of our simple nonlinear market model. This effect is as important in the capital markets as the laser is in

Probability

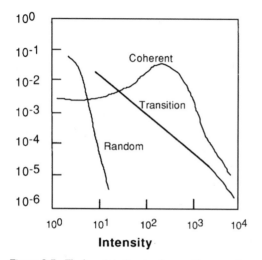

Figure 2.5. The laser transition involves a wide range of probability distributions governing the intensity of the laser beam. Likewise, market state transitions can substantially affect return probabilities.

science and engineering. In the stock market, recent empirical evidence by Brock and his colleagues confirms that simple moving averages can be used to forecast periods of above average returns with below average risk.

Complexity and the Emergence of Life

With a laser or a fluid, one can externally control the amount of energy flowing through the system. The experimenter can "tune" the system and take it above, below, or precisely to the critical threshold of the state transition. However, some systems may evolve on their own to a critical state. Currently, one of the hot areas of research on complex systems is focusing on the origins of life and the evolution of complexity in biological and social systems. Computer simulations of the logical processes that emulate life have become recognized as an important new field of research.

Conway's Game of Life uses cellular automata which are the simplest example of a nonlinear dynamic system. The behavior of these elementary logic structures also undergo transitions from "do-nothing" states to states characterized by periodic motion and ultimately to "chaotic" regimes. Researchers speculate that life may have evolved into a self-organized critical state (i.e., the critical point between unstructured states and chaos).

Christopher Langton of the Santa Fe Institute organized the first workshop on artificial life in September 1987 at the Los Alamos National Laboratory. The event was attended by about 150 researchers from a variety of disciplines with a common interest in simulation and modeling of biological phenomena. Langton, who coined the term "artificial life" organized the session to pull together research that had previously been highly fragmented.

The scope of the artificial life workshop included more than just research on "life as we know it"; rather, it included the analysis of "life as it could be." Topics of interest included: the origin of life, molecular self-assembly, growth, development, evolution, animal behavior, insect-colony dynamics, ecological dynamics and cultural evolution. Symmetry breaking occurs in the feeding pattern of ant colonies. The relevance of this to financial market behavior is being studied by Dr. Alan Kirman at the European University in Florence, Italy.

One of the concepts proposed by Langton is that life is complexity evolving at a critical point at the edge of chaos. The critical transition state between the "do-nothing state" or periodic motions state and a state of macroscopic chaos is the point at which Langton suggests the "dynamics of information has gained control over the dynamics of energy." Nor is Langton alone in the belief that life evolves in the critical region. Norman Packard also arrived at this conclusion as did Stuart Kaufmann, a physician and research biologist at the Santa Fe Institute. Packard is a principal of the Prediction Company in Santa Fe which is currently seeking to develop short-term nonlinear market forecasting tools for trading purposes.

Artificial life isn't exactly a new concept. The pioneers of early computers, such as John von Neumann, had a deep interest in the subject of *cellular automata*, which are programs for creating patterns on a computer screen based on tables of rules. John Conway invented the Game of Life based on the concept of cellular automata. For example, a two-dimensional cellular automaton may be defined to paint a cell on a computer screen black (alive) if it has either two or three adjacent cells which are black. If there are less than two adjacent cells, the cell dies of loneliness; if there are four or more adjacent cells, the cell dies of overcrowding. These simple rules can evolve into complex structures as they are iteratively applied to a random starting configuration.

Stephen Wolfram noted that all cellular automata rules can be categorized into four classes. Class I includes rules that lead to uninteresting patterns which fail to evolve, but die out rather quickly. Class II rules may lead to recurring patterns, but the oscillations are periodic and hence no more interesting than watching a pendulum progress through its predictable motion. Class III rules produce chaotic results in which the evolution of structures would not last long enough to be of interest. Class IV however includes rules that didn't fit nicely into the other classes; here there was emerging structure that was persistent, ever changing and evolving, recombining, and growing in complexity. Wolfram observed that these classes were analogous to the behaviors seen in nonlinear dynamic systems.

The most interesting behaviors found in the computer world of artificial life occur in the Class IV region which is analogous to the unstable transition threshold at the edge of chaos. Here the flattening of the "potential well" leads to fluctuations that follow a power law in terms of the frequency at which large, long-lasting fluctuations occur. In the stock market, the fluctuations represent the returns from investments. With life and evolution, the fluctuations may represent the biomass of a species where the fluctuations represent the origin, growth and eventual extinction of the species.

If life is evolving in a self-organized critical state, it follows a power law distribution. A few species may grow to a very large size, as found in Michael Creighton's *Jurassic Park*. Some species will survive seemingly forever, reproducing and successfully adapting to the environment. Interestingly, religion teaches rules of interaction between individuals with the goal of attaining everlasting life. The Game of Life teaches us that rules of interaction are indeed vitally important in the survival and evolution of a "life form." Too little or too much interaction could lead to death or instability and early extinction. Just the right conditions lead to the critical state where fluctuations of infinite duration are theoretically possible, though in practice are limited by the finite size of the energy flow through an ecosystem.

Even as social complexity increases, threats to social evolution continue to emerge in the form of drugs and disease. AIDS is prevalent in many countries. In some countries, the prevalence of this disease is higher among the urban professionals than among the rural population where social and sexual interaction is less prolific. As individuals, we are all increasingly dependent on social order in a world where few are self-sufficient. Hence the moral fiber of society is also of fundamental importance for long-term social development and continued economic growth. Long-term growth and evolution of global economies are integrally related to simple rules interactions among the key players.

Can cellular automata be put to use in the financial markets? Peitgen observes that "cellular automata have become a very important modeling and simulation tool in science and technology, from physics, chemistry, and biology, to computational fluid dynamics, in airplane and ship design, to philosophy and sociology." He discusses in detail the relationship between cellular automata and the *Pascal triangle* and shows that a one-dimensional cellular automaton can be related to the addition of even and odd binomial coefficients.

In effect, by coloring odd entries black, and even entries white, the Pascal triangle begins to look like a *Serpinski gasket* which is one of the interesting structures of fractal geometry. The Pascal triangle is also closely linked to the binomial distribution of probability theory of which the Gaussian or normal distribution is a special case. Hence simple rules of feedback, or interaction among simple computational elements can lead to surprising complexity which is inherently related to the concepts of fractals and probability theory. We will see later that the capital markets also exhibit a fractal structure.

The interaction between the individuals of a society is a key factor in the theory of social imitation that determines the macroscopic state. The stabilities and dynamics of the social group depend on the degree of coupling among the individuals making up the social group. Without enough interaction, the social group will remain disordered. With strong interactions, coherent and chaotic states may emerge. At the critical point, large, long-lasting fluctuations will occur. Therefore, the state transitions in nonlinear systems share the same fundamental properties, regardless of the details of the analysis. Our particular nonlinear model is robust enough to capture the essential features of nonlinear dynamic systems.

The Global Economy: A Complex and Adaptive System

There is a growing level of interest in using the concepts of nonlinear dynamics to develop new models of the global economy, which may well be the most complex of systems that affect our lives directly on a daily basis. The dynamics of the international currency markets have been studied by academic researchers and there is evidence of strong nonlinear dependencies. That doesn't mean that there are any simple models that predict the path of currency fluctuations, only that the methods of nonlinear dynamics may ultimately prove to be useful in better understanding global markets if not predicting them any better than say our ability to predict the weather far into the future.

According to physicists Farmer and Sidorowich, "To someone schooled in nonlinear dynamics, economic time series look very far from equilibrium, and the emphasis of economic theories on equilibria seems rather bizarre." They go on to observe, "the use of the word equilibrium in economics appears to be much closer to the notion of attractor as it is used in dynamics rather than any notion of equilibrium as it is used in physics."

These comment in the proceedings of a workshop on Evolutionary Paths of the Global Economy at the Santa Fe Institute in 1987 illustrate a cultural divide between physicists and economists.

The Santa Fe Institute workshop on the global economy was one of the earliest events sponsored by the institution. A look behind the scenes at the movers and shakers who were responsible for the conception and growth of this institute is provided in Waldrop's recent book. One goal was to take a fresh look at economic issues and explore the potential applications of the new tools of nonlinear dynamics to complex economic systems, including the global economy.

John Reed, Chairman of Citicorp, was one of the workshop sponsors. He was particularly interested in global capital flow and debt. Reed was concerned with the limited accuracy and predictive utility of contemporary economic models. As a financial manager, he faced large risks and uncertainties while being responsible for making near real-time decisions. He was looking for new tools that could help characterize the dynamics of the global economy and provide a rational basis for business decisions.

According to David Pines, one of the organizers of the workshop, along with Philip W. Anderson and Kenneth J. Arrow, the workshop sought the involvement of scholars with the following characteristics:

1. confidence;

2. an open mind;

3. a willingness to learn;

4. a sense of adventure; and

5. a sense of humor.

The workshop succeeded in attracting a distinguished set of physicists and economists. And while not successful in solving John Reed's immediate business problems, the conference at least recognized the potential relevance of new analytic techniques and legitimized the search for nonlinear models of systems as complex as the global economy.

As the quote from Farmer and Sidorowich demonstrates, the workshop provided a frank exchange of views. Waldrop observes that "the physicists could only be awestruck at their counterparts' mathematical prowess—awestruck and appalled." He quotes one physicist's views of the economists as follows:

> They were almost too good.... It seemed as though they were dazzling themselves with fancy mathematics, until they really couldn't see the forest for the trees. So much time was being spent on trying to absorb the mathematics that I thought they often weren't looking at what the models were for, and what they did, and whether the underlying

assumptions were any good. In a lot of cases, what was required was just some common sense. Maybe if they all had lower IQs, they'd have been making some better models.

At the same time the economists were surprised by the style of the physicists which was "a little rigorous thinking, a little intuition, a little back-of-the-envelope calculation."

One of the economists who had spent considerable time delving into physics and had already made significant applications of the basic concepts of nonlinear dynamic systems was W. Brian Arthur of Stanford University. He was the lead-off speaker at the workshop and spoke on the subject of *positive returns* or self-reinforcement mechanisms at work in economic endeavors.

The concept of positive feedback is central to all nonlinear dynamic systems in the fields of physics, chemistry, and biology. All of the earlier examples we have explored involve some self-reinforcing mechanism which leads to the emergence of structures in states far from equilibrium. Hence Brian Arthur's concept of positive feedback in economic markets is of special interest.

In the economy, there are numerous examples of positive feedback, self-reinforcement, or, in Brian Arthur's economic jargon, increasing returns. One is the emergence of the VHS standard for video recording equipment. Of the two early contenders, the Sony Betamax and VHS, one gained a dominant market share in spite of the fact that both were technically sufficient to meet consumer needs. However, as one of the two incompatible technologies gained popularity, the remaining consumers in the marketplace were influenced to go with the leader and further reinforced the dominance of VHS.

Whereas conventional economic theory emphasizes diminishing returns or negative feedback and stability, the concept of *positive feedback* has not gained widespread acceptance. Positive feedback can lead to instabilities and multiple equilibrium points. This makes prediction more complicated at best and often impossible. How the system evolves to one stable point instead of another may depend on small random forces or slight variations in initial conditions.

Other examples of positive feedback are easy to find. Once Microsoft gained an edge with MS-DOS as the operating system of choice for personal computers, it became the dominant provider of microcomputer software. Not only did it capture the dominant position with respect to the operating system market, it also enjoys an advantage in applications that run under the operating system.

As the market for local area computer networks emerged in the early 1980s, Novell established a product with the best cost performance characteristics, and became the leading provider of computer network operating systems. However, being first is not a guarantee of market dominance. Visicalc™, the first spreadsheet on the market, was displaced by Lotus 1-2-3™, an "integrated" spreadsheet product. Once business users tailored their spreadsheet to the Lotus 1-2-3™ format, they became locked into this environment. To change would require conversion of all their existing spreadsheet files, retraining all the users, purchase of new documentation, and so on. Real or imagined, a perceived advantage in the market can lock in a product for an extended period.

Peter Lynch advises his readers against investing in "the next anything." Frequently, new business ideas are touted as "the next McDonalds," or "the next Microsoft," or "the next Blockbuster Entertainment." However, the leader of a market niche normally has the element of feedback working in his favor and against the competition. Unless the competitor truly offers a better product, better value, or some other major advantage, the market is likely to stick with a name it knows and is satisfied with.

Another example of positive reinforcement is the dominance of the gasoline powered automobile. While other fuels are possible, it would be very difficult to establish the production, distribution, and retailing channels for an alternative to gasoline. Without such distribution mechanisms, there is little incentive for automobile manufacturers to invest in development of vehicles designed for alternative fuel technologies.

At some point, limitations in supply or other developments may result in alternative fuels gaining popularity. However, as long as a dominant mode is "locked-in," it is very difficult to set a competing trend in motion. Feedback within the marketplace leads to a selection process which, for better or worse, creates long-lasting economic trends that are very difficult to reverse. Hence the reason for tenbagger and twentybagger stock returns is not just the whim of investors but the underlying fundamentals of the marketplace for goods and services. As long as the economy is growing, there will be an adequate supply of big winners to provide substantial gains for the patient investor.

Complexity and the Emergence of Bull Markets

The capital markets are another example of social complexity. They have existed for hundreds of years, more or less in the form we know them and longer, depending on how defined. In recent years, with the collapse of communism and a global race toward privatization, stock markets have emerged in nations that previously had banned such activity. Capital markets are a key part of the global economy.

If complexity theory can help us understand the origins of life, and the global economy, surely it can also help us recognize the origins of bull markets. Our nonlinear market model explains why at times the markets can in fact become more ordered, structured and predictable (i.e., bull or bear markets emerge). Empirical data from both practitioners and researchers supports this theoretical prediction.

While the origins of life are difficult to grasp even at the simulation level, the origins of bull market are easy enough to recognize. Our nonlinear market model involves an unstable state transition where large, long-lasting fluctuations must be expected. Below this critical point, the market is in equilibrium, a "do-nothing state" with expected returns following a normal distribution near the neighborhood of zero. However, above the critical point, there is "symmetry breaking" and the probability of large returns increases dramatically depending on the prevailing fundamentals.

Our nonlinear model of market state transitions involves two control parameters. The first is a measure of whether investor sentiment is above or below the critical flash point for group think; the second is a measure of the prevailing fundamental bias. The first measures the degree of feedback among market participants. Given that there is a high degree of interaction or coupling of opinions, the market is apt to move in large steps. However, the number of steps higher versus lower is determined by the prevailing bias in fundamentals.

This theoretical model shares many of the features we have observed in complex systems from other fields. In particular, it assumes that as the flow of money becomes large enough (i.e., the market is sufficiently far from equilibrium), there is a critical threshold above which a state transition occurs from disorder (true random walk) to more ordered or structured state (trending markets). In particular, the coherent market hypothesis maintains that under the right combination of control parameters, the risk-reward outlook for market returns becomes inverted (i.e., there is a strong likelihood of above average returns with below average risk) or, in other words, a bull market will emerge.

Is there any evidence that bull markets do emerge under these conditions? The answer is yes, absolutely! Brock shows that simple moving averages can be used to identify periods of above average returns with below average risk. However, the returns are not as large as theoretically predicted. Hence it should be possible to develop better technical and fundamental rules to zero in on coherent markets. Practitioners have done just that.

An analysis by Dr. Martin Zweig in *Barron's* (February 4, 1985) and updated later (*Barron's*, February 11, 1991) suggests that there are two important conditions near the beginning of every major bull market over the last 60 years. Zweig developed a trading signal that was based on two factors. The first was the ratio of advancing stocks to declining stocks on the New York Stock Exchange. If this ratio averaged 2:1 or better over a two-week period (which is not a very frequent occurrence), he defined the market to be in a breadth stampede. The second factor is an extremely positive reading in an indicator of Federal Reserve Board policy. Typically this requires two easing actions such as cuts in the discount rate or reserve requirements for member banks.

When both factors occur within a period of three months of each other, Zweig defines the event as a *double-barrel buy signal*. Table 2.1 summarizes the subsequent returns for the S&P 500 and the Zweig Unweighted Price Index (which is very similar to the Value Line Composite Index). Of interest is the fact that this signal caught all of the largest bull markets during the past 60 years. While the signal misses an early part of each move, there is enough persistence in the uptrends in each case to produce positive returns over the subsequent 3-, 6-, 12-, and 18-month periods following a double-barrel buy signal.

What is also interesting is that if the overlapping periods in 1932 and 1933 are annualized as a single period, then the average annualized returns

Table 2.1. Double-Barreled Buys vs. S&P 500, 1926 to 1988 (% Change in Index After Signal)

Date of buy	1 month	3 months	6 months	12 months*	18 months*
7/21/32	+48.7	+35.0	+40.6	+85.5	+85.5
5/26/33	+16.4	+20.8	+ 7.5	+ 4.4	+ 1.9
4/16/38	− 5.1	+14.1	+25.0	+ 4.1	+20.0
9/14/42	+10.3	+10.2	+29.4	+39.1	+42.9
7/13/49	+ 3.7	+ 8.1	+12.8	+12.9	+42.8
2/05/54	+ .8	+ 8.9	+15.5	+40.5	+61.8
1/24/58	− 2.5	+ 3.4	+11.8	+34.3	+43.0
12/4/70	+ 1.9	+ 9.5	+13.2	+ 8.5	+22.7
1/10/75	+ 7.9	+15.4	+30.6	+30.8	+44.6
1/23/85	+ 1.2	+ 2.6	+ 8.6	+15.2	+34.6
2/05/91					

SOURCE: Reprinted by permission of *Barron's*. © 1991 Dow Jones & Company, Inc. All rights reserved worldwide.

*12- and 18-month returns for 1932 buy signal are cut off on 5/26/33 in order to avoid overlap with the latter signal.

of all of Zweig's signals are approximately 25 percent for the S&P 500 while the standard deviation of returns is on the order of 10 percent. This is remarkably consistent with the theoretical forecasts of the coherent market hypothesis. What Zweig calls a breadth stampede can be interpreted as evidence of market sentiment conducive to positive feedback, or *crowd behavior*. This coupled with a very liberal (stimulative) Federal Reserve policy as a measure of positive fundamentals meet the conditions for the emergence of a coherent bull market. This evidence supports the concept that there are state transitions in the capital markets, which lead to more structured and predictable behavior in market returns.

Obviously, there is only a small sample of data. The conditions for runaway bull markets don't occur that often. So we must be careful not to jump to far-reaching conclusions. However, it's nice to see that there is some evidence that what theory suggests should happen, has happened with remarkable consistency. And by the way, Zweig's most recent signal also turned out to be correct; the latest signal really was a bull market in spite of historically high valuations!

3

Indicators of Chaos: Diagnostic and Predictive Tools

The physicist Doyne Farmer glances at his audience. More than 200 Wall Street analysts and money managers stare back, their eyes both eager and hostile. They want Farmer to deliver. If he's right, the stock market is predictable and orderly. If he's wrong, this is yet another hoax; they've heard these promises before and seen them turn to dust. Their restless shuffling as Farmer takes the stage is vaguely threatening. The previous speaker was heckled off the stage by red-faced analysts shouting "bull---."

JIM JUBAK
"Can Chaos Beat the Market," *Worth*, March 1993

Fuzzy Day 1992: The "Woodstock of Chaos" for Financial Quants

Doyne Farmer is the dean of chaos theory; he is also a gambler. He has taken time off from his pursuit of esoteric nonlinear theories in physics to study the gaming tables in Las Vegas, looking for slight imperfections and imbalances in roulette wheels that can shift the odds in his favor. Now he heads the Prediction Company, developing a nonlinear trading strategy for the commodity and financial markets. Farmer was a key speaker at Fuzzy Day 1992. Each year the Society of Quantitative Analysts (SQA) in New York is host to Fuzzy Day. Members and guests devote a full day to exploration of emerging technologies which may in the future have practical applications for the professional investment community. The May 1992 program was on "Chaos and Nonlinear Prediction: Financial Market Applications." As Arnie Wood of Martingale Asset Management observed, it turned out to be "a Woodstock event." Certainly the meeting hall was overflowing as over 200 financial "quants" gathered for the event and the colorful, computer-generated fractal graphics added a certain psychedelic effect.

SQA president Bruce Smith, a portfolio manager with the State of New Jersey's Department of Treasury, had assembled an all-star cast of chaos theorists and practitioners, as well as multi-media displays of fractals and strange attractors. The speakers included physicists, mathematicians, and financial professionals. All had published significant works or were practitioners making use of chaos theory in their investment endeavors. An air of excitement prevailed in the crowded meeting room of the Twin Towers Marriott under the shadow of the World Trade Center.

Jubak captures the mood of the audience at Fuzzy Day 1992. It was a tough crowd and Farmer rose to the occasion. No, he didn't deliver the Holy Grail—that magic get rich quick chaos formula. Nor did he offer up much hope that such a formula exists at all. But he did present convincingly the concept that even if a small part of the market's dynamics are predictable, that can be used to make a lot of money.

Doyne Farmer is one of the leading researchers in the field. He cut his teeth on problems involving nonlinear dynamics at the Los Alamos National Laboratory in New Mexico. He has published extensively on chaos, fractal structures, and empirical time series analysis. Currently, he leads a group of seven physicists, all specialists in nonlinear systems analysis, in the pursuit of forecasting models for the financial markets. His Prediction Company has been retained by O'Conner Associates specifically for investment application development. So when Doyne spoke at Fuzzy Day, everyone listened.

Farmer earned the respect of the crowd by defining his terms. *Fractal, fractal dimension, chaos, nonlinear,* and *noise* are all terms used rather loosely and may mean different things to different people. Defining these terms carefully was time well spent. We will also endeavor to define such terms in this chapter relying in part on the work of Farmer and other speakers at Fuzzy Day 1992.

Farmer suggested that the physics of fluid turbulence went through a period similar to where the financial research is now. Back in the 1970s, papers attacked *turbulent fluid flow* as a random process. In fluid dynamics, there is a critical state transition from laminar flow to turbulence, controlled by the *Reynolds number* (a Reynolds number well above a critical threshold predictably leads to very turbulent fluid flow). Early work thought of turbulence as completely random; more recent work shows large-scale and small-scale structure. Near the critical transition threshold there is low-dimensional chaos.

Farmer suggested that determinism and randomness can coexist. A nonlinear system may be 95 percent random and 5 percent low-dimensional (i.e., predictable) dynamics. Given the low standards of predictability that are required in financial markets (i.e., the goal is to do better than the random walk benchmark), even a five percent predictable component can be very profitable. In Farmer's words you "don't need much low-dimensional stuff to get rich."

The problem in financial markets is to find the hidden structure. This is akin to finding the vortices in a highly turbulent fluid or the major weather patterns in a satellite photograph. Once you get to that point you hope to construct a nonlinear model and make short-term predictions which on average will be better than any predictions possible with linear methods. Farmer's Prediction Company is developing nonlinear models to make short-term market forecasts.

Farmer's analogy between fluid dynamics and the capital markets is particularly interesting. The state transitions in fluids are directly analogous to the market state transitions predicted by our simple nonlinear market model. After Fuzzy Day 1992 ended, I asked Farmer if he had looked for state transitions in his analysis of financial time series. He said he hadn't. Unlike fluid flow problems where the experimenter is free to change pressure (Reynolds number component), Farmer suggested he had no ability to do that in financial markets. Yet the Fed often adjusts interest rates, depending on its perception of the economic environment, and capital markets may frequently be transitioning between high-dimensional (unpredictable) states to more coherent, low-dimensional (more predictable) states.

In the physical sciences, there is a subculture interested in *open systems* (i.e., those far from equilibrium). Prigogine's Nobel prize in 1977 recognized the importance of work in this area. In systems which exhibit state transitions, the issue is not simply whether or not there is low-dimensional chaos; rather the problem is how to identify the conditions under which disordered behavior may at times become more ordered. What are the conditions necessary for the evolution of life? What are the conditions (economic Reynolds number) for bull and bear markets in the jargon of traditional investors?

In a letter to the editor of *Physics Today* in February 1979, I suggested that "the market may be considered an open system in which an adequate flow of money will create a transition from disorder (random walk) to order (cooperative or crowd behavior)." Such state transitions involve major changes in the risk-reward profile of each state as predicted by our nonlinear market model. While the investor can't control Fed policy, clearly the Fed's actions create a persistent bias that is closely watched by traditional investors as a clue to the prevailing risk-reward outlook for the stock and bond markets.

So far, no one has been able to predict the path of turbulent fluid flows. However, the aviation industry has compiled a respectable if not perfect safety record because the Reynolds number enables aeronautical engineers to design aircraft wings for the reliable lift provided by laminar flow and pilots are trained to avoid operating under conditions that lead to turbulence and loss of lift.

Likewise, so far, no one has been able to predict the future path of the stock market, even for short periods into the future. Farmer's methods represent the best hope for doing so. If he is successful, it would be a revolutionary achievement with major benefits for short-term traders and market makers. However, it is not the only way to apply nonlinear dynamics to the investment process.

An alternative goal in capital market research should be the identification of the economic Reynolds number which reliably predicts transitions from random states or high-dimensional chaos to more coherent, low-dimensional chaotic states. Traditional money managers rely on heuristic market Reynolds numbers such as price-to-earnings ratios, price-to-book ratios, dividend yield levels, and so on to avoid the most turbulent market periods and stocks. By successfully predicting market state transitions, more accurate assessments can be made of the market's risk-reward profile over periods of time of greater interest to intermediate traders and long-term investors.

We will look at state transitions and stochastic forecasting methods in later chapters. The remainder of this chapter describes some of the concepts and techniques applicable to the field of deterministic chaos theory. While there has been little success to date in the development of successful short-term deterministic prediction tools, some of the key concepts, such as chaotic attractors, are also applicable to our nonlinear stochastic model.

Dynamical Systems: The Limits of Predictability

Dynamics is a branch of physics concerned with the behavior of systems. Newton's laws of motion, first stated more than 300 years ago, together with knowledge of the initial conditions of a system, provide a basis for prediction of the state of the system into the future. It was widely assumed that if the initial conditions of every atom were known, with enough computational power, one could predict arbitrarily far into the future.

Quantum physics threw out this idea. The *uncertainty principle* of quantum mechanics states that it is impossible to pinpoint the initial conditions of any system perfectly. There is a tradeoff between the location and momentum uncertainties, such that the product of these is on the order of Planck's constant. While this is a very small number, conceptually it represented a very large change in how physicists were forced to view the world.

While quantum mechanics deals with the microscopic world of atomic systems, another revolution has been brewing in the past two decades which is of greater relevance on our everyday level of experience. Much as quantum mechanics places bounds on our ability to predict precisely the future of an atomic system, we now must accept that we can't predict very far into the future, even with some relatively simple systems that we see in the world around us.

Chaos theory, or more generally, the *theory of nonlinear dynamic systems* has seen an explosion of research in recent years, as evidenced by an exponential growth in the number of publications in both research journals and popular articles. James Gleick popularized this emerging new science with a highly readable description of an otherwise abstract topic. Gleick's timing was impeccable, his book hitting the street shortly after Wall Street's Crash of 1987 which gave impetus to financial research related to chaos theory.

Chaos involves, by definition, a loss of predictability or knowledge of prior history at an exponential rate. For example, if a system is in a state with uncertainty, N_0, at time t_0, then its future state, N, will show a growth of uncertainty determined by

$$N = N_0 e^{ht} \tag{3.1}$$

where h is the *Lyapunov exponent* of the system. A positive value of h implies exponential growth in uncertainty and hence represents an indicator of chaos.

Figure 3.1 illustrates the growth of uncertainty in a chaotic system as trajectories in phase space diverge at an exponential rate. This can occur in low-dimensional systems and implies that relatively simple nonlinear models may also be able to account for chaotic dynamics. Since uncertainty grows exponentially even for simple models of chaos, long-term forecasting becomes impossible. However, for systems such as the financial markets any improvements in short-term forecasting could be extremely important.

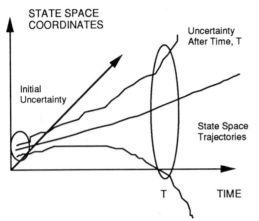

Figure 3.1. An exponential growth in uncertainty is an indicator of chaotic dynamics.

We have introduced a number of concepts that are inherent in the language and methods of dynamic systems and chaos theory. *Phase space, dimension,* and *Lyapunov exponents* are all part of the jargon of nonlinear systems and are typically described in great detail in the growing list of books on this subject. Here we will include basic definitions, enough to make clear how these concepts are being used to analyze financial markets and to present results that are important to practitioners.

Phase Space: Chaotic and Strange Attractors

A *phase space* or *state space* is another way to represent information contained in a time series. One reason for drawing a state space is to avoid the need for drawing a chart that is extremely long. For example, the time history of a simple pendulum leads to a periodic chart as shown in Fig. 3.2a where the amplitude of the cycle dies down to zero due to friction forces. Figure 3.2b shows a corresponding phase space portrait where the x axis represents the position of the pendulum, and the y axis represents its velocity at that point.

For a pendulum, the velocity is just the rate at which the position changes with time. The pendulum's position could also represent the price of a stock or the return from the market averages. In that case, the velocity of the pendulum represents the change in price over time or rate of return. From this point of view, the phase portrait of the pendulum simply shows returns as a function of price, as orbits in phase space.

PENDULUM
TIME SERIES

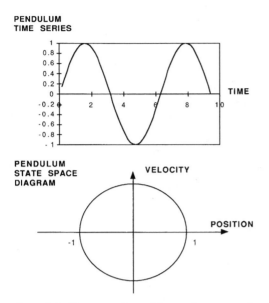

PENDULUM
STATE SPACE
DIAGRAM

Figure 3.2. The motion of a pendulum can be represented as either a time series or as elliptical trajectories in state space.

Unfortunately, the pendulum's orbit in phase space isn't as useful for predicting stock market fluctuations as it is for predicting the behavior of clocks and other physical problems. There is a school of thought that the market's behavior is not unlike a pendulum motion, in which valuation levels swing from extremes of under valuation and pessimism to overvaluation and optimism. However, a nonlinear pendulum, which exhibits chaotic motion is a far better model of market action than the simple linear pendulum. Furthermore, the element of chance or noise further complicates the analogy of the pendulum and financial markets.

In physics, there are two broad categories of dynamic systems. *Conservative systems* do not lose energy. In contrast, *dissipative systems* lose energy through mechanisms such as friction in the pendulum example. Dissipative systems tend to spiral toward a stable or fixed point attractor in phase space, unless additional energy is pumped in from an external source.

Dissipative systems which are far from equilibrium, therefore, represent a class of dynamic systems in which there is a flow of energy that keeps the system in motion. This is the class of problems that we are most interested in since the market represents a flow mechanism, with money always flowing from buyers to sellers. Depending on the supply and demand factors, a market may either move toward a point attractor in state space or follow a stable elliptic trajectory.

One of the key properties of a dissipative system in physics is that its motion is not invariant under time reversal. In the case of a dissipative pendulum, the motion in state space gradually spirals inward to a state of rest as friction converts kinetic energy to heat. The reverse process of heating a pendulum will not cause it to widen its trajectory in state space. A dissipative system, therefore, requires a constant input of energy to maintain a given trajectory in state space. The analogy here with the markets is that there are costs of doing business in the financial markets; money is always being taken out by brokers charging commissions, managers charging fees, and governments collecting taxes. A market requires constant replenishment in the form of investors with new capital to maintain a given pattern in state space.

A closed trajectory in state space represents periodic motion. The motion of the dissipative pendulum describes a curve spiraling inward toward the fixed point at which the pendulum has come to rest. The fixed point represents an "attractor" of the system in state space; regardless of the initial energy and trajectory of the pendulum, it's motion converges toward the attractor.

The pendulum represents a very simple example of a dynamic system and is useful to illustrate the concepts of trajectories in state space. Other dynamic systems follow more complicated trajectories and may be characterized as having more complicated attractors. These systems do not follow simple periodic motions. Chaotic systems governed by strange attractors, for example, may exhibit motions in state space which never repeat exactly even though the global motion is confined to a particular region of the space.

One of the best known attractors is the *Lorenz attractor*. At Fuzzy Day 1992, SQA President Bruce Smith presented a videotaped interview with Dr. Lorenz describing his research in the early 1960s on the characteristics of this set of nonlinear differential equations. The state space representation of orbits on the Lorenz attractor is shown in Fig. 3.3. This model was originally used by Lorenz in connection with attempts to make weather forecasts. Since those early days, the Lorenz attractor has been widely studied by numerous researchers. It is a prime example of low-dimensional chaos.

One of the applications of the *Lorenz attractor* has been in the area of laser physics. In fact, the problem of the transition from ordinary random light to coherent laser light can be set up as a set of three nonlinear differential equations that correspond to the Lorenz equations. Depending on the control parameter values, the system may or may not exhibit chaotic fluctuations. This connection with the laser is of special interest since the laser model also underlies the coherent market hypothesis.

Transitions from random walk to coherent or chaotic states was illustrated previously in Chap. 1 as being governed by a two well potential function. We did not begin with the more complicated set of laser equations

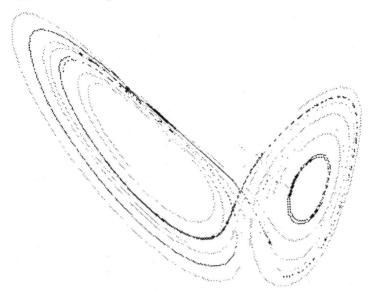

Figure 3.3. Orbits for the Lorenz attractor are not periodic, yet they are confined to a limited region of the state space. The Lorenz attractor is an example of a low-dimensional chaotic attractor, that is based on a set of three coupled nonlinear differential equations.

which correspond to the Lorenz attractor. However, if one looks at the trajectories in state space that are associated with the Lorenz attractor, it is evident that the system tends to spend more time at the extremes of the range of motion than near the middle. This is the same type of behavior seen in the two well potential which constrains the dynamics to the extremes and away from the middle of the well.

The utility of concepts such as state spaces comes in characterizing the motion of chaotic systems. State space portraits take on *fractal structures* in which there is a self-similarity across different scales or levels of granularity at which we study the motion. In the stock market, for example, we may be interested in hourly, daily, weekly or monthly time series. However, just looking at the data, there may not be any distinguishing features based simply on the interval of time over which the data was sampled. This self-similarity characterizes some chaotic systems; it also characterizes random systems in that noise looks the same across a wide spectrum of characteristic times.

Many of the diagnostic tools for detecting chaos amount to measuring different characteristics of the phase space portrait of a time series. Among these is the estimate of the dimension of the dynamic system. In our example of the pendulum, our phase portrait was constructed in two dimensions and that is enough to characterize its motion. In general it may be necessary to construct higher dimensional state spaces to adequately capture the dynamics of some complex systems. Some systems involve fractional dimensions or fractal characteristics. Dimension is a measure of the complexity; fractals are a measure of the "strangeness."

Fractal Structure: Evidence of Market Nonlinearity

Michael Barnsley, co-founder and president of Iterated Systems, Inc. in Norcross, Georgia, specializes in fractal compression. His firm recently entered into an agreement with Microsoft, Inc. to commercialize the technology. The approach basically involves storing fractal algorithms which recreate a picture, rather than a voluminous bit pattern that exactly replicates the image. Self-similarity between large-scale objects and fine-grained details allow reuse of algorithms on different scales and compression ratios of 2000:1 have been demonstrated. The process can be done with special purpose chips or even in software on a PC in just a few minutes.

Barnsley hasn't applied his fractal replication process to the problem of market forecasting. However, at Fuzzy Day 1992 he suggested that simple linear models are not the way to go. Just looking at time series data suggests that there is structure in time series. Even simple jagged patterns are more apt to provide representations of market time series than straight line predictions.

Michael Barnsley characterizes fractal geometry as an extension of classical geometry. The latter provides "a first approximation" to the structure of physical objects, while fractal geometry can be used "to make precise models of physical structures from ferns to galaxies."

At Fuzzy Day, Michael Barnsley described how it has taken five years of intensive research to go from simple fractal geometries such as a Serpinski triangle to more complex pictures. His company, Iterated Systems, has grown from 3 employees in 1987 when they were first learning to represent simple, self-similar structures such as ferns, to 87 employees in 1992. He claims the highest density of fractal geometers in the world among his workforce and they now can achieve compression ratios of 2000:1, which is the expansion factor of predicted output versus input data.

Barnsley suggested that some fractal algorithms looked suspiciously like stock charts. He suggested that stock market researchers need to match the data with models that have the same characteristics as the data, not to try to fit smooth curves to jagged time series. For example, a coastline is complicated; there is no advantage to trying to model it with polynomial-based curves.

As an example of a fractal structure and the underlying structure, Barnsley explained the basis of his chaos game. The corners of an equilateral triangle define three equally spaced points. Starting at an arbitrary point, the rules of the game are to move halfway toward a particular point depending on the outcome of a roll of a die. For example, a 1 and 6 may correspond to point 1; a 2 and 5 may correspond to point 2, and a 3 and 4 correspond to point 3. The roll of the die is random. However, after enough rolls, the pattern of points begins to trace out the Serpinski triangle, the underlying attractor of the dynamics of this simple system.

Barnsley's approach to image replication is based on modifications to the rules of the chaos game. By means of rotations and rescaling of simple objects he is able to replicate complex patterns with simple algorithms rather than storing the complex pattern itself on a bit-by-bit basis. Each chaos game or algorithm has its own set of rules and corresponds to a unique picture. A computer allows use of processing power rather than memory to recreate the picture rapidly based on the rules or the attractor.

Another of the Fuzzy Day speakers, David Sarfatti, President of Fractal Markets, Inc., described the use of fractals in option trading. Sarfatti suggested that the trading process is loaded with nonlinear effects. Markets are "self-aware." But if they are too self-aware, they will shut down.

According to Sarfatti, there is a need to consider the intrinsic time scale of a process. In game theory, there is no time scale. With macroeconomics, data typically comes out on a monthly or quarterly basis. With options, however, traders are interested in a much shorter time scale. They are interested in tic data and moment by moment fluctuations and they are interested in volatility. Options premiums increase as volatility increases.

Traders buy low volatility and sell high volatility. At least that is the simple goal of many options traders. They use charts to look for periods of abnormally low volatility and buy, assuming that volatility will again increase in the future. Likewise they sell periods of high volatility, assuming that it will again relax back to normal levels in the future. In effect, this assumes that volatility in state space follows a simple pendulum pattern, swinging from highs to lows and back again.

Sarfatti suggested that periods of high volatility are preceded by "periods of intense fractal activity." Unfortunately he didn't define what that meant or how it should be measured. However, by using some measure of this "fractal activity" to predict "impending volatility" and comparing that with the "implied volatility" of traditional option models, Sarfatti suggests that one could achieve the inverse of fractal compression and expand kilobucks into megabucks.

Farmer defines a fractal as something that exhibits "structure" across a range of scales. For example if you look at something with a microscope you find interesting features across a wide range of magnification factors. While neither Farmer nor Barnsley related fractals directly to the stock market, the idea of self-similarity is essentially captured in the power law distribution associated with self-organized criticality. Assuming that stock market fluctuations follow a power law distribution at a point of self-organized criticality (or for that matter, a Fed induced critical state) then there is the possibility that anomalous fluctuations on a short time scale will evolve and grow into critical fluctuations on a longer time scale far more frequently than would be expected from just a random noise process.

This idea is also at the heart of the *Elliott wave concept* popularized by A.J. Frost and Robert Prechter, Jr. The Elliott wave principle is based on the idea of self-similarity across a wide variety of time scales. A bull market is made of three major upleg cycles interrupted by corrections. However, each of these cycles is also made up of three smaller upleg cycles and the correction is made up of two major downward cycles interrupted by an upward cycle. This structure is assumed to be repeated across different time scales which are known as the *degree of the wave*. This is clearly reminiscent of the chaos game in which simple rules are replicated on a variety of scales to build up a complex pattern. The Elliott wave is a good descriptor of market patterns which aren't straight lines, but rather made up of jagged sequences.

Mandelbrot suggests that nature is full of objects which aren't exactly cones, spheres, or straight lines. Rather they involve patterns that can better be described as something between simple integral-dimensional objects. For example, a sheet of paper is a two-dimensional object, but after it is folded, it takes on a bit of a three-dimensional shape. Folded many times, it may be better described as a three-dimensional object, but that is not quite precise either since it is really a folded two-dimensional object.

Fractals come in both *deterministic* and *statistical* forms. Barnsley's work focuses on the former and has found important applications in the compression of information for storage and transmission. Random fractals deal with probabilities and in particular the structure of the fat tails on some probability distributions. Financial and economic series frequently show fat-tailed distributions, and hence random fractals may well be more important than deterministic counterparts.

Fractal structures typically exhibit structure across a range of scales. For example, a ball of yarn looks quite different depending on the scale on which it is examined. It resembles a mathematical point when viewed from far away. Closer, it has the appearance of a solid sphere, a three-dimensional object. However, at very close range, it appears to be comprised of strands of material which are one-dimensional objects. The strands in turn are made up of fibers, and so on down to the atomic level where the individual molecules of the material again begin to look like mathematical points.

In economics and financial markets, the structure of price changes has a similar look across many time scales. Hourly plots of stock market data look similar to daily, weekly, and even monthly plots. Here it is difficult to find structure on any particular time scale, other than the fat tails on the price change probability distributions. However, the deviation from a true normal distribution is evidence of an underlying fractal structure.

Edgar Peters, another speaker at Fuzzy Day 1992 and author of *Chaos and Order in the Capital Markets*, suggests that there is an underlying nonlinear or fractal structure in the capital markets. This structure may be ignored as a first approximation. However, the *fat tails*, by definition, mean that there are more large price changes or financial landslides than would be expected by chance alone. This, in turn, raises the possibility that nonlinear models and methods of analysis can be successfully developed and used to advantage by practitioners.

Peters also notes that the stable Paretian distribution originally presented by Mandelbrot appears to capture the *fat tail effect*. In his critique of our coherent market hypothesis (CMH), Peters notes that within the framework of the CMH the average state of the market may well be the unstable transition state. We agree with this notion of an "average" state, assuming the average is made up of periods of time in true random walk, or in the chaotic or coherent states which surround the unstable transition region.

In any event, the market as a dissipative system, reacts to a flow of money quite differently in each of its states. The true random walk would not produce a fractal structure or self-similarity in any structure other than noise across time scales. However, in the unstable transition region or above transition in chaotic or coherent states, there would indeed by a degree of structure or order (i.e., trend persistence which is picked up by Peters' rescaled range analysis).

Fractal Dimension: Estimates of Complexity

Dimension is easy to understand in Euclidean geometry. A point has a dimension of zero. A line has a dimension of one, a plane a dimension of two, and so on. However, the dimension of a fractal structure is more difficult to characterize. It is a concept used to describe the degree of complexity for a particular dynamic system and is related to the number of *degrees of freedom* or dynamic variables needed to build a model of the system's motion. For example, a point attractor has dimension zero since motion always converges to a point regardless of where it originates. A limit cycle, which is described as a circle in phase space, has a dimension of one, since only a single variable is needed to completely specify its state.

However, chaotic systems have more complicated motions in phase space and they are also more difficult to characterize in terms of degrees of freedom. In these situations, the integral dimensions of Euclidean geometry must be replaced with fractional or fractal dimensions. Attractors in phase space which have nonintegral dimensions are called *strange attractors*.

Chaotic motion refers to the nonperiodic, random-like motion of a system. *Strangeness* refers to the geometry of the attractor in phase space which governs the motion. A few examples are in order. Moon suggests that "in some sense, we are entering the second phase of the Newtonian revolution in dynamics, and new geometric concepts such as fractals must be mastered if one is to use the results of the new dynamics in practical problems."

A simple example of a fractal structure is the *Cantor set*, presented in Fig. 3.4. The set is constructed by discarding the middle third of each line in the prior iteration. As the number of iterations becomes infinite, the length of the line segments approaches zero. However, this "dust" has a finite fractional dimension, less than that of a line (one dimensional), yet greater than that of a point (dimension zero).

To determine the dimension of a fractal, one approach is known as the *capacity dimension*. Here the problem is to determine how many small boxes are needed to package the fractal structure in question. For example, the number of boxes of size e, needed to cover a straight line is simply $1/e$. To cover a two-dimensional surface with small boxes of size e will require

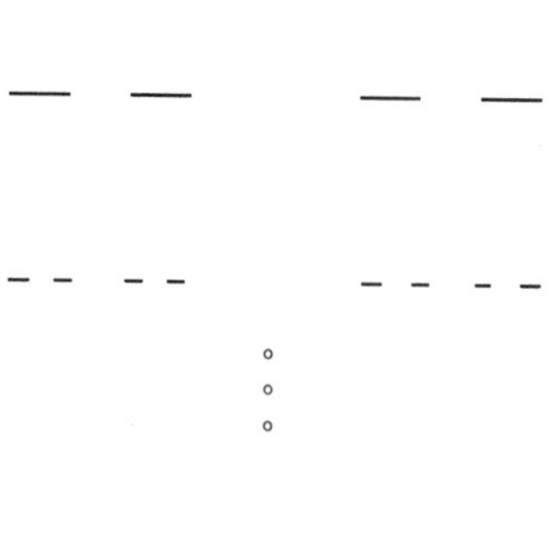

Figure 3.4. The Cantor set represents a simple fractal structure. It has a fractal dimension greater than a point yet less than a line.

approximately $1/e^2$ boxes. Increasing the approach inductively to higher dimensions suggests that the number of boxes needed to cover a d-dimensional surface will be $1/e^d$. Therefore, the capacity dimension is defined by

$$d_c = \lim_{e \to 0} [\log n\ (e)/\log(1/e)] \qquad (3.2)$$

If this number is not an integer, the term *fractal* is often used to characterize the associated geometry.

For the Cantor set, the capacity dimension is log 2/log 3. Two boxes are required to cover each line segment of the set and the size of each box is 1/3. Therefore $n(e) = 2$ and $1/e = 3$ and the ratio of the logarithms works out to be 0.63092. This makes sense intuitively as the Cantor set is something less than a line yet more than a point. Using the same approach, the Serpinski triangle has a fractal dimension of log 3/log 2.

There are other ways to characterize the dimension of a fractal structure. The pointwise dimension is based on the probability $P(r)$ of finding points in phase space within a distance, r, of some point on a trajectory in phase space. The pointwise dimension at a particular point, x_i, is then defined by

$$d_p = \lim_{r \to 0} \log P\ (r, x_i)/\log r \qquad (3.3)$$

This dimension estimate can then be averaged over some part, M, of interest in phase space.

Correlation dimensions are based on the work of Grassberger and Proccacia. Brock focuses on the application of this indicator in economic and financial situations. Computation of the correlation dimension involves determining the distance between pairs of points on a trajectory in phase space and counting the number of pairs within some distance, r. The computation is performed by constructing a sphere or cube at each point x_i in phase space and counting the number of points in each sphere. Therefore

$$C(r) = \lim_{r \to 0} 1/N^2 \sum_i^N \sum_j^N H\ (r - [x_i - x_j]) \qquad (3.4)$$

where $H(s) = 1$ if $s > 0$ and $h(s) = 0$ if $s < 0$. Unlike the pointwise dimension calculation, the sums are performed around every point and the dimension estimate then becomes

$$d_g = \lim_{r \to 0} \log C\ (r)/\log r \qquad (3.5)$$

The correlation dimension is the basis for statistical hypothesis testing.

Rescaled Range Analysis: Evidence of Persistent Trends

Edgar Peters' method for searching for structure in financial time series is known as *rescaled range analysis*. This was originally developed by hydrologist Harold Edwin Hurst who developed the method to study flooding of the Nile River in Egypt. Hurst was involved in the Nile River Dam Project near the beginning of the century and was searching for a way to manage the discharge of the dam to ensure a constant amount of water each year.

Hurst postulated that the range of fluctuations in river levels, normalized by the standard deviation of the fluctuations, would follow a power law of the form

$$R/S = aN^H \tag{3.6}$$

where R is the range (i.e., maximum influx relative to average less minimum influx relative to average), S is the standard deviation of the observations, a is a constant, N is the number of observations, and H is the "Hurst" exponent.

If the river influx is a random process, the Hurst exponent would be 0.5. In other words, the range divided by the standard deviation would scale according to the same process that underlies the random walk problem. However, values of H between 0.5 and 1.0 indicate that there is a greater degree of persistence than would be expected from chance alone. Likewise, with values between 0 and 0.5, there would be less persistence than would be expected from chance.

For the Nile River, Hurst found an exponent of 0.9. Apparently, the influx data for the Nile are highly trend persistent, an effect which Mandelbrot characterized as the *Joseph effect* (i.e., seven good years followed by seven years of famine). In the financial markets, Peters has found Hurst coefficients substantially higher than 0.5 as well. For example, the S&P 500 index, Peters found a Hurst exponent of 0.78. Hence the stock market, as the Nile River tends to produce periods of consistently above average returns followed by periods of below average returns. Peters results are illustrated in Fig. 3.5.

The Hurst exponent is related to the correlation coefficient, C, according to

$$C = 2^{(2H-1)} - 1 \tag{3.7}$$

Hence a Hurst coefficient of 1 implies perfect correlation while 0.5 corresponds to uncorrelated noise. A Hurst coefficient below 0.5 is indicative of less persistence than expected by chance.

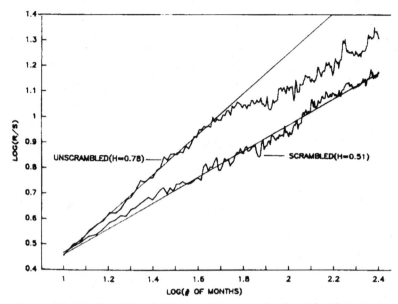

Figure 3.5. Edgar Peters' Rescaled Range analysis suggests that there is fractal structure in the stock market. Peters has proposed the fractal market hypothesis to account for nonlinear capital market dynamics. (*Reprinted with permission from* Financial Analysts Journal, *November/December 1992.* © *1992 Association for Investment Management and Research, Charlottesville, VA. All rights reserved.*)

Stability Analysis: Lyapunov Exponents

Another key diagnostic indicator of chaos is the *Lyapunov exponent.* Fuzzy Day 1992 featured professor Allan Wolf of the Cooper Union in New York City as a luncheon speaker.

Dr. Wolf is known for his work on an algorithmic approach for extracting Lyapunov exponents in empirical time series. Lyapunov exponents are a necessary but not sufficient condition for chaos.

Wolf spoke of type A chaotic systems (low-dimensional, potentially predictable system) and type B chaotic systems (high-dimensional, unpredictable system). His approach works well for type A systems. However, with low-dimensional problems one should be able to construct simple theoretical nonlinear models of the underlying process (e.g., the Lorenz attractor is governed by three coupled nonlinear differential equations) in which case the Lyapunov exponents can be determined from the theoretical model.

Wolf has compared theoretical Lyapunov exponents with empirical results and found agreement within about 10 percent for known attractors.

Wolf's algorithm for the computation of the Lyapunov exponents is available for use on personal computers. He has provided over 500 copies of his software package to researchers in various fields. Unfortunately, according to Dr. Wolf, less than 10 percent make proper use of the algorithm.

At Fuzzy Day 1992, Dr. Wolf delved into the uses and abuses of diagnostic tools for testing for chaos in time series. His comments were largely directed at applications made in the physical sciences. However, they are also particularly apt in financial time series where there is little evidence of low-dimensional chaos (i.e., type A chaos which, by definition, is governed by a few degrees of freedom and is not corrupted by noise). Dr. Wolf is particularly interested in low-dimensional chaos in simple toys.

Examples of low-dimensional chaotic systems are the Lorenz attractor which has a fractal dimension of 2.06. Wolf also had numerous other examples of type A chaotic systems, most of which were simple physical toys that exhibited complex motions, unpredictable, never repeating, yet capable of being modeled by a few differential equations. One example, the Wildwood pendulum, describes the motion of a magnetic pendulum moving around five fixed magnets near its base. Here time series analysis conforms nicely with theoretical model predictions.

Lyapunov numbers characterize how the phase space trajectories of a dynamic process evolve. In general, there may be more than one Lyapunov number, depending on the dimension of the problem, but as long as the largest number is greater than zero, there is the potential for exponential growth in uncertainty. Hence Lyapunov numbers are an important diagnostic indicator of chaos.

The method developed by Wolf to compute Lyapunov numbers is based on a calculation of the distance separating adjacent trajectories in phase space. If the initial distance between the trajectories is N_0, then after a small interval of time, the new distance, N, is given by Equation 3.1. If the Lyapunov number is $h < 0$, the trajectories will converge at an exponential rate; if $h > 0$, the trajectories will diverge exponentially.

For most physical problems, trajectories in phase space will diverge only in particular neighborhoods of phase space. If a system is bounded globally, then trajectories in phase space must bend back and converge over some larger region. Therefore, the calculation of Lyapunov number, h, will yield different results at different points in phase space. Hence an iterative process is required to perform the calculation and the results are averaged together.

The procedure for performing Lyapunov number calculations developed by Wolf picks a particular trajectory in phase space and computes the ratio of $d(t)/d_0$, where d_0 is the distance to some nearby trajectory. The process is repeated if the initial trajectories move too far apart. Results are then averaged over time so that the Lyapunov number in a particular dimension is

$$h = (1/(t_N - t_0)) \sum_{k=1}^{N} \log_2 [d(t_k)/d_0(t_{k-1})] \qquad (3.8)$$

An average greater than zero is an indication of the potential for chaos.

Wolf's algorithm for computing Lyapunov exponents works well for type A chaotic systems but not for type B, which involve many degrees of freedom, and may be strongly influenced by noise. The algorithm tracks nearby points in phase space and determines how rapidly the trajectories diverge. As the points become so far apart as to be causally unconnected, a new set of points is picked and the process is repeated. This is computationally very intensive, but will converge to a number (the average rate of divergence for all sets of points).

Unfortunately the amount of data required to perform Lyapunov calculations is very large. For example, Wolf suggests that at least 30 points are required for a single trajectory. He also suggests that at least 30^d points are needed for a system of dimension, d. For a Lorenz attractor with dimension slightly higher than 2, only about 900 points are required. However, a problem with dimension 4 would require nearly a million points and so forth for higher dimensional systems.

Many researchers have claimed evidence of chaos with far less data to back up the claim. As Wolf puts it, they "get the software on Tuesday, run it on Wednesday, and publish on Thursday." Most researchers fail to test whether their results are independent of the parameters used to reconstruct the state space. If results vary with these parameters, they are of questionable significance.

While Wolf expressed considerable skepticism in the application of his algorithm for high-dimensional problems, he was even more skeptical of diagnostic tests of the fractal dimension. A few tips here from Wolf were to first provide graphic illustrations of the time series and state space. If these pictures look "dirty" to the eye, the problem is probably a high-dimensional one for which the algorithms for dimension estimates won't work.

One problem with dimension estimates is that chaos is typically associated with fractional dimensions. Hence the error bars around dimension estimates need to be at least less than ±0.5 and ought to be ±0.1. Unfortunately this level of accuracy can't be achieved for most empirical time series. Actual error bars are more likely to be on the order of ±1.0, or even higher.

Wolf concluded that the diagnostic testing of time series is still in its infancy. Current methods simply aren't applicable to type B chaos which is where financial data appear to fall. A quick scan shows that if the data is a mess, the algorithms won't work. Equally important, if the data is neat and clean, there should be simple theoretical models of the dynamics and the algorithms aren't needed.

In spite of Wolf's warnings, financial researchers have sought to compute dimension and Lyapunov estimates with modest amounts of data. For example, dimension estimates for the S&P 500 have ranged from as low as 2.3 by Peters, to approximately 6 by Sheinkman and LeBaron. Our own model suggests that financial data is always noisy (many degrees of freedom) but that there is at times, the coupling among these subsystems constrains the randomness to a double well attractor, which is a well studied problem and covered extensively by Moon.

For example, the correlation dimension of the Lorenz attractor is 2.06 and the two well potential or Duffing oscillator has a correlation dimension of 2.14 for a particular driving frequency. The latter is also the attractor underlying chaotic states within our nonlinear market model. However, the attractor in our nonlinear model may change as a result of changes in the control parameters. Furthermore, with the S&P 500, there is no periodic forcing function; the random forces are assumed to be delta correlated and the correlation coefficient replaces the magnitude of the periodic force.

Kolmogorov's Theorem: It Pays to Be Smart

Kolmogorov is the Russian mathematician who was instrumental in the initial development of probability theory. Some of his work was addressed at Fuzzy Day 1992 by Professor John Hubbard, a mathematician at Cornell University. Dr. Hubbard is a pure mathematician who is involved in topology and geometry.

Dr. Hubbard showed a videotaped presentation of the Mandelbrot set and zoomed in toward one particular point. The computer presentation was based on work performed at the Fractal Research Center and the Cornell Supercomputer Facility and illustrated the remarkable degree of complexity that can arise from even the simplest processes. Twenty years ago, people didn't realize that very simple processes could give rise to pictures of extraordinary complexity. Furthermore, standard statistical tests are incapable of finding this complexity.

Dr. Hubbard suggested that one could adopt either of two views with respect to complexity. One is that it is an awful situation: even the simplest things appear to be incomprehensible. The other view is to be hopeful; even if the data looks like a mess, there could be a very simple pattern behind it. Barnsley's work is clearly along the lines of the hopeful. Wolf's comments were just the opposite; the situation with high-dimensional, type B chaos is just awful. There's never enough data to say anything with any degree of confidence.

Kolmogorov brought out the notion of complexity in a statistical sense. He worked on the notion of how dense the information content of a string is. This can be thought of as the ratio of the program size that will print out the string, compared to the size of the string itself. Most strings never have a density much greater than 1, or much less than 1. A high-density string could be thought of as information rich; however, everything of interest is information poor. These notions carry over to the information in state space. An attractor in state space is just a picture that has a certain degree of complexity.

As examples of the density of information in a string, Dr. Hubbard suggested that living systems are specified by their DNA. A rabies virus has 20,000 base pairs of DNA; the fruit fly has 100,000 base pairs; the human has a billion base pairs; the frog has 43 billion and the water lilly has hundreds of billions. A person also has about 1000 trillion cells; the density is about 10^{-6}. In contrast a random sequence has a density of 1.

Professor Hubbard suggested that the Fuzzy Day group should be interested in the information density of the Dow Jones Average. Unfortunately, Dr. Hubbard confessed he had no idea of what that might be whatsoever. What Dr. Hubbard did offer was the idea that standard statistical tests are unlikely to discover anything about the simplicity that may underlie a string. He indicated that Kolmogorov's theorem explicitly rules out the ability of any process to infer whether a system is information rich or poor.

According to Dr. Hubbard, speaking at Fuzzy Day 1992:

> You aren't going to discover the pattern in the Dow Jones Average if you are stupid. But if you are smart, maybe you can. I personally view this [Kolmogorov's] theorem as extremely helpful. It sort of says "hey, it's worthwhile being smart." Because if you do these things the dumb way, you see, its not going to work. That's what's really being said by this theorem. If you just apply dumb procedures you are just not going to find out anything.
>
> You have to start out with a preconceived idea of what the structure of the market is and then build a model that builds in the structure and then you might try to adjust a few parameters. You cannot just hope to apply statistics and hope that patterns come out. The patterns just won't come out. Its also true that if patterns did come out all the stockbrokers would immediately know about it, everybody would discover it and nobody could profit from it.

We agree with Dr. Hubbard's idea that you need to start out with a preconceived model that has structure build into it. Clearly, if the market undergoes state transitions, the dynamics are governed by a different attractor in each state. Averaging data together from different states would hide any structure that may be present in each state.

State Space Reconstruction and Nonlinear Prediction

Our model of nonlinear market dynamics suggests that there are a number of market states, each with distinct attractors and associated risk-reward profiles. It further assumes that there is more involved than just deterministic processes that lead to complex behavior. The element of chance as well as coherent, chaotic, and unstable behavior characterize the markets. This is the rule rather than the exception in the complex systems we explored in Chap. 2. State transitions are a key characteristic of systems far from equilibrium However, statistical tests will not necessarily pick up the information inherent in such state transitions.

While our simple nonlinear market model exhibits many of the important features of nonlinear dynamic systems, there are an infinite number of nonlinear models that could be used. For example, J. Doyne Farmer and John J. Sidorowich observe that "finding a good representation is largely a matter of trial and error." In fact most of the work ongoing by researchers in the area of nonlinear financial modeling is based on methodologies that seek to fit models to empirical data. Typically, this involves the assumption that the time series is stationary (i.e., governed by a single attractor in state space which does not vary in time).

Under conditions of a stationary problem, the normal procedure is to reconstruct a state space from the empirical data. While there are a variety of ways to do this, normally a d-dimensional state vector is created by taking measurements at d points in time, each delayed by an interval ranging from T to $(d-1)T$. The delay interval, T, is arbitrary but should not be too large or the elements of the state vector become causally unrelated. The delay interval can be varied parametrically to search for the best results. The embedding dimension, d, can also be varied parametrically if the dimension of the attractor is unknown and should be greater than the dimension of the attractor.

After a state space representation has been constructed, a predictive model must be fit to the data. With powerful computers available at relatively low cost, a large set of candidate models can be evaluated in a reasonable amount of time. Farmer and Sidorowich suggest that polynomials are a good representation "because their parameters can be linearly fit to minimize least squares deviations, and because they arise naturally in Taylor expansions." We agree. In effect our nonlinear market model, presented in Chap. 1 can be expressed approximately in polynomial form. In fact we refer to our model as a simple, nonlinear model exactly for this reason. An inifinite number of other possible models could be constructed. However, the added benefits are not at all clear.

Our goal is not to make short-term predictions. Rather, it is to identify the applicable probability distribution governing fluctuations. In either case the control parameters or coefficients of the nonlinear model must be estimated to make either stochastic or deterministic predictions. This can be done by either inferring the coefficients based on fitting predictions to past data or relating the coefficients to other measureable factors that theoretically control the dynamics of the system. Empirical time series analysis attempts to do the former. A preconceived theory attempts to do the latter.

A popular nonlinear modeling technique is the use of neural networks. Neural networks seem to be unique and esoteric. In fact they are just another method of generating a nonlinear function to make short-term predictions. Neural networks have been used for both market timing and stock selection purposes. Tools exploiting this technology are commercially available from a variety of vendors.

Neuralware from Neural Ware, Inc. in Pittsburgh, advertises its product as "the Cadillac of neural network development systems." Neural Ware products have found applications in support of a variety of problems in business, industry, and government. Financial modeling, forecasting, and risk management are just one area of focus. Neural Ware also offers courses specifically related to the application of this technology in the area of market timing.

David Aronson of the Raden Research Group in New York offers professional investors its Automated Trading Logic Synthesizer (ATLS) as a tool for "developing multi-indicator nonlinear predictor-based trading models." Raden also offers consulting support to help clients tailor the technology to specific applications.

While neural networks have received much publicity in financial market applications, other technologies are also finding applications. For example, case-based reasoning technology has been offered by Cognitive Systems, Inc. of Boston, for intelligent retrieval of data from financial data bases. While this is more of a decision support tool than a nonlinear predictive model or black box, unlike neural networks which offer no explanation of forecasts, this approach provides well explained conclusions based on reasoning from prior similar experiences.

New technologies and tools are being rapidly developed and offered to investment professionals. Reviews of these tools can be found in magazines such as *Futures, Technical Analysis of Stocks and Commodities*, and *Wall Street and Technology. Business Week, Worth*, and *The Economist* have also addressed the subject of nonlinear prediction. Special conferences also offer opportunities for updates on technology. These may be expected from organizations such as the Society of Quantitative Analysts in New York, and the International Neural Network Society in Washington, DC.

While our intent is not to endorse any specific products, nonlinear prediction and decision support tools are rapidly becoming a competitive resource and discriminator for professional money managers. For example,

Dean Barr of LBS Capital Management in Shelter Harbor, Florida recently described the application of neural networks in stock selection and sector rotation at an SQA conference. He has successfully used this technology to achieve above average performance with below average risk, managing several hundred million dollars for institutional clients. LBS is also collaborating with Dr. Andrew Lo of MIT on neural network technology applications.

Summary

Nonlinear models are not difficult to define for the capital markets. The real problem comes in the estimation of the control parameters of the model (i.e., the coefficients of the nonlinear function). Here there are two choices. One is to assume no knowledge of the underlying dynamics and to infer the parameters purely from fitting the model to historical data. The other approach is to base the control parameter estimates on a preconceived theoretical model of the dynamic process.

Most researchers of financial time series analysis assume that the problem is stationary (i.e., doesn't change with time). That's the equivalent of assuming that a golfer will always use a single iron for all shots. That just isn't the case with most golfers and most nonlinear systems. A lot of statistical data on random light doesn't help one understand a coherent laser beam. President Bush's popularity in the Gulf War vanished when the economy began to slump.

Seasons change and so do weather patterns. The prudent sailor may choose to avoid trans-Atlantic crossings during hurricane season rather than attempt to predict the onset of a storm or avoid the path of the storm after it develops. While this is possible for the recreational sailor, those who always need to be on the open oceans are in need of the best predictions possible.

Nonlinear systems typically involve state transitions. For example, a fluid does not become turbulent until a set of conditions are met. These conditions, such as fluid velocity, pressure and characteristics of the environment in which the fluid flows are captured in an empirical measure known as the Reynolds number. Below a critical threshold, the fluid flow is laminar (i.e., smooth and predictable). Above the critical threshold it becomes turbulent or chaotic.

Chaos can be either good or bad. An aircraft wing must be designed for predictable lift under a wide range of dynamic conditions. Here the advent of turbulence is clearly undesirable, as it implies a loss of predictability and hence control over the desired behavior of the system. In other situations, chaotic dynamics is the preferred state. For example, the complex, unpredictable behavior of a living organism is normal. If an animal digresses to periodic, predictable behavior, it may not be able to adapt to its surroundings and compete in the "fitness" race. The zebra that fails to run unpredictably will quickly fall prey to the lion, ever vigilant for such abnormal behavior in a herd.

Diagnostic tools have been developed to determine whether a dynamic system is chaotic. Methods have also been developed to forecast the conditions under which the onset of chaos can be expected. Researchers of financial time series have focused primarily on diagnostic tests of chaos. However, there is some financial research regarding prediction of the conditions necessary for the onset of chaos, as for example, Maurice Larrain of Pace University whose suggests that there is orderly progress toward disorder in interest rates.

Most diagnostic tests assume either that the problem is stationary, or that the conditions describing the market do not change substantially over time. However, if periods of chaotic behavior are mixed in with random periods, then the diagnostic tests would suffer. Another problem is the limited availability of data in economic and financial situations, and the lack of repeatability or experimental control over an economy or financial market.

The aeronautical engineer is free to tune the wind tunnel and to redesign the aircraft's wing, repeating the diagnostic tests and predictive experiments as often as necessary to have confidence in the results. In contrast, the researcher of financial data has only a single time series for a given market and the amount of data available particularly for economic variables is far less than corresponding problems of the physical sciences. More important, the amount of data is small relative to what is needed to draw firm, statistically significant conclusions from the diagnostic tests.

In spite of severe limitations with the availability of financial data, the issue of prediction is vital to investment practitioners. Most efforts have focused on the development of short-term forecasting tools. The payoffs are large for traders or market makers where even a slight edge can lead to substantial rewards. However, equally important is the issue of prediction of the conditions necessary for the onset of chaos. What is the Reynolds number in the financial markets that describes the conditions necessary for the onset of chaos.

The state transitions that occur in nonlinear systems contain information. The entire computer industry depends on the ability of nonlinear electronic devices to switch between states. Likewise state transitions in the financial markets can be used to make investment decisions. The conditions for the emergence of bull markets in Chap. 2 illustrate the latter problem, where the combination of control parameters determine the emergence of either linear, chaotic, or coherent behavior. Predictive analysis related to control parameters does not seek to forecast the path of the market, but rather to predict the conditions under which the market may undergo a state transition and become chaotic.

Practitioners often use simple indicators to avoid the onset of chaos in the behavior of their investment portfolios. For example, value investors, by definition, steer clear of stocks with high price-to-earnings or high price-to-book multiples. Some have developed quantitative rules of thumb such as the P/E ratio divided by the earnings growth rate as a criteria for designing an investment portfolio that is least likely to encounter turbulence during rough market periods. This is not unlike the use of the Reynolds number in designing an aircraft wing. The point of such tools is not to predict either the path of the stock prices or the distribution of velocities within the turbulent fluid. Rather these indicators based on control parameters are used to predict the potential onset of chaotic market action or turbulent air flow over the aircraft's wing.

More sophisticated nonlinear modeling tools are now available at moderate costs and have been used by a growing number of professional investors. However, nonlinear tools require a considerable investment in development of specific applications. These tools cannot just be plugged in and turned on. The application of the technology requires insight into the underlying nonlinear dynamics.

4

Random Walk:
Just the First Step
Down Wall Street

Navellier's portfolios only seem to be full of risky stocks. There are stocks you've never heard of, often with wild price histories and earnings swings. Navellier is not looking for big companies that show a decade of consistent ten percent earnings growth. In fact, he's looking for the erratic company that has disappointed at one time or the one whose performance can't be predicted. But Navellier holds that this seeming risk is actually the key to extraordinary returns. The risk indeed is less than it seems, and the upside surprises are actually predictable. An investor can have it both ways, Navellier is arguing, if he is smart enough. Instead of seeking to eliminate risk, Navellier yearns to transform it into a source of consistent profits.

ANDREW FINEBERG,
"Mr. Perfect," Worth, *June 1993*

Louis Navellier:
Mr. Perfect

Louis Navellier is "Mr. Perfect." As noted by Andrew Fineberg, "His stocks go up 35 percent every year; maybe he does have it all figured out." Navellier publishes a market letter from his office in Incline Village, Nevada and has had one of the hottest track records in the recent bull market. Fineberg goes on to observe, "Louis Navellier thinks he has it all figured out. In fact, he believes that he's built the ultimate stock picking machine, a mathematical model that lets him perch on the edge of danger, right at the side of the cliff."

According to the *Hulbert Financial Digest*, Navellier's *MPT Review* has the highest performance rating over the past eight years with a total return of 748 percent. That represents a 30.6 percent annualized rate of return after allowance for commission costs. Over the same period, the Wilshire 5000 index gained 191 percent for a 14.3 percent annualized rate of return. Equally important, Navellier ranks highest on a risk-adjusted basis. This performance has not gone unnoticed and Navellier now manages some $600 million from his offices near the picturesque Lake Tahoe.

So what's going on here? Navellier's stated approach to investing is rooted in *modern portfolio theory*. Developed in the late 1950s, MPT as it is widely called, is the brainchild of Harry Markowitz who did his work at the University of Chicago. Markowitz won the Nobel prize in 1990 in recognition of his contribution to economic theory. Yet MPT has hardly captured the fancy of active managers. In fact, the theory is based on the efficient market hypothesis which maintains that beating the market is impossible without also taking proportionately higher risks.

How has Navellier harnessed this dusty academic model so successfully to capture big bucks on Wall Street? Has he just been lucky? MPT is concerned with the risks as well as the rewards of investing. According to Robert Hagin, a leading practitioner with MPT credentials, there are four basic types of MPT-based applications:

1. security valuation;
2. portfolio optimization;
3. performance measurement; and
4. asset allocation.

These functions rest on the theoretical foundations of the efficient market hypothesis, efficient capital market theory, and the capital asset pricing model.

As a finance major at the University of California, Navellier studied modern portfolio theory. The theory deals with both the performance and the riskiness or volatility of securities, individually and as baskets or portfolios of individual stocks. Quantitative measures of performance relative to the market average, known as *alpha*, and risk relative to a market average, known as *beta*, are fundamental aspects of the theory. Different investors have different risk tolerances. Hence MPT seeks to measure both the risk and performance of individual issues and to construct portfolios that optimize performance within the constraints of acceptable individual risk tolerance levels.

The *efficient market hypothesis* maintains that it is impossible to use technical and fundamental analysis to actually trade and beat the market. However, the *capital asset pricing model* maintains that a predictable relationship exists between the level of portfolio risk and the performance to be expected. Low risk takers should expect modest returns; higher risk is likewise expected to be rewarded by higher portfolio returns. These are the rational expectations of investors in efficient markets and the goal of active managers should be to construct portfolios of stocks that meet these goals for investors with specific objectives. One way to achieve these goals is through various asset allocation mixes between security classes with different risk-reward profiles.

A key aspect of MPT is the quantitative measurement of performance and risk. The widely used academic approach to this process is typically based on taking five years of historical data to evaluate how an individual stock is performing relative to the overall market, and how volatile it is relative to the market. The goal of academic work is to take a long enough sample of data so the measures of risk and reward can be approximately stationary (i.e., parameters that do not vary over time). Ideally, these numbers would be absolutes or invariant descriptors of particular securities that one could rely on to make investment decisions.

What occurred to Navellier, was that five years was too long period of time over which to take these measurements. If a stock has already outperformed the market for five years, how much longer is it likely to continue doing so? He tested alternative periods for making the same measurements of performance and risk. Finally, after trying a number of alternative time periods, he settled on a year's worth of monthly data. Longer periods tend to lag too much behind the actual prospects of a company. Shorter periods tend to produce too much volatility in the performance and risk measures and result in too many transactions.

In "The Secret to Unlocking the Modern Portfolio Theory," Navellier describes the heretical concept that by using the key variables of MPT, but measuring them over shorter, more responsive time periods, and focusing on the smaller, less efficiently priced securities, it is in fact possible to substantially outperform the market and to do so without taking inordinate risks. In his early work using a hand calculator covering the period between 1977 and 1979, Navellier found that the top 10 percent of OTC stocks having the largest alphas (gains in excess of market returns) and the lowest volatility (standard deviation of returns), did in fact beat the market. Navellier states that "I was shocked by the outstanding performance!"

Navellier's key measure of utility is a stock's alpha divided by its standard deviation. He calls this his risk-reward ratio and publishes a "buy list" of the top such stocks in his monthly market letter. This is one of the secrets. The other is a strong emphasis on fundamental research. Navellier focuses on a number of fundamental screens as well as the risk-reward ratio. Projected earnings growth, profit margin expansion, net annual profit margins, analysts' earnings revisions, and sales growth are all key factors that are used to further screen the "buy list" down to specific portfolios.

Hence Navellier's approach is founded in both technical analysis (the risk-reward ratio) and fundamental analysis. These are the two control parameters in our nonlinear market model. The coherent market hypothesis predicts that there will be market periods and individual stocks where the risk-reward ratio is turned upside down. Above average performance with below average risk is theoretically possible within the framework of nonlinear dynamics. Navellier's stock screen, based on the ratio of performance relative to risk, provides direct confirmation of this theoretical prediction.

Hence it appears that Navellier's track record may well be more than a matter of luck. It is completely consistent with the nonlinear market model presented in Chap. 1. While Navellier is not a physicist and has not espoused any interest in chaos theory or nonlinear dynamic systems theory, his empirical work provides another example of a market practitioner discovering an anomaly in the risk-reward principle.

Nonlinear theory helps explain why some practitioners may have more than luck behind their performance records. Of course, theory can also help project how a system will work when the macroscopic economic environment changes. As stocks continue to become overvalued, the biggest winners of the past may be less persistent in extending their gains into the future. This could hurt the performance of approaches such as Navellier's as a result of both lower performance and higher trading costs. However, Navellier's approach would pick up whatever is in a coherent bull state in any particular climate. For example, Navellier notes that while he is not a market timer, if the beta factor of his buy list declines, it is an indication of weakness in the overall market.

The random walk model and the efficient market hypothesis are at the heart of MPT. Likewise the capital asset pricing model is a first step toward defining the relationship between risk and reward within the context of MPT. We will look at the linear random processes and extend our discussion to nonlinear stochastic models as well. The latter include models such as physicists Earl Callen's and Don Shapero's Theory of Social Imitation which offer new insights into why practitioners such as Louis Navellier are probably more than just lucky in their performance results.

The random walk model of stock price behavior dates back to the beginnings of the century when Louis Bechalier published his doctoral thesis in France. Five years later, Albert Einstein formulated the celebrated *theory of Brownian motion* to account for the behavior of microscopic particles erratic fluctuations in a fluid. Bechalier proposed that the prices of financial assets were essentially a game of chance. This concept, radically new at the time, failed to catch on until nearly 60 years later, when it was rediscovered and gained widespread acceptance under the banner of the efficient market hypothesis (EMH). Ironically, while the EMH maintains that new information is discounted instantaneously by the capital markets, the same evidently is not true in the market for new academic ideas.

The widely accepted academic formulation of market dynamics is cast in the framework of probability theory. The random walk model has gained a degree of acceptance among practitioners as well primarily in the area of option valuation. However, there are serious limitations with some of the assumptions underlying the random walk model. In fact, even as the proponents of the efficient market hypothesis were framing their new found approach to market analysis, critics such as Benoit Mandelbrot were pointing out in 1963 the deviations between the forecasts of the random walk model and the actual behavior of speculative markets.

Mandelbrot suggested that speculative markets did not follow a Brownian motion process. He argued that "the empirical distributions of price changes are usually too "peaked" to be relative to samples from Gaussian populations. That is, the histograms of price changes are indeed unimodal and their central "bells" remind one of the Gaussian ogive. But there are typically so many "outliers" that ogives fitted to the mean square of price changes are much lower and flatter than the distribution of the data themselves." The second key factor that Mandelbrot pointed out was that the second moment of the probability distribution did not tend to any limit. In other words, the volatility of prices varied widely from one period to the next.

Mandelbrot suggested in 1963 that speculative markets could be better characterized by a class of probability distributions known as *stable Paretian*. He showed that the fat tails on the time histories of price changes in the cotton market corresponded well to this class of probability distribution. In effect, the stable Paretian distribution corresponds to the behavior of systems that evolve to a critical state. This class of probability models is described in further detail in the Appendix.

Another statistical approach to which we have alluded is the rescaled range analysis of E. Hurst which has also been popularized for financial market applications by Edgar Peters in 1991. This approach is an empirical method for generalizing the random walk and it bridges the gap between the efficient market hypothesis of classical quantitative analysis and the new world of nonlinear dynamics.

Our nonlinear market model offers new insights on the risk-reward profiles that must be expected in the capital markets. Unlike the simple, linear relationship expected from the capital asset pricing model, we offer an alternative interpretation of the data in which the linear model splits into a two-state pricing model. This approach may be a more realistic way to examine the risk-reward relationships that exist in the market, and can help explain how practitioners such as Navellier can perch precariously at the edge of chaos and still enjoy superior risk adjusted performance levels.

Efficient Market Hypothesis and the Random Walk Model

Investing need not be a complicated process. As a result of long-term economic growth, anyone can purchase shares of stock in American or international corporations and have reasonable expectations of enjoying profitable returns at some point in the future. According to a study by Lawrence Fisher and James Lorie in 1964 there is about an 80 percent probability of success by simply picking stocks at random and holding them for several years. However there is risk. Stocks fluctuate in value and create negative returns or loss of principal as well as positive returns.

While it is human nature to seek the lucrative returns associated with stocks, fears of the downside have motivated investors to seek ways to avoid the most dangerous bear markets. The Crash of 1929 led to a three-year bear market in which the portfolios and net worth of many leveraged investors were totally wiped out. The bear market of 1973 to 1974 involved losses of more than 40 percent for the average portfolio without leverage. The Crash of 1987 saw a 20 percent decline in a single day.

Market technicians and chartists have long been seeking systems for predicting the future path of stock prices by reading chart patterns for evidence of cycles or trading signals. However, the utility of these endeavors has been the subject of hot debate and ridicule within academic circles. According to Burton Malkiel, the sole purpose of technical analysis is to "green" the brokers by generating trading ideas. Early academic work showed no benefit to investors using technical analysis. This has changed in recent years, but was one of the key foundations of the efficient market hypothesis.

The efficient market hypothesis (EMH) maintains that future price changes can't be predicted from past price changes. This is the weak form of the hypothesis and it takes direct aim at the practice of technical analysis or market forecasting. More strict interpretations of market efficiency suggest that fundamental information as well as technical analysis is discounted by the market too quickly to enable short-term profits. The semi-strong form of the hypothesis maintains that all public information is fully discounted. The strong form goes the full measure and suggests that both public and nonpublic information is fully reflected in prices. These versions of the EMH call into question fundamental securities analysis as well as technical analysis, although the case has been made that markets are efficient because of fundamental analysis.

The EMH is related to the coherent market hypothesis (CMH). To be sure, the CMH suggests that markets are not always truly efficient. Periods of instability must be expected when prices transition between the bullish and bearish states associated with chaotic markets. However, in periods of true random walk and even over short periods in chaotic markets, the CMH corresponds to the EMH with regard to market efficiency. Hence our purpose is not just to challenge the EMH, but to point out potential extensions that are possible with the nonlinear market model. These extensions also apply to MPT and help explain why practitioners have in fact successfully outperformed the market without simply taking proportionately more risk.

The random walk model was proposed for financial markets shortly after the turn of the century by a French mathematician, Louis Bachelier. His work predated Albert Einstein's formulation of the random walk theory of Brownian motion by several years.

In a random walk process, each step is made independently of preceding steps. For example, the staggering of a total drunk is sometimes used as an illustration of random motion where all sense of direction has been lost. Bachelier's work suggested that stock changes were no more orderly than a mindless drunks ambulatory efforts.

Bachelier's work failed to generate significant interest until some 60 years later when it was rediscovered in the early 1960s by Paul Samuelson of MIT. In the late 1950s and early 1960s, there was renewed interest in study of stock price fluctuations using a new tool—the computer. Work by Roberts in 1959 at the University of Chicago suggested that "classical patterns of technical analysis can be generated by a suitable roulette wheel or random number table." M.F.M. Osborne of the U.S. Naval Research Laboratory in Washington, DC suggested that the price changes expressed in logarithmic form did conform to the random walk model.

The increasing availability of the computer and higher level programming languages ushered in a new era of interest in the random walk model and statistical testing. One of the issues researchers faced was that of the differencing interval. The random walk model is normally expressed in terms of price changes over some interval of time. For example, daily, weekly, or monthly intervals are frequently used. However, intraday changes or longer time periods could also be examined, depending on one's time frame of interest. Early research assumed fixed intervals; this left open the possibility that different results might be seen on different time scales.

Tests of variable-time trading rules were also conducted. These approaches sought to predict future price changes on the basis of past price patterns or events. In 1961, Sidney Alexander of MIT tested a filter approach which evaluated returns after price changes had exceeded a pre-specified filter or threshold. For example, a buy signal may be triggered if a stock price advances by five percent. It is then held until it declines by at least five percent. All smaller moves are assumed to be noise and, therefore, ignored. While there appeared to be some evidence of short-term trends, when the effects of trading costs were considered, any excess returns above the buy and hold tended to vanish.

Another study by Hendrick Houthakker of Harvard also found some evidence of trends based on a variable-time decision rule. Houthakker proposed that price movements occurred in "runs" or a sequence of price changes in the same direction. By setting stop-loss limits and letting profits run, one could hope to capture excess returns above market. His test of trading rules on wheat and corn futures did indicate some nonrandom price trends.

Other tests in the early 1960s tended to support the random walk model over short-term price change intervals. However, the longer the differencing interval, the greater the deviation from random behavior. For example, Cootner found that with a one-week differencing interval, price fluctuations did exhibit random behavior. However, when the interval was increased to 14 weeks, price changes did not follow a random walk.

In 1965, Eugene Fama analyzed the Dow Jones 30 industrials over differencing intervals ranging from one to 16 days. He failed to find any evidence of trends over these time periods. Other tests also suggested that any short-term excess trading profits were less than the commission costs. Fama's work became regarded as the definitive study, if not confirming the random walk precisely, at least showing that past prices could not be used to make trading profits in excess of the costs of trading.

Also in the mid-1960s, Robert L. Hagin tested a variety of additional trading rules and strategies as part of his PhD thesis. He found no basis for expecting profits to exceed trading costs for a set of 790 stocks, compared with the relatively small sample represented by the Dow. For this larger universe Hagin found "no systematic behavior in stock prices that could be used for profitable prediction when the data were studied with differencing intervals of between one and 16 days."

Hagin also studied price and volume combinations. Using the same large data file of 790 actively traded stocks, he found no evidence that knowledge of preceding volume changes, coupled with price change information, offered any basis for capturing returns in excess of a passive strategy. Hagin also examined breakout patterns. This research addressed the question of whether large price changes are followed by additional large price changes.

Here results suggested that "there is some evidence that 'large' price changes occur in succession, but the direction of the change is random." Hagin concluded based on these and other tests that there is no evidence of other than random price behavior over short periods of time—less than 40 days.

Are the markets truly efficient? Louis Rukeyeser recently posed this question to practitioners John Templeton and Peter Lynch at a black tie anniversary gala for his *Wall Street Week* program on public television. Peter Lynch responded that the markets were always pretty efficient; he said he normally expects to hold a stock at least three years before he expects to make any real money with it. John Templeton said the market was never efficient. He suggested that investors always tend to extremes of optimism and pessimism which leads to over valuation and under valuation of stock prices.

Within the context of our nonlinear market model, both answers can be considered correct. The market may almost always be efficient on a short-term basis, with prices fluctuating in an unpredictable random walk. However, over a longer-term horizon, investor psychology may be biased by economic fundamentals leading to persistent price trends that can carry valuations from one extreme to the other in irregular cycles. These cycles may be more predictable than the short-term random fluctuations or noise which affects the markets.

Modern Portfolio Theory: The Academic Baseline

The award of a Nobel prize in October 1990 to Harry Markowitz, William Sharpe, and Merton Miller recognized work in several important areas of investment theory, including the concepts of risk and reward as related to investment valuation. Markowitz was recognized for his modern portfolio theory. Sharpe had developed the capital asset pricing model. Miller's work extended Markowitz's ideas into the domain of corporate financing. Hence the efficient market hypothesis has found recognition even as the new paradigm of nonlinear dynamics is fundamentally challenging some of the concepts underlying the efficient market hypothesis.

Harry Markowitz's *Portfolio Selection* was published in 1952. This classic work established him as the founder of modern portfolio theory though widespread acceptance of his work took decades. He defined the analytical process by which the benefits of diversification on overall portfolio risk could be measured. Markowitz suggested that the goal of portfolio management is to maximize what he called *expected utility* which is a measure of both the returns and level of risk that an investor is comfortable with.

In the context of modern portfolio theory, portfolio management is more than a matter of selecting the best stocks for maximum return. Rather the goal of active management is defined to be maximum returns within the constraints of an acceptable level of risk. For example, fixed dollar investments such as U.S. Treasury bills or money market funds have relatively low returns but also have relatively low risk and, therefore, may be the optimum solution for risk averse investment objectives. At the other extreme, stocks typically are the highest risk investments and also tend to provide the highest long-term expected returns. Stock portfolios may be the optimum solutions for investors with long time horizons, looking for maximum appreciation potential.

Whereas Markowitz's portfolio theory requires estimates of the return and volatility for each stock in a portfolio, William Sharpe introduced the concept of risk and return relative to that of the overall market. The concept of market risk and return are separated from the performance of individual stocks.

Sharpe's capital asset pricing model is summarized in Fig. 4.1. Here the x axis represents the volatility of a security or portfolio relative to that of the overall market. This relative volatility is known as the *beta factor*, and a beta of 1 means that the stock or portfolio is just as volatile as the overall market. In contrast, a beta of 2 means the stock is twice as volatile as the market while a beta of 0.5 implies an issue is half as risky as the market.

In addition to relative volatility, Sharpe introduced the concept of relative returns in excess of what would be expected from the market.

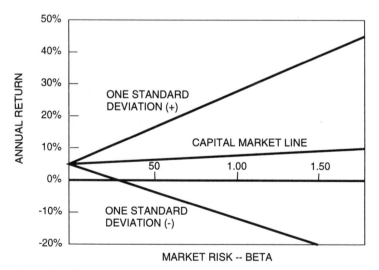

Figure 4.1. The capital asset pricing model relates the expected return from stocks to their volatility or risk in linear fashion. According to this basic tenet of modern portfolio theory, above average returns can only be attained by taking above average risks in rational markets.

This measure is called *alpha*. An alpha greater than zero implies that the stock has been more rewarding than the overall market. Its returns cannot be accounted for in terms of simply the market's returns and relative volatility.

Sharpe also broadened Markowitz's analysis to include asset classes other than stocks. For example, short-term government securities such as U.S. Treasury bills can be viewed as riskless assets. Portfolios can then be constructed as weighted averages of high risk and riskless asset classes to produce any desired volatility and the expected return would follow the capital market line (i.e., the straight line linking expected returns of riskless securities with the expected return of the overall market).

The capital market line in Fig. 4.1 illustrates the classical linear model of capital asset pricing. The two lines around the capital market line show the standard deviation of returns around the average. Assuming a market portfolio provides a 10 percent rate of return with a 20 percent standard deviation, one would expect about two thirds of the market's returns to fall between 30 percent and –10 percent. Extending these points to a nominal five percent expected return from risk-free assets leads to a *risk funnel.* Clearly, high beta stocks and portfolios have a far greater standard deviation of returns than low beta stocks and vice versa for low beta stocks.

William Sharpe's CAPM concept was cast in terms of the returns investors could realistically attain in efficient markets. The other side of this coin is the costs to the borrowers or issuers of stock. The Modigliani-Miller hypothesis generalized the CAPM concept by suggesting that efficient markets adjust the cost of capital so as to minimize the importance of a firm's internal decisions with regard to the level of debt and equity used to finance a business.

Hence, modern portfolio theory has become the baseline theory that captures the behavior of financial markets. However, it is not as widely accepted as may be suggested from the recent prizes and awards bequeathed upon its founders. At the root of the problem is the nature of the empirical evidence supporting the linear capital market line. The excess return generated from stocks with progressively higher betas is at best elusive. While over long periods of time there does appear to be a positive correlation, there are extended periods over which the relationship does not hold. Furthermore, even over the long run it appears that low beta stocks do better than would be expected, while high beta stocks do not compensate adequately for the excess risk.

Capital Asset Pricing in Chaotic Markets

The validity of the capital asset pricing model (CAPM) was tested by Fisher Black, Michael Jensen, and Myron Scholes in 1972. They examined all 1952 stocks listed on the New York Stock Exchange over a 35-year period covering 1931 to 1965. For each year, the stocks were put into 10 bins based on that year's estimate of the beta coefficient. The highest beta bin included the 195 stocks with the highest betas, the next bin included the 195 stocks with the next highest betas, and so forth.

Figure 4.2 summarizes the monthly returns of each portfolio over the entire 35-year period covered by the study. Both the empirical and theoretical capital market lines are shown for the period covered. The results are in fact highly linear. However, the empirical results follow a somewhat shallower slope than the theoretical model predicts. This implies that low risk stocks did better than expected, while high-risk stocks did not offer as much return as the theory predicts.

The finding that low risk stocks did better than expected supports the CMH. Our nonlinear model suggests that stocks in coherent bullish states will display well above average returns with moderate risk. Navellier's screen is one way to identify coherent stocks; his buy list constitutes only the top 6 percent of the stock universe he screens. These are further narrowed down by means of fundamental analysis. Hence the number of stocks likely to exhibit coherent results may only be a small fraction of the total market. However, it is encouraging that even when diluted by the large mass of

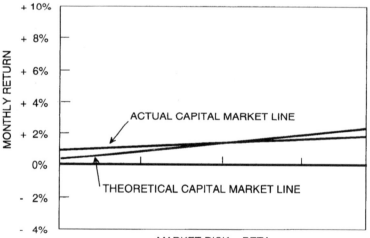

Figure 4.2. Empirical studies of capital market lines showed higher returns with low risk stocks and less returns from high risk stocks than expected from the theoretical risk and reward relationship predicted by the capital asset pricing model. This supports the coherent market hypothesis which suggests that some stocks and market periods produce above average returns with below average risk.

efficiently priced securities, the impact of low risk, high return securities is still significant.

Black, Jensen, and Scholes also presented their results over shorter time spans. Figure 4.3 shows the results for two-year periods overlaid on the same graph. The interesting feature of this presentation is that there is a very wide spread in the slopes found over any two-year period, depending on whether the market averages were performing well or poorly. Likewise there are periods in which the capital market line is nearly flat.

Hence even though the long-term average may support the theory over the period shown, the behavior over shorter time spans differs dramatically from the long-term average. This type of behavior could simply be the risk funnel associated with a bell-shaped return probability distribution. How-

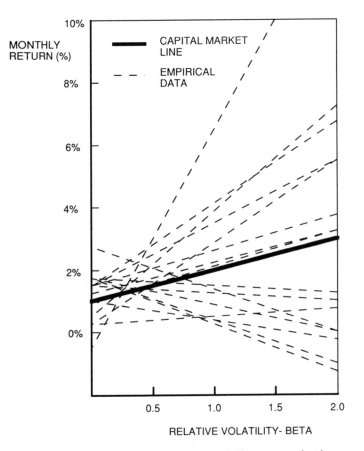

Figure 4.3. Variations in the slope of the capital market line in empirical studies are assumed to be the normal standard deviation of returns around the most probable level. (*Empirical data based on Black, Jensen, and Scholes, 1973.*)

ever, it is also consistent with our nonlinear model in which there are states with distinctly different risk-reward profiles than would be associated with the simple bell-shaped curve. If the probability distributions associated with market returns are not normally distributed, the CAPM theory is directly affected. For example, fat-tailed distributions as proposed by Mandelbrot would have undefined second moments which would lead to the wide variations in the short-term capital market line.

The bimodal distribution in our nonlinear market model would lead to a bifurcation of the capital market line. Both a negative sloping line and a positive sloping line as shown in Fig. 4.4 would be expected to describe

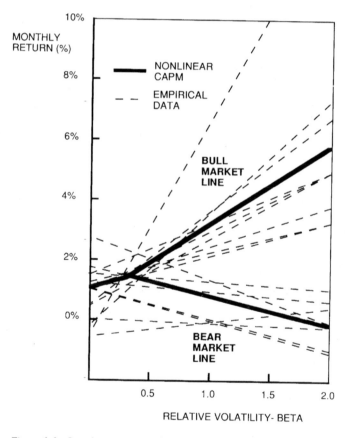

Figure 4.4. Capital asset pricing in chaotic markets would expect returns to be stable around either of two quasistable market lines. The relative stability of the bull and bear market lines depends on prevailing fundamentals. If fundamentals are strongly positive than the bear market line would virtually disappear, and vice versa if fundamentals are strongly negative. (*Empirical data based on Black, Jensen, and Scholes, 1973.*)

returns more accurately in periods of chaotic markets with possible abrupt state changes between these states. In a coherent market, the bull market line would be far more probable than the bear market line (or vice versa, depending on prevailing fundamentals).

The period covered by the Black, Jensen, and Scholes study began in depressionary lows and extended through the bull markets of the 1950s and 1960s. This was clearly a period in which there was a strong positive bias in returns. More recent attempts to replicate these findings have not shown the same positive slope even though the markets have made substantial progress over the past three decades. In fact the observations of some recent studies are that the beta factor is not necessarily a good indicator of investment returns.

This is not unexpected in view of the nonlinear market model. Risk is more difficult to quantify in the world of nonlinear dynamic systems. For example, the distributions described by Mandelbrot have no second moment or standard deviation. Our two-state chaotic market model can lead to stable states having either positive or negative slopes in the capital market lines. Hence the capital market line is not an invariant, but rather depends on the control parameters governing the market states. Both technical (investor sentiment) and fundamental factors determine the market states which have widely differing risk-reward profiles and associated capital market lines.

In spite of these considerations, the framework of MPT is nevertheless useful for discussing risk in chaotic markets as well as true random walk states. However, the relationship between risk and reward is more complex than the simple linear capital market line. The variables that control the relationship between risk and performance can be defined within the framework of our nonlinear model.

Nonlinear models can also help identify the types of market conditions needed for specific investment strategies to be effective. For example, Navellier's approach has been highly successful in a long-term coherent bull market, but may be less successful in a long-term random walk market. In the latter situation, the persistence of trends would be lower and trading costs would be higher. The period of time the market is expected to remain in a given state in a chaotic market depends on the potential barrier separating the two low regions of the potential well. This is known as the *first crossing problem* within the domain of Markov processes, and is discussed further in the Appendix.

Both MPT and nonlinear dynamics involve the basic concepts of random processes. Hence to further develop our nonlinear model of market dynamics we review some of the basics of random processes in the Appendix. The random walk model, at the heart of MPT is a key problem in the theory of Markov processes. However, Markov processes are not limited to the linear random walk. Our nonlinear market model is based on an extension of the random walk into the nonlinear domain. In order to examine further the characteristics of nonlinear market states, we review the concepts and methods of probability theory in the Appendix. This includes a discussion of bistable processes and the first exit time problem which enables us to quantify the question of trend persistence.

Summary

Risk is difficult to define in the capital markets. While the simple capital asset pricing model offers a gross relationship between the beta factor and market returns, it doesn't fit empirical data as well as might be expected. Returns from low beta stocks tend to be higher than they should, while returns from high beta stocks don't provide as much return as expected from the linear model. This supports the coherent market hypothesis which maintains that above average returns are possible without taking above average risk.

Our nonlinear market model offers an alternative capital asset pricing model for chaotic markets. This would be represented by two straight lines rather than one. An upward sloping *bull market line* and a downward sloping *bear market line* can be fit to actual empirical data as well as the single line. The nonlinear market model suggests that returns tend to either cluster well above the linear capital market line or well below it. Unlike the risk funnel created by the standard deviation lines in which most data would be expected to cluster closest to the linear capital market line, our nonlinear (bifurcated or split) capital asset pricing model suggests that returns are stable at levels well above the straight line fit or well below it in chaotic markets. Only in periods of true random walk would returns be stable near the middle region.

The two lines for capital asset pricing in chaotic markets are not necessarily equally probable. Depending on prevailing fundamentals, the bullish line may be more probable than the bearish or vice versa. In a coherent bull market, the bearish line essentially vanishes or becomes statistically unlikely. However, regardless of how strong fundamentals are, the slope of the bull market line will not change very significantly. The slope of the bull market line would be at the low point of the bimodal potential well, at about a +25 percent annualized rate of return for the S&P 500 market index, not counting dividends.

In a chaotic market, there is a risk of an abrupt switch between a bull market state (and associated line of the two-state CAPM model) and the bear market state. The average time for this to happen depends critically on the potential barrier separating the two states, which in turn depends on the control parameters (i.e., sentiment and fundamentals). A mania can be defined as a situation where the market is actually in the less probable of the two states. For example, a bullish state could persist even after fundamentals weaken. However, under these conditions, the chances of an exit from the less probable to the more probable state is increased substantially.

A stock selection strategy such as featured in Louis Navellier's *MPT Review* or Jim Collin's *OTC Insight* is designed to catch those issues that are on the bull market line. Stocks in coherent bull markets may stay in this state indefinitely. However, if fundamentals weaken, the probability of an abrupt jump to the bear market line increases. As stocks switch states, they would be dropped from the portfolio. As long as the bull market line is a stable state and more probable than the bear market line, the strategy would be expected to work; in a true random walk market, the bull and bear market lines collapse back to a single linear risk, reward line. Navellier's strategy of being "perched on the edge of danger," is reminiscent of the edge of chaos concept espoused by researchers in the field of artificial life.

Just as the most interesting "a-life" forms appear to be found in the critical state at the edge of chaos, the most interesting stocks also appear to be perched at the edge of chaos. These are the issues that you are afraid to buy for fear of being the greater fool. They are stocks far from equilibrium. They have large flows of money into them, and often they are subject to large short-term fluctuations. However, these issues also appear to perform best on average, at least when the overall market provides a net positive bias. Navellier's portfolios are perched in a stable state on the bullish capital market line. They won't stay there forever and when issues fall off his buy list, they are soon dropped from the portfolio and replaced with other stocks exhibiting the desired risk-reward profile. Hence the cost of this turnover can be significant, especially with smaller, less liquid over the counter issues.

Sometimes Navellier's stocks do take a drubbing. In bear markets, his portfolio does fall off the precarious edge on which it is normally perched. Fortunately, recent bear markets have been short lived, and his stocks have bounced back quickly. However, leverage is not advisable unless you are also a nimble market timer. Navellier's 40 percent downside fluctuation in the Crash of 1987 period is one reason why. When the flow of money is interrupted, the market may transition abruptly between bullish and bearish states. The stocks that did best may also have the furthest to fall. Hence a close eye on fundamental developments is warranted for the investor inclined to invest at the edge of chaos.

Relative strength investing is usually associated with growth stocks and can be compared to the draw shot in golf. Here the ball is deliberately aimed away from the target with a predictable spin. The experienced golfer knows that the spin will carry the ball back to the desired target line. With a growth stock in a bullish state, short-term returns may be well above levels that are sustainable over the long term. The growth investor knows that the profit margins may not be sustainable, competition will come along, unexpected developments may interrupt growth. The stock may drop sharply at some point if such factors torpedo earnings expectations. However, the relative strength investor seeks to get the maximum distance from these stocks before their growth and stock price action slows to more sustainable levels.

5

Synergetics: Beyond Chaos and Random Walk

Buffet is a beacon of simplicity and sanity–and probably a genius. Rationality and common sense, actually uncommon sense, are his guiding lights.

ANDREW KILPATRICK,
1992, Warren Buffet,
The Good Guy of Wall Street

Warren Buffet is an uncommon investor. His common sense has taken him from a newspaper route at age 13 to a personal fortune worth over $4 billion. According to *Forbes*, Buffet is one of the 10 richest men in America, largely due to his stake in an investment partnership, which he founded in 1956, and Berkshire Hathaway which has become a holding company for his investments.

A $10,000 investment in 1956 in the Buffet Partnership, Ltd., reinvested in 1969 into Berkshire Hathaway, has grown to over $40 million by 1991. This 4000-fold return dwarfs the performance of passive indexing. Over 13 years, the Buffet Partnership produced a 29.5 percent annualized rate of return while Berkshire Hathaway has increased in value at about 25 percent per year.

Today Berkshire Hathaway has over $11 billion in total assets, including large stakes in brand names such as Coca-Cola, Wells Fargo, American Express, Capital Cities/ABC, Gillette, and General Dynamics. While Peter Lynch was reputed to have "never met a stock he didn't like," Buffet's success is largely based on a relatively few highly successful decisions.

What's Buffet's secret? According to Andrew Kilpatrick, "He made most of these investments at distressed times and bargain prices. He held on for the long term, through good times and bad, for a sunnier day."

Unlike the Navellier approach of buying stocks on the bull market line of our nonlinear capital asset pricing model, Buffet's strategy is just the opposite. He buys stocks that are on the bear market line. Over the short term, this can look bad, since the bear market line is a stable state, virtually ensuring negative trend persistence. However, if long-term fundamentals are positive, there will be a transition from the bear market line to the bull market line. How long this will take is a random variable which depends exponentially on the height of the potential barrier separating the two states.

Of course, Buffet is not a chaos theorist. Rather he bases his judgment on simple common sense. Buffet's annual reports have become legendary for their common sense, wit and insights into the business world. Known for simplicity and efficiency, the annual meetings are short on formality and long on informal discussion. Buffet himself is one of the lowest paid executives of a major corporation. There is no promotion of Berkshire Hathaway either through fancy logos, Wall Street promotions, or fancy offices.

While there is little emphasis on business style, there is earnest work going on at the World Headquarters of Berkshire Hathaway. Buffet looks for opportunities to buy profitable businesses that have fallen out of favor with the rest of the market. According to Buffet in *Fortune*, December 19, 1988, "Great investment opportunities come around when excellent companies are surrounded by unusual circumstances that cause their stock to be misappraised."

Clearly there is a firm conviction behind Buffet's approach that the markets will not always price major firms in a rational manner. This again is heresy within the framework of the academic efficient market hypothesis where there is a basic premise that rational investors in an efficient market will drive the market price of any security into a point of stable equilibrium which fully reflects the prospects of the company.

In contrast, our nonlinear model suggests that there will be multiple stable states in which the markets may establish pricing equilibrium points. These stable states either represent a strong bullish or bearish bias among market participants. It is clear that some companies deserve to be in stable bullish states, while others deserve a negative fate in the marketplace. What is particularly interesting about our nonlinear model is that it predicts that even fundamentally sound companies will at times fall out of favor. Likewise, fundamentally unsound companies will at times become the darlings of the investment community.

The word "mania" comes to mind when a business without positive fundamentals becomes overvalued in the market based on wild fantasies about future prospects. Inevitably these situations fall out of favor when marketplace realities prick the bubble that has dominated the market's collective perceptions. The opposite situation is also predicted by our nonlinear model. A fundamentally sound business may fall out of favor and enter a bearish state with respect to market performance. Buffet's approach is to patiently wait for the latter type of mania and to pick up high quality companies in industries with stable growth potential and sound management at distress sale prices. He doesn't need a lot of these situations to make a lot of money.

Buffet's approach takes advantage of two of the primary characteristics of nonlinear dynamic systems. First is the fact that markets are far from equilibrium. The stable states in the financial markets are sustained by a flow of capital. When a stock is in favor it attracts additional investors, momentum players, who keep the price in a steady growth state. However, when the prospects of a company falter, and the market action switches to the mirror image of negative returns and bad news, the process will also feed on itself and drive prices far lower than a short-term setback may justify.

The imitative behavior that occurs in social groups including financial markets is one of the fundamental problems that has been the subject of research in nonlinear systems. Specifically, the work of the German physicists at the University of Stuttgart, Hermann Haken, Wolfgang Weidlich and Gunther Haage under the banner of synergetics, has led to quantitative models of social behavior. Similar concepts have been published by American physicists, Earl Callen and Don Shapero under the title *A Theory of Social Imitation*. Both of these approaches apply the Ising model of the ferromagnet to describe the polarization of opinion in social groups. The same method underlies our nonlinear market model and can help us understand how the polarization of opinion among investors can predictably lead to the types of investment opportunities that Warren Buffet has been capitalizing on.

While our quantitative models may at first glance appear to be complicating the elegantly simple investment philosophy of the market contrarian, our goal is to demonstrate why practicing contrarians, such as Warren Buffet, haven't simply been lucky. Knowing that, we can invest with the confidence that is necessary to implement a strategy over the long run, as needed to successfully implement any investment plan.

Synergetics: The Basic Concepts

Having discussed linear deterministic, nonlinear deterministic, and linear stochastic models, the domain of nonlinear stochastic models is the only one that remains to be explored from a theoretical viewpoint. This area offers the best potential for investment applications with long-term horizons where short-term deterministic forecasting isn't possible even in principle, and linear stochastic models are inadequate.

Hermann Haken is the editor of the Springer-Verlag series on *synergetics*, the name he has given to the Stuttgart school of nonlinear dynamic systems research. He is a laser physicist by training, but his interests in synergetics take a far broader perspective. In 1975, Haken described a wide range of examples of "cooperative" behavior in complex systems, including lasers, nonlinear waves, tunnel diodes, fluid dynamics, neuron networks, and the behavior of interacting social groups.

All of these diverse systems share the property of transitions from disordered, random states to more ordered states. The laser transition is one of the most widely studied examples of a complex system, far from equilibrium in which there is a transition from disordered, random light, to ordered, coherent laser light. Particularly remarkable to early researchers such as Haken, these state transitions in systems far from equilibrium shared many of the properties of similar transitions in systems that are in thermal equilibrium.

There is no reason to think that a system far from equilibrium would share any of the properties of systems in thermal equilibrium. Hence it came as a surprise that the laser's behavior at the critical threshold showed the same large, long-lasting fluctuations as a magnet at the critical Curie temperature. Haken showed how simple, nonlinear models could help explain the characteristics of such state transitions in systems far from equilibrium. Hence the wide range of examples in his work.

For example, a magnet can exist in either a disordered state where the molecules do not line up and there is no net external magnetic field. However, under the right conditions, the molecules polarize and align with their neighbors. The conditions necessary for this to happen are well understood. First, the coupling between molecules must be large enough. It is with a ferromagnetic material such as iron. Second, the influence of random thermal noise must be small enough so as not to disrupt the tendency of the molecules to align. The latter condition implies that the temperature of the material must be below a critical threshold.

The critical threshold in a bar of iron has well-known properties, including the appearance of large, long-lasting fluctuations in the magnetic field. This is the same characteristic we described in the previous section on the probability distribution governing self-organized critical systems. The power law distribution occurs in magnets at the critical transition threshold, as well as sand piles, earthquakes, and other examples previously presented.

Haken showed how a simple nonlinear model captures the essential features of state transitions in a wide range of phenomena in the fields of physics, chemistry, biology, and sociology. The latter example is of special interest since it offers insights into the nonlinear dynamics of social groups from a theoretical viewpoint. The quantitative models of social imitation in turn help us understand from a fundamental statistical viewpoint why collective thinking and action in social systems such as the capital markets will inevitably produce profitable investment opportunities for the occasional investor with uncommon sense.

Analogies between the behavior of social groups and problems in physics have been of interest for some time. W. V. Smith of IBM's Watson Research Laboratory pointed out the similarity of behavior in a research environment and solid state physics as early as 1968. A goal of the research laboratory is to support gifted people who are the "nucleation centers" around whom productive results are most likely to emerge; however, the research must also support the larger goals of the business need which it is designed to support. This interaction between individuals coupled with interaction of larger organizational objectives illustrates the dynamics underlying a variety of social systems.

Wolfgang Weidlich provided a detailed mathematical model of polarization of opinion is social groups in 1971. His motivation was to understand the intense, long-lasting polarization of opinion that occurs in political environments such as the French student revolution of the mid-1960s. He used the Ising model of the ferromagnet and reinterpreted the control parameters and state variables to provide a statistical model of biases in public opinion. In 1975, Callen and Shapero generalized this application of the Ising model to a wide variety of examples such as birds flying in flocks, fish swimming in schools, and people conforming to the dictates of fads and fashions.

In this chapter, we examine the synergetics approach, in general, and then take a closer look at the theory of social imitation. The synergetics framework is particularly attractive for the financial markets since it involves both low-dimensional attractors and the element of chance. The low-dimensional attractor or potential function is primarily defined by two control parameters which can be related to investor sentiment and economic fundamentals. A third parameter defines the degrees of freedom or complexity of the system in the disordered state.

However, the most compelling reason for looking at Haken's models can be based on the correspondence principle of physics. Any new theory in physics must correspond to established theories in the limiting situations where existing theories have proven themselves to be effective. In the capital markets, this means that replacing the random walk model and the normal, Gaussian distribution with a better model must inherently have the ability to produce the bell-shaped curves that tend to roughly describe the price changes that occur in most markets. Ideally, the new model would also shed light on deviations from the linear random walk model.

Potential functions are used in a wide array of problems, including those dealing with the element of chance as described in the Appendix. For example, in quantum mechanics there is an array of simple potential functions for which the Schröedinger equation can be solved and used to make statistical predictions for atomic systems. Nuclear physics has its own set of potential functions that govern the behavior of nuclear problems.

Haken showed that the concept of a potential function also is useful in describing state transitions in systems far from equilibrium as well as nonphysical systems. He adopted this approach to illustrate some of the fundamental properties of state transitions both for deterministic systems and problems where the element of chance dominates. Our nonlinear model of market states is based on the idea that nonphysical systems can also be characterized by potential functions.

A potential well with a single low point splits or bifurcates into a well with two low points under the right combination of control parameters. The Appendix shows that in random processes the question of stability can be analyzed by means of a potential function. Potential functions are widely used to analyze stability since the slope of the potential well determines the force field at a given point of the well.

With deterministic problems, the potential well can be used to predict the state of the system into the future. When random forces are substantial, this is no longer possible. In the latter case the potential function can be used to determine the probability of finding the system in a particular point in state space in the future.

Our nonlinear market model introduced in Chap. 1 suggests that there is no one correct answer as to market stability. Rather there may be a set of models corresponding to different market states. No single investment strategy will be effective in all of these states. For example, a trend-following strategy may be effective in a coherent or chaotic market but not in a trendless period of true random walk. The technical and fundamental control parameters determine the shape of the potential function associated with each market state which, in turn, determines the features of the probability distribution associated with the market's fluctuations while in a particular state.

It becomes possible, in principle, to determine the probability distribution governing market fluctuations to the extent that an active manager can assess the control parameters. This distribution varies in nonlinear fashion as the control parameters are changed. Under some conditions, the classic bell-shaped curve of the random walk will indeed govern market dynamics. However, at the critical transition, there is a high probability of large long-lasting fluctuations. Above the critical threshold the risk-reward ratio may become inverted in a coherent market when there is a strong fundamental bias or may yield multiple equilibria in a chaotic market.

Our goal in describing the market states predicted by the nonlinear model is one of explanation. However, as we look at the methods of some practitioners in later chapters, we will see that investment decisions may be based on looking at indicators of market state transitions. Certainly our model suggests that some markets may be closer to true random walks on average than others. Likewise some may be closer to the critical state on average where the power law distribution governs fluctuations. At times, markets may become coherent and offer unusual profit opportunities, while at other times a dangerous chaotic market may spawn abrupt changes between widely separated stable states.

Order in Complex Systems

Synergetics is defined as the science of multicomponent or complex systems in which the elements of the system interact. Under the right set of conditions they may cooperate with each other rather than behaving independently. In physics, chemistry, and biology the elements of a complex system may be vastly different. Likewise the interactions between elements may vary widely. Nevertheless, early researchers such as Hermann Haken found close analogies between a wide range of problems, independent of the microscopic details. The macroscopic similarities include state transitions, instabilities, critical fluctuations, and self-organization. This macroscopic level description is the basis for the interdisciplinary nature of the field of synergetics. Our goal is to apply the basic concepts of synergetics profitably in the financial markets.

In physics and chemistry, the elements composing a system are typically the elementary particles or more complex molecules. Interactions at a microscopic level are due to the fundamental forces of nature. With chemical reactions the forces resulting in chemical bonds are the results of the elementary particles and their composite interactions as molecular units. These interactions may be quite complex and difficult to analyze at the microscopic level even for a relatively few molecules.

On a macroscopic level, physical and chemical systems can often be characterized by relatively few variables such as temperature, pressure, and density. However, the macroscopic state of a system may undergo phase transitions as the control parameters reach certain critical points. Often such macroscopic state changes may be described in Haken's words as transitions "from disorder to order" as with a bar of iron passing from an unmagnetized state to a polarized state with an external magnetic field. A state transition may also occur from one ordered state to another; for example, the magnet may switch polarity, either spontaneously or as a result of some external force.

Haken coined the term *order parameter* to describe the macroscopic state of a system. An order parameter might be the magnetic field associated with a bar of iron, the electric field strength of a laser, or the magnitude of the electrical current in a superconductor. *Control parameters* might include variables such as the temperature of the system and macroscopic external forces that bias the order parameter. For example, Table 5.1 summarizes examples of order parameters for a wide range of systems which undergo state transitions between disordered (random) states and more ordered (coherent) states.

We have added the financial markets to Haken's list of examples. Here the returns from a market may serve as the order parameter, while control parameters are yet to be determined. However, as indicated in Chap. 1, they will be related to traditional market technical and fundamental analysis and indicators.

The goal of synergetics as a new branch of science is to identify the appropriate order parameters and control parameters for a give problem. Then the dynamics of the order parameters must be modeled by appropriate equations of motion.

Table 5.1. Examples of Order Parameters in Complex Systems

Discipline	System	Order parameter
Physics	Ferromagnet	Magnetic field
	Superconductor	Pairwave function
	Tunnel diode	Capacitance charge
	Laser	Electric field
Chemistry	Fluids	Benard cells
	Liquid crystals	Molec. alignment
	Chemical reac.	Molecular density
Biology	Neuron networks	Firing rate of cells
	Phys. clocks	Molecular density
	Forest	Density of trees
	Populations	
Sociology	Political	Density of animals
	opinions	Number of people
Finance	Stock market	S&P 500 Index

SOURCE: H. Haken, *Cooperative Effects*, North Holland, 1974.

Deterministic Equations of Motion: Linear and Nonlinear Oscillators

In our nonlinear model, we think of the returns from a market index or a particular stock as a physical particle that is being buffeted by random forces. The position of the particle corresponds to the returns that a financial market has generated. The random walk model of Brownian motion states simply that the particle's position will cover a progressively wider range in proportion to the square root of the time it is observed. In the financial markets, this just means that we are likely to see larger returns (either up or down) simply by holding a security for a longer period.

If there were no random forces, the position of a particle in a force field would be governed by Newton's laws of motion. *Newton's law* states that there is an equilibrium between the force, F_0, acting on a particle of mass, m, and the acceleration, a, of the particle, according to

$$ma = F_0 \tag{5.1}$$

Since acceleration is also the rate of change of the velocity, v, of the particle, this relationship may also be expressed as

$$m \, dv/dt = F_0 \tag{5.2}$$

The force, F_0, in general may consist of a "driving" force, F, and a "frictional" force which is proportional to velocity, v, according to

$$F_0 = F - \mu v \tag{5.3}$$

which, in turn, yields

$$m \, dv/dt + \mu v = F \tag{5.4}$$

If the force, F, is associated with a spring, it will vary linearly with the displacement of the spring from equilibrium

$$F(q) = -kq \tag{5.5}$$

This is *Hooke's law*. The minus sign expresses the characteristic that the force tends to bring the mass back to the equilibrium position.

Now we may express Newton's law as

$$m \, d^2q/dt^2 + \mu dq/dt = F(q) \tag{5.6}$$

where $v = dq/dt$. If the mass is small and the damping is large we can drop the second order derivative. Likewise, by selecting an appropriate time scale, we may eliminate the damping constant and simply write

$$dq/dt = F(q) \qquad (5.7)$$

This is the equation of motion of the heavily damped harmonic oscillator.

Our derivation is based on the example of a physical mass connected to a spring. However, equations in the form of Equation 5.7 also occur in other disciplines. In chemistry, q might represent the density of molecules of a given type being produced in a chemical reaction, or it might represent the rate of multiplication of bacteria in a culture. In a financial market, q could represent price and dq/dt the rate of change in price over time.

At this point we introduce the concepts of potential energy, V, and work, W. Work may be defined as force times distance. Climbing a ladder requires work in an amount equal to the weight of the person (gravitational force) times the height of the ladder. A closely related concept is that of a potential energy function, V, which is the negative of the work, W. For example, there is a potential for falling off the ladder, in which case the individual does no work, but gravity exerts a force on the person over the height of the ladder.

Over an infinitesimal distance, dq, an infinitesimal amount of work would be performed against force $F(q)$ as follows

$$dW = F(q)dq \qquad (5.8)$$

This representation is important where the force varies with position. Here, the individual infinitesimal work elements must be integrated over the path over which the mass is moved.

Likewise, the potential, V, may be expressed as

$$F(q) = -dV/dq \qquad (5.9)$$

Therefore, the case of a linear restoring force in Equation 5.5 may equivalently be expressed by the potential function

$$V(q) = 1/2 \, kq^2 \qquad (5.10)$$

This is shown in Fig. 5.1.

So far, we have built a linear deterministic model. We know that this is inadequate for predicting the behavior of the financial markets. However, it is the first step toward developing a general nonlinear stochastic model.

The next step toward a more sophisticated model is to add a nonlinear term to the force field, F. For example, adding a cubic term leads directly to

$$dq/dt = -kq - k_1 q^3 \qquad (5.11)$$

POTENTIAL: V(q), k>0

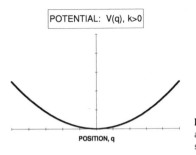

POSITION, q

Figure 5.1. The heavily damped harmonic oscillator is a simple deterministic model of the dynamics of linear systems.

With this slight modification there is a dramatic change in the potential function as shown in Fig. 5.2.

When $k > 0$, the potential function is essentially the same as we have for the linear situation. The potential well has a single low point and the force field tends to restore the system to this low point. However if $k < 0$ and $k_1 > 0$ there is a bifurcation or split in the potential well. Now the point $k = 0$ becomes quasistable while two new points of stability emerge at $q_{1,2} = \pm \sqrt{|k|/k_1}$.

The potential associated with the nonlinear force field is

$$V(q) = 1/2\ kq^2 + 1/4\ k_1\ q^4 \qquad (5.12)$$

This is the Duffing oscillator or double well potential function which we encountered previously. It is one of the simple, low-dimensional chaotic attractors of deterministic chaos theory. The bifurcation of stable states is shown in Fig. 5.2 as a function of the control parameter, k.

In the bistable potential well of Fig. 5.3, a particle at rest in one side of the well or the other would simply stay there forever. Likewise, a particle at rest at exactly the quasistationary point, $q = 0$, would stay there indefinitely as well. However, in the latter case, any minor fluctuation would tend to

POTENTIAL: V(q), k<0

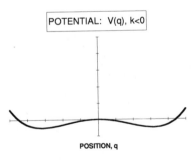

POSITION, q

Figure 5.2. The potential function for a nonlinear oscillator can lead to chaotic motion. The bistable well has been studied extensively and is an example of a low-dimensional model of nonlinear dynamics.

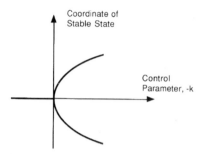

Figure 5.3. The bifurcation of the single bottom potential well to the double bottom well occurs as a function of the control parameters governing the system.

drive the particle away from the metastable point to a more stable point (lower point of the potential well). At these stable points, any slight perturbation would be damped out quickly and the particle would return to rest.

The process by which the potential function splits into a double bottom well is known as *symmetry breaking instability*. Although the well is still symmetric, for the example shown, the particle must end up in one side of the well or the other, thereby breaking symmetry. Near the critical transition from a well with a single stable point to the double bottom well, the potential function flattens out. A particle that is displaced from the origin would fall back down the well more and more slowly, an effect known as *critical slowing down*.

In effect, the critical transition represents a point of instability. Even small random forces could trigger large, long-lasting fluctuations of the particle in the well. Our interpretation is that the particle represents market returns. The linear potential implies an efficient market with a simple, single equilibrium (which may be displaced from zero). However, the nonlinear case involves a symmetry breaking state transition in which the most stable point for returns moves as a matter of necessity far from the linear stability. At the critical point the market will exhibit critical slowing down (large, long-lasting fluctuations in returns).

In general a potential function, $V(q)$ may be expressed in a Taylor series expansion

$$V(q) = c_0 + c_1 q + c_2 q^2 + c_3 q^3 + \ ... \ + c_m q^m \qquad (5.13)$$

where the coefficients of the Taylor series are

$$c_0 = V(0)$$

$$c_1 = dV/dq|_{q=0}$$

$$c_2 = 1/2 \ d^2 V dq^2 |_{q=0}$$

$$c_m = 1/m! \ d^m V / dq^m |_{q=0}$$

and the expansion is taken about the point $q = 0$.

At the point of equilibrium, $dV/dq = 0$. Assuming the first coefficient is also zero (since the absolute height of the potential well is unimportant) we see that the behavior of the potential well is determined by the next nonvanishing term in the power series. If the coefficient c_2 is greater than zero, the system is stable; if c_2 is less than zero the system is unstable. If $c_2 = 0$ we have an instability and the potential depends on the next higher term.

Hence at critical points, slight nonlinear effects which would normally be unimportant can dominate the behavior of a system. The French mathematician Rene Thom studied the behavior of potential functions as a general mathematical problem. His work become popularly known as catastrophe theory since it dealt with bifurcations, instabilities and behavior near critical points.

Catastrophe Theory: Multiple Stabilities

J. Barkley Rosser observes that, "Somehow it is ironic that sharply divergent opinions exist in the mathematical House of Discontinuity with respect to the appropriate method for analyzing discontinuous phenomena. Different methods include catastrophe theory, chaos theory, fractal geometry, and synergetics theory. All have been applied in economics in one way or another. Ironically what we must consider is the bifurcation of bifurcation theory into competing schools."

The principal architects of *catastrophe theory* have been Rene Thom and E. Christopher Zeeman. Their work popularized the study of singularities or critical points in nonlinear systems. Essentially, Thom's work provided a classification of elementary "catastrophes." Figure 5.4 summarizes the picturesque names and characteristics of the lowest order critical states, including the dimension of the state space, X, the dimension of the control parameter space, C, the *catastrophe germ* or lowest nonzero term of the Taylor expansion of the potential around the critical point.

For example, the potential associated with our nonlinear model has a state dimension of 1, the returns from a market index. We are concerned with two control parameters, investor sentiment, and the fundamental bias. According to Zeeman, a dynamic system governed by a cusp dynamic structure will exhibit any of five behavior patterns including:

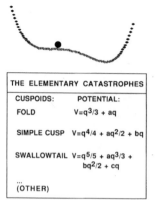

THE ELEMENTARY CATASTROPHES

CUSPOIDS:	POTENTIAL:
FOLD	$V = q^3/3 + aq$
SIMPLE CUSP	$V = q^4/4 + aq^2/2 + bq$
SWALLOWTAIL	$V = q^5/5 + aq^3/3 +$ $bq^2/2 + cq$
(OTHER)	

Figure 5.4. Our nonlinear market model is related to one of Rene Thom's elementary catastrophes.

1. bimodality;

2. inaccessibility;

3. sudden jumps (catastrophes);

4. hysteresis; and

5. divergence.

Bimodality occurs when the system spends most of its time in either of two widely separated states. The barrier between the states is the inaccessible region which is relatively unlikely to be occupied. In the market, this condition implies a trend: investors will either be generating large positive returns or negative returns. A sudden jump from one state to the other represents a market crash.

Crashes, like earthquakes, can occur on different size scales, with not all of them making the news. According to Per Bak, a power law distribution covers the number of crashes of particular size. Hysteresis occurs in physical systems such as a magnet in which the polarization may oscillate back and forth between the two states of the bimodal system. Divergence occurs when the system is near the critical point and slight changes in the path could lead to a large divergence in the future path of the system state variable.

Hence our market model is a relatively simple nonlinear model within the broader mathematical framework of critical states. Thom's classification system can be extended further. However, when the sum of control dimensions and state dimensions exceeds 11, the number of categories becomes infinite and the classification system loses its utility. Thom referred to these as *nonelementary* or *generalized catastrophes*.

Our nonlinear model is just one example of a possible large set of potential functions which will arise with different assumptions on the nature of the dynamics. However, it should also be recognized that catastrophe theory itself is not the only way in which discontinuities can arise. Not all systems will have continuous potential functions which underlie their dynamics. Hence catastrophe theory is only one facet of the larger mathematical world of fractal structures. Nevertheless, it is useful to illustrate how even elementary models within the nonlinear domain can capture important concepts that are totally absent in the linear world. Concepts such as symmetry breaking are crucial to understanding market trends, manias, panics, and crashes.

Our model is only one point in the larger universe of nonlinear models that can be constructed within the domain of catastrophe theory and fractal structures, in general. We could focus on refining it by considering other potential functions or exploring other types of fractal structures which may underlie the chaotic aspects of the market's dynamics. Extensive ongoing research on nonlinear market dynamics will undoubtedly result in improved models. However, our interest is not in refining the model by means of extensions in deterministic directions. Rather we wish to extend the model by adding the element of chance to the otherwise deterministic formulations of catastrophe theory. This key contribution of Hermann Haken's synergetics makes it particularly well suited to the development of a nonlinear market model.

Chance and Necessity:
The Fokker-Planck Equation

The simplest equations of motion for the order parameter or state variable of a complex system which combines both the element of chance and deterministic forces are the *Langevin equations* which may be expressed, in general, as

$$dq_i(t)/dt = F_i(q_1, \dots, q_n) + f_i \qquad \text{with } i = 1, 2, \dots, n \qquad (5.14)$$

where f_i are fluctuating random forces and $F_i(q_1, \dots, q_n)$ are either linear or nonlinear functions of the order parameters $q_i(t)$.

One simple example is the Langevin equation for Brownian motion which can be expressed as

$$dq_i/dt = p_i/m$$

and

$$dp_i/dt = -\mu p_i + f_i \qquad (5.15)$$

where i = 1, 2, 3 for three physical coordinates, q_i is the position of the microscopic Brownian particle, and p_i is its momentum.

In Equation 5.14, there is both a deterministic component, μp_i, and a random component, f_i, in the force. The net motion of the particle is illustrated in Fig. 5.5. The deterministic part of the motion is damped with time according to e^{-at} while the random fluctuations contribute the erratic deviations from the e^{-at} trajectory.

For an ensemble or collection of experiments, it becomes meaningful to talk of an "average" behavior of the Brownian particle. Each time the particle is initially placed at the same starting point it will trace out a new path due to the random forces. The characteristics of the random forces may then be expressed in terms of the ensemble average of numerous experiments. Typically, the random forces have vanishing mean values and are uncorrelated with order parameters. The random forces are self-correlated over short periods of time.

The variance of the ensemble mean is defined as

$$s_i(t) = [(q_i(t) - [q_i(t)])^2] \tag{5.16}$$

Figure 5.6 shows a representative set or ensemble of paths of the Brownian particle around a particular deterministic trajectory. This type of behavior is typical of a combination of linear deterministic force with random forces. A more complicated situation occurs when the deterministic forces are nonlinear.

We have seen that nonlinearities introduce bifurcations into the behavior of a complex system. This implies that there may be critical points near which the path of the order parameter may follow entirely different trajectories for slight changes in initial conditions.

Even small random forces may lead to very large differences in the ultimate state of the order parameter. Under these conditions, the individ-

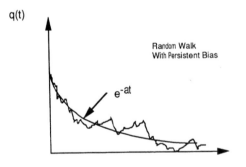

q(t)

Random Walk
With Persistent Bias

e^{-at}

TIME, t

Figure 5.5. Brownian motion can involve drifts as well as diffusion processes.

Coordinate, q

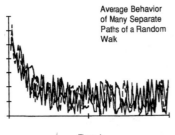

Average Behavior
of Many Separate
Paths of a Random
Walk

Time, t

Figure 5.6. An ensemble of paths of a Brownian particle
represents the outcome of a set of experiments.

ual paths within an ensemble of experimental trajectories may deviate
significantly from their mean value. As shown in Fig. 5.7, the ensemble
mean values no longer meaningfully describe the sample paths.

An alternative approach to the Langevin equations is the *Fokker-Planck
equation*. Langevin equations are expressed in terms of the order parameter
of the system as the independent variable. This is appropriate since we are
interested in modeling the dynamics of the order parameter. However,
when random forces are important, a probabilistic formulation of the
dynamics becomes appropriate. The Fokker-Planck equation develops the
dynamics within a probabilistic framework.

The Fokker-Planck equation is presented in the Appendix as a function
of key parameters including the drift and diffusion coefficients. Figures 5.8
and 5.9 illustrate the probability distributions that correspond to the two

Coordinate, q

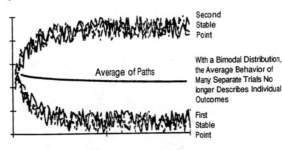

Second
Stable
Point

Average of Paths

With a Bimodal Distribution,
the Average Behavior of
Many Separate Trials No
longer Describes Individual
Outcomes

First
Stable
Point

Time, t

Figure 5.7. An ensemble of paths in a nonlinear state can show
a wide divergence in outcomes as a result of slight changes in
initial fluctuations.

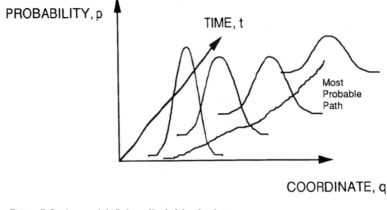

Figure 5.8. A normal "bell-shaped" robability distribution
corresponds to linear Brownian motion (Fig. 5.6).

hypothetical ensembles described previously in Figs. 5.6 and 5.7. The first
case is the linear situation; the second case involves a bifurcation and
bimodal probability distribution.

The Fokker-Planck may be derived from a *master equation.* The master
equation represents a continuity equation in which the rates of transition
between elements of the complex system achieve a balance such that the
change in density of a state represents the difference in the rate at which

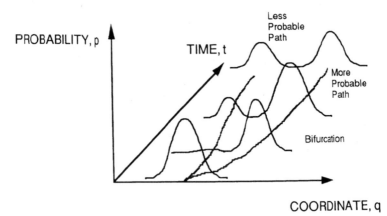

Figure 5.9. A "bimodal" robability distribution corresponds to
nonlinear Brownian motion (Fig. 5.7).

elements transition into the state less the rate at which elements transition out of the state. We explore this further in Appendix B for the case of social systems where the assumptions underlying the macroscopic system behavior are directly applicable to our nonlinear market model.

The theory of polarization of opinion social groups presented in the Appendix underlies our nonlinear market model. It helps explain why there are a significant number of bearish market manias which lead to the golden buying opportunities exploited so effectively by investors such as Warren Buffet. We will see that in a chaotic market state, there is a chance of a bearish mania in which investors sell a quality stock even though the fundamentals may not justify such a course of action.

Summary

In Chap. 1, we discussed the fact that there are predictably more big winners in a coherent market state than expected purely from a Gaussian noise or diffusion process. This can be vitally important to the active manager. Practitioners such as Peter Lynch know the positive impact that even a relatively small number of tenbaggers can have on an otherwise diversified portfolio. Even small deviations from a Gaussian model can dramatically increase the likelihood of finding big winners.

In this chapter, we have shown how our nonlinear market model, based on the concepts of synergetics and, more specifically, on a model of polarization of opinion in social groups, also assures a significant number of manias in the marketplace where price move against fundamentals. The implication for investors is that there will be predictable, numerous situations in which investors either bid up fundamentally unsound companies or sell off financially sound companies. There may initially be good reason for selling a company whose short-term prospects have weakened. However, our nonlinear model suggests that once a stock enters a bearish state, it may persist in that state even past the point warranted by fundamentals.

Warren Buffet has a simple strategy. He looks for quality companies that have fallen out of favor with investors on a short-term basis, but otherwise have sound fundamentals and, therefore, excellent long-term prospects after short-term problems are fixed. Once he has found such an opportunity, he buys at far below fair value and holds for the long run. At some point, the stock will again transition from the bearish or out of favor state to a bullish state. In fact, over the long run, the stock may spend time in each of the states predicted by the nonlinear model. However, if the fundamentals are sound, on average it will spend more time in the coherent bull state than the other less desirable states. By investing when the stock has been beaten down, one is virtually assured of well above average returns over the long run.

Unfortunately, most people are loathe to buy a stock when it is unpopular. There are always good reasons not to buy it. The collective wisdom of the marketplace has spoken, after all, decimating the price. It takes strong conviction to make a commitment to an issue that is out of favor. The key is fundamentals. If a company has a strong balance sheet, it can survive short-term setbacks. In contrast, a company that is burdened by excessive debt may or may not survive.

One ought not to buy a stock simply because it has fallen out of favor. There may be reasons why the stock will never come back. However, knowing that even high quality companies will predictably fall out of favor more often than chance alone would dictate, suggests that it is well worth looking for short-term bearish manias that provide long-term profit potential. Likewise the investor willing to bear the risk of selling a stock short may find ample opportunities of the market having bid up stocks beyond what the fundamentals justify.

6
Megatrends and Manias: The Fundamental Difference

We are often asked why our books seem so "positive" and why we do not describe more of the problems facing humankind.

Headlines about crime, drugs, the Brazilian rain forest, AIDS, chemical warfare, corruption, and double-digit deficits assault us daily, causing us to wonder whether any good can exist side by side with so much of the bad? If the evil, ignorance, and negativity we all read about are true, how can any positive trends be valid?

The people reporting the bad news are doing their job. We respect them for it. And we admire the activists whose life's work is to right the world's wrongs. Our mission is a different one. Because the problems of the world get so much attention, we, for the most part, point out information and circumstances that describe the world trends leading to opportunities.

JOHN NAISBITT AND PATRICIA ABURDENE
Megatrends 2000

Naisbitt's Megatrends:
A Booming Global Economy

Naisbitt coined the term *megatrends*. His best-selling book with that title, published in 1982, identified 10 fundamental changes or megatrends in our society and the larger global economy. Among these, the first on his list was the transformation of the industrial society to the information society: "While the shift from an agricultural to an industrial society took 100 years, the present restructuring from an industrial to an information society took only two decades."

Another megatrend on Naisbitt's list is the increasing globalization of the economy. After World War II, the American economy was the showplace of the world, including a 25 percent share of the world's manufacturing. This included a dominant share of the automobile, steel, and consumer electronics industries. However, competition from abroad has changed this picture dramatically. And it's not just the Japanese that have become industrial powers. South Korea, Brazil, and Singapore are all relatively new, important players.

Nasbitt also observed a trend away from centralization to decentralization. For example, in America there has been a growing assertiveness of local government vis-à-vis the Federal government. The American Medical Association is growing weaker while the specialty medical groups are adding members and gaining strength. The major television networks are losing viewers to new specialized channels for news, weather, and sports. A large rise in new magazines has occurred with regional specialty magazines at the forefront of this trend. Regional airlines are also competing against the large established carriers.

In a more recent update, *Megatrends 2000*, Naisbitt and coauthor Patricia Auberdene have added "a booming global economy" to their list of megatrends for the decade ahead. "We are in an unprecedented period of accelerated change, perhaps the most breathtaking of which is the swiftness of our rush to all the world's becoming a single economy." The American economy is now so intertwined with that of the other major industrial states that it is difficult to separate out the contributions of each entity. However Nasbitt's view is that this is unnecessary. They see this as a healthy development which has resulted in "more democracy, more freedom, more trade, more opportunity and greater prosperity."

Within the growth of the global economy there are backlashes in the form of protectionist policies. However, Nasbitt and Aburdene see these as weak, reactionary developments. The "big, powerful, overarching megatrend is toward worldwide free trade, underneath which we witness the much weaker counter trends of protectionism." They also see no limits to growth: "Everything that comes out of the ground will be in oversupply for the balance of this century and probably much longer." For example, the world is becoming more energy efficient while producing more than ever before. "Interest rates will be contained because there is plenty of capital in the world today, and there is worldwide competition in the renting of money, worldwide competition in the price for renting money."

At a time when most of the developed nations are experiencing slow growth, at best, if not outright recession, Naisbitt's analysis is clearly an upbeat prognosis. Many think of the world economy as a *zero-sum game* (i.e., if Japan gains, someone else has to lose). Naisbitt's observes that "All economies can grow. Everyone can win." These views are much more consistent with the idea that the global economy is an *open system*. As long as there are adequate physical resources, and the availability of credit, the economies of all nations can grow.

The concept of megatrends underlies the results of some of the most successful investment practitioners. A megatrend is not a state of static equilibrium. Rather it is a state of dynamic equilibrium. As Edgar Peters aptly observes, "Equilibrium in a system means the system's death." Dynamic equilibrium occurs in "open systems" which are far from static equilibrium, where a flow of some sort has created structure. In the global economy there is a flow of credit, which is also the flow of information.

Global telecommunication networks support the global economy with real-time multinational voice and data networks. News flows instantaneously from remote points of the globe from transportable satellite terminals. Financial transactions follow the sun around the globe as different markets begin trading where the more eastern markets left off. And like the global economy, the capital markets are also "open" systems in which equilbrium points are dynamic, created and sustained by the global flow of capital.

Open Systems: No Limits to Growth

Rolf Landauer, a physicist and fellow of IBM's Watson Research Laboratory, was the first to recognize the basic similarity between state transitions in open systems far from equilibrium and systems that are in equilibrium. In November 1978, he published an overview article on how random noise affects open systems. Landauer observed:

> Systems such as the gas jet, which require a constant flux of energy to sustain a steady state, are called "open" systems. Stability questions in such open systems are not new, but in the last decade have become fashionable as a result of new viewpoints. Several conference proceedings attest to this interest. The 1977 Nobel Prize for Chemistry, awarded

to Ilya Prigogine, recognized work in this area. There has also been a growing concern with the effect of noise and fluctuations on stability.

Dissipative systems are those which "burn" matter or energy and hence require a flow of some sort to maintain a particular dynamic behavior. The stability of such systems is of great interest and we have seen that questions of stability are important both with random and deterministic processes.

Landauer's article came a month after the October Massacre of 1978. His main point was that open systems, far from equilibrium, are more suscep- tible to "noise" or random fluctuations, than systems in static equilibrium. In a letter pointing out that capital markets may also be viewed as "open" systems far from equilibrium, we suggested that markets at the critical state are also as a matter of necessity more susceptible to random news:

> Rolf Landauer's comments on the influence of noise on "open systems" are well illustrated by recent fluctuations of historic proportions in the stock market. The market may be considered an open system in which an adequate flow of money will effect a transition from disorder (random walk) to order (cooperative or crowd behavior). Near the critical threshold it is highly susceptible to noise (random ecconomic or political news).
>
> The concept of the second-order phase transition in equity markets is new. It implies that the market is not always efficient, that is, the impact of random economic and political news is not always discounted (damped) quickly. In particular, a virtual lack of damping near transition implies a highly inefficient market, characterized by large, long-lasting fluctuations.

The October Massacre of 1978 illustrates the types of fluctuations that may occur in an open system far from equilbrium. In effect, the collective thinking and action that occurs in markets is a manifestation of the nonlinear forces that occur in a diverse range of complex systems.

Landauer's response to the suggestion of market fluctuations as an example of his basic assertion was to offer another example of social imitation of greater interest to physicists than market fluctions:

> The evaluation of scientific work has become much like the stock market; the influence of the opinions of others provides a coupling leading to positive feedback, and to a strong dominance by fads and fashions. Just as the investor can no longer ask: "Which company will do well?" but must ask, "Which company will others think will do well?" the scientist who asks, "What are the important problems?" instead of, "What will others think are the important problems?" takes a serious risk with contract-granting agencies and with his chances for invited papers.

Research, itself, falls into communities of interest and a high degree of polarization of opinions as to what constitutes important problems. These collective opinions, in turn, determine the flow of research funding which reinforces the research community's perception of what's important. Hence the theory underlying open systems and state transitions is not merely a curiosity for those scientists whose life's work may ultimately rest at the mercy of the fads and fashions within the scientific community.

As one example, the whole field on nonlinear dynamic systems was relegated to insignificance for decades. Now this area has come into prominence and is a fashionable topic. Interestingly, the science of complexity offers qualitative insights and quantitative models of the imitative behavior within scientific circles and elsewhere.

The *theory of social imitation* offers a mathematical model of the polarization of opinions in social groups based on an analogy with molecules in a magnetic material. It shows how the coupling between individual molecules (individuals) together with an external bias and random thermal forces all interact to determine the likelihood of finding the system in any particular state.

Market States:
Risk-Reward Profiles

Our nonlinear market model's forecasts depend explicitly on the particular values of two control parameters related to investor sentiment and economic fundamentals. These determine the probability distributions and potential wells that are associated with each of the most interesting market states. For example, the megatrends which Naisbitt so elegantly describes would fit well within the coherent market states of our nonlinear market model. However, our model also predicts that there will be manias, panics, crashes, and quieter periods of true static equilibrium or random walk.

The true random walk (efficient market) is characterized by a lack of feedback or crowd behavior among market participants. Under these conditions, fundamentals will have a much smaller influence than during crowd behavior. Usually random walk markets occur after a coherent bull market has carried prices sharply higher and investors come to their senses, "slowly and one by one," as observed by Charles Mackay. These trendless markets can be frustrating for traders and lead to whipsaws in trading signals generated by technical analysis.

A transition from random walk to crowd behavior is marked by instability. Large, long-lasting price fluctuations are probable during transition. According to researchers such as Per Bak, the critical state is the basis for the fat tails on the probability distribution governing market dynamics. Our view is that the critical state may often represent a good "average" behavior, but not necessarily the only possible state that a market may enter. Coherent markets occur when crowd behavior dominates investor sentiment and there is a strong bias in fundamentals as well. The theory of social imitation suggests that under these conditions, the risk-reward outlook becomes inverted. As long as fundamentals remain positive, these are periods of below average risk and above average return. In effect, there is a single stable state under these conditions, however, the state is far from equilibrium and requires a flow of money to maintain stability. This state would predictably produce even more big winners (or losers) than expected in the critical state.

Chaotic markets occur when crowd behavior produce multiple stable states but fundamentals don't provide a clear preference for one state over the other. Usually, the most dangerous chaotic markets occur when crowd behavior has carried stocks sharply higher over an extended period, fueled by bullish fundamentals. If fundamentals turn even slightly negative, the probability for the market to abruptly transition (i.e., crash) from a stable bullish state to a stable bearish state increases exponentially.

Table 6.1 summarizes the expected return and standard deviation forecast by the nonlinear model as a function of the two input variables, k and h. Here, the third parameter n, the degrees of freedom is assumed to be 186, roughly the number of independent industry groups. The first state is the well-known random walk which occurs when sentiment is below the flash point for crowd behavior (which occurs at $k = 2.0$). Under these

Table 6.1. Risk-Reward Forecasts

Market	Sentiment (k)	Fundamentals (h)	Expected return	Standard deviation
Random walk	1.8	+ 0.02	+8%	10%
	1.8	0	0	10
	1.8	− 0.02	−8	10
Transition	2.0	+ 0.02	14	12
	2.0	0	0	16
	2.0	− 0.02	−14	12
Coherent bull	2.2	+ 0.03	+27	8
	2.2	+ 0.02	+25	11
Chaotic	2.2	+ 0.01	+16	18
	2.2	+0.005	+10	21
	2.2	0	0	23
	2.2	−0.005	−10	21
	2.2	− 0.01	−16	18
Coherent bear	2.2	− 0.02	−25	11
	2.2	− 0.03	−27	8

conditions, the expected return increases or decreases in proportion to the fundamental economic bias, but not very much. Assuming a neutral bias, there would be no return from stocks in a random walk market with a modest risk of about 10 percent.

The transition to crowd behavior occurs when $k = 2.0$ At this point, crowd behavior begins to create large, long-lasting market moves and sentiment may swing from one extreme to the opposite. Any bias in fundamentals will have a much larger effect than during a random walk market, and the risk with neutral fundamentals is also much higher: 16 percent standard deviation, compared to 10 percent in a random walk market.

A coherent bull market occurs when there is both strong crowd behavior and a strong positive bias in fundamentals. For example, the fundamental bias of $h = 0.02$ which provided an 8-percent return in a random walk market, would provide a 25-percent return when the positive feedback of crowd behavior amplifies the markets response to this positive situation. Risk remains low at 11 percent, for a ratio in return divided by risk of better than 2:1. With even better fundamentals, risk drops below 10 percent. However, the return expected increases only slightly to 27 percent. No matter how strong fundamentals are, we can't expect much more than a 25-percent annualized rate of return from the stock market averages.

A chaotic market occurs when there is strong polarization among investors, but the fundamental bias is not as clearly positive or negative as needed to produce a coherent market. If fundamentals are neutral, the model predicts a 23-percent standard deviation, more than double the risk of a random walk market. If there is a fundamental bias, there can be a sizable positive or negative expected return, but risk is high and the ratio of return to risk is typically less than one.

A coherent bear market is also theoretically possible. This is the mirror image of the coherent bull market. Fortunately, there aren't very many instances of this type of market. However, it may be the best model of the Crash of 1929 and the 1973 to 1974 bear market, both of which involved extended periods of negative performance.

Control Parameters: Technical and Fundamental Factors

The control parameters of the nonlinear model (i.e., the sentiment or "technical" variable, k, and the "fundamental" parameter, h), can be based on either subjective opinions of market sentiment and fundamentals or on quantitative models. In fact, some traders seem to prefer a technical approach while others prefer a fundamental approach. Others keep an eye on both technical and fundamental parameters.

For example, in *Market Wizards*, Jack D. Schwager interviews a number of highly successful traders to isolate the factors that contribute to their success. The practitioners he talked to included both technically oriented traders who made extensive use of charts as well as fundamentally oriented traders. However, most successful traders interviewed by Schwager appeared to in one form or another consider both factors.

For example, the commodity trader, Michael Marcus indicated that the underlying chart must show that the market is moving in the same direction as fundamentals before he is interested. Further he observed that fundamentals should indicate an imbalance of supply and demand, an indication of the market being far from equilibrium. When a potential trade meets these conditions, Marcus expressed a willingness to commit to five or six times the position size he normally would bet.

Another trader interviewed by Schwager, Bruce Kovner suggests that charts are absolutely crucial as alerts to existing market disequilibria. He looks for situations where the markets are not confirming the consensus view: this leads to large, long-lasting flows of money as people are forced to bring their perceptions and portfolios in line with market realities. His position is that both technical and fundamental factors are important, with fundamental factors increasing in importance as a result of the enormous increase in use of technical tools by a whole new generation of computerized traders.

Paul Tudor Jones is another successful trader who is frequently featured in *Barron's* interviews. Tudor suggests that trading range expansions are clear signals that the market is getting ready to move in the direction of the expansion. Trader Larry Hite suggests that if the market doesn't respond to important news the way one would expect, it is telling you something very important.

Peter Lynch suggested that there is nothing he enjoys more than curling up with a long-term chart book. However, he also does his fundamental homework before making a commitment to stocks. As a long-term investor, he is forced to ride out some large downward fluctuations. His criteria for when to sell is not to use a stop-loss determined by price; rather he keeps his eye on the fundamental story underlying his reason for initially buying a stock. As long as the fundamental story remains intact, he advises holding a stock no matter how much it falls, and even adding to the position. However, Lynch also recommends selling a stock as soon as there is a change in the fundamental story; and he doesn't wait for the stock to bounce back a little before he gets out.

Marty Zweig's two sacred rules are:

1. don't fight the Fed; and
2. don't fight market "momentum."

He tracks an array of indicators in each of these categories and creates a weighted average to assess the risk-reward outlook. His Fed indicators and Tape indicators can also be interpreted as the control parameters of our nonlinear model. While Zweig is not interested in chaos theory, our nonlinear models suggest that the empirical tools underlying his long-term track record are more than a matter of luck.

Warren Buffet is not a trader, but he does his fundamental homework. He looks for steady growth opportunities in major industries with products and services for which there is a fundamental need. However his market timing is also consistent with our nonlinear model which suggests that even when fundamentals are sound, the market may enter a state of bearish mania, driving down prices without real justification. These periods may be few and far between, but if you recognize them for what they are and have the courage to act on them, you don't need many to become hugely successful.

Louis Navellier's and Jim Collin's technical screening methods are closely tied to our nonlinear market model which predicts that there should be stocks of above average performance with below average risk. However, both Navellier and Collins also focus on the fundamentals associated with their selections. This attention to fundamentals as well as the technical screens is crucial for avoiding the bullish manias that can accompany high performance stocks.

Even Dick Fabian, the telephone switching maven, professes to track only the simplest of technical measures—the long-term moving average price breaks. However, Fabian's approach implicitly involves selection of specific funds which have managers who are worrying about picking the best stocks and diversification of the portfolio. Hence even the switch fund investors are implementing a strategy which involves both technical and fundamental factors, in search of the coherent trends that can develop in the capital markets.

Random Walk: The First Step

A true random walk market is a trader's worst enemy. The market may remain in this state indefinitely, not making big moves in either direction, but locked in a range. However, these market states can lead to high transaction costs and little in the way of returns.

Random walk is the "first step" in the general nonlinear model. In fact, as originally shown by Wolfgang Weidlich, the probability distribution simplifies considerably when nonlinear forces are small, and becomes

$$f(q) = (1/g\sqrt{\pi}) \exp(-q^2/g^2)$$

where the variance

$$g^2 = 1/(2-k)n.$$

This represents the normal or Gaussian probability distribution associated with a snapshot in time of a random walk process.

The nonlinear problem can't be solved in closed form for the general time dependent case. When the nonlinear forces are small enough to be ignored, the usual time dependent random walk distribution is obtained in which the standard deviation widens in proportion to the square root of time.

Note that as k approaches 2 in the equation above, the variance of the normal distribution becomes large. While the approximation above loses its validity as k approaches 2, there is a fundamental instability inherent in the nonlinear model at this critical threshold in the transition from random walk to crowd behavior.

One way to view the stock market, or more precisely, the return from a market index is to think of it as a ball trapped in a potential well, buffeted by random forces. Using this model, the random walk state can be thought of as a ball trapped in a well with a single bottom with a low point near zero, as shown in Fig. 6.1. Random forces cause the ball to fluctuate unpredictably

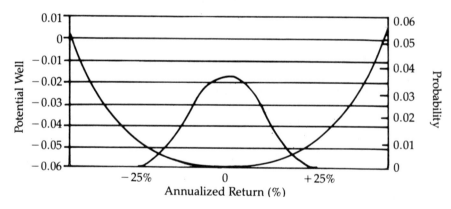

Figure 6.1. Returns are likely to fluctuate narrowly about a single stable equilibrium point in a true random walk market. (*Reprinted with permission from* Financial Analysts Journal, *November/December 1990.* © *1990 Association for Investment Management and Research, Charlottesville, VA. All rights reserved.*)

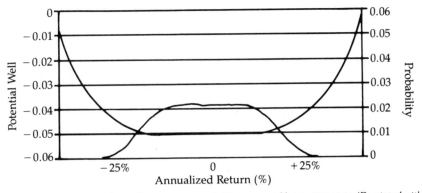

Figure 6.2. Large, long-lasting fluctuations are probable in an unstable transition state. (*Reprinted with permission from* Financial Analysts Journal, *November/December 1990.* © *1990 Association for Investment Management and Research, Charlottesville, VA. All rights reserved.*)

in the well and its future position can't be predicted from knowledge of its past positions. However, the most likely place for the ball to be is near the center of the well.

Fundamentals may shift the low point of the well to the right or the left. This would allow for a small positive or negative expected return, depending on the fundamental bias. However, without the magnification effects of crowd behavior, the market isn't likely to provide a large net return in either direction and chances are you'd be better off in a risk-free money market fund.

Unstable Transition: The Critical State

Transitions from disorder to order have well-defined characteristics regardless of the type of system or details of the microscopic interactions among subsystems. These characteristics include "critical fluctuations" and "critical slowing down" in the fluctuations of the order parameter which for the stock market we have defined as the return from a market index. The influence of random noise is much larger and longer lasting than comparable forces in a typical random walk market.

In the stock market, the transition from random walk to crowd behavior is marked by an instability in investor expectations. Sentiment may swing from one extreme to another in response to even minor economic or political news. Unlike an efficient market where new developments are discounted quickly, an unstable transition is highly inefficient due to a lack of the usual damping forces that are present in a random walk market.

During transition, wide variations in the returns may occur for individual industry groups. Some sectors may look highly attractive and attract significant interest from investors. Other groups may be totally out of favor and show large negative returns. On average, the market may show little net gain while individual groups show widely varying results.

Thinking of the market index as a ball in a potential well, Fig. 6.2 shows a flat well with a wide, near uniform probability distribution. This implies that annualized returns are more probable across a wide range. The ball, representing the return from a market index, is free to swing over a wide range, as though there are no restraining forces until sentiment and prices reach extremes. The types of fat-tailed distributions that can be expected in the unstable transition are described further in the Appendix.

Since random forces have a large, long-lasting impact, a transition market can best be characterized as being inefficient. In contrast, in either a random walk or coherent market, new developments are discounted quickly, though the market's reaction is usually strongly biased in a coherent market.

The case shown is for neutral fundamentals. If there is a fundamental bias, it will have a large impact during a period of instability. For example, a bullish bias in fundamentals ($h = 0.02$) would shift the expected return from zero to a healthy +14 percent—nearly double the impact of the same positive fundamentals during a random walk market. This reflects the increasing influence of the coupling of opinions among investors, leading to positive or regenerative feedback, in which a trend, once established tends to reinforce itself.

Coherent Megatrends: The Most Rewarding Markets

The most interesting market state for investors and traders alike is the coherent market. This occurs when there is both crowd psychology at work as a result of large flows of money and a strong bias in economic fundamentals which gives the market a preferred direction. In effect the equilibrium of the market splits from the single stable point of the random walk market, to two new stable points far from static equilibrium. However, the strong fundamental bias makes one of these points far more likely than the other. In effect there is only one stable state, but it is centered at a point far from equilibrium that corresponds to large returns or price trends.

A coherent market is one where a variety of practitioners' trading rules kick in. "Don't fight the trend" is one example. These are powerful trending markets, driven by large flows of money. The rally of January 1975 comes to mind as an example of a coherent bull market. August 1982 is another more recent example. In both of these cases, there was collective action which showed up in volume and breadth figures. The price trend was consistent with the easing of interest rates by the Federal Reserve. While there were short-term fluctuations in both directions, these fluctuations centered around a large positive rate of return.

Even in coherent bull markets, short-term volatility will always mask the underlying trend in prices. A 25-percent annualized rate of return is only about 0.1 percent per day, while daily volatility is typically on the order of 1 percent per day. The market's short-term price action may not be statistically significantly different from what is seen in a period of true random walk. However, even a small daily bias will compound into a large return over a six- or twelve-month period. Of course, technical measures such as price breaks above the moving average will capture the trending market and generate appropriate buy signals. Unfortunately, after a long basing period, or true random walk market, and the associated whip saw results of trading, it may be difficult to act on the first signal in a new bull market which often generates the best results.

Within the framework of our nonlinear model, as the degree of crowd behavior or group-think increases (k = 2.2), investor sentiment will become increasingly polarized. If fundamentals are neutral, the potential well splits into a double bottom configuration with each side of the well separated by a potential barrier in the center. This makes the extremes far more likely than the center. A big market move is more probable than flat or sideways market action.

Usually, crowd behavior is stimulated by a strong bias in fundamentals. For example, if fundamentals are very positive (h = 0.02) as shown in Fig. 6.3, one side of the potential well becomes much lower than the other side.

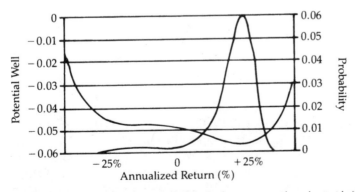

Figure 6.3. A coherent bull market state can generate large returns with moderate risk. (*Reprinted with permission from* Financial Analysts Journal, November/December 1990. © *1990 Association for Investment Management and Research, Charlottesville, VA. All rights reserved.*)

The probability distribution also becomes strongly skewed, favoring positive outcomes over negative moves. Under these conditions, the expected return from the stock market is unusually large, while the risk becomes unusually low.

In effect, the risk-reward ratio is "inverted" or turned upside down in a coherent bull market. Historically, the market has averaged returns of 10 percent a year with a 20-percent standard deviation. During a coherent bull market, the theoretical model forecasts a 25-percent return with a standard deviation in the neighborhood of only 10 percent. This narrowing of the width of the probability distribution is analogous to the narrowing in the width of the spectral distribution function of laser light. In both cases, the result is a more orderly or predictable state of the system. In the laser, this effect is many orders of magnitude or factors of 10; in the stock market, it is far less pronounced, but large enough to make a real difference in your investment results.

Most of the market's long-term gains can be attributed to coherent bull markets. You have to be fully invested during these periods or risk under performing the market averages. The rest of the time the stock market offers more risk than reward in the form of chaotic markets and periods of true random walk. Passive indexing captures all the coherent stocks in a given universe and also guarantees a fully invested portfolio during coherent market periods. As long as there is a positive fundamental bias, the passive indexing approach is guaranteed to include the post profitable stocks and market periods.

If fundamentals are bearish during crowd behavior, the nonlinear model forecasts the mirror image of the coherent bull market. Now the bearish side of the well is the most probable outcome. Even small negative developments can push the ball from a bullish state to the bearish side of the well. However, the reverse is not likely to happen since the well has a very steep uphill barrier as you move from the bearish to bullish side.

Chaos: The Most Dangerous Markets

Chaotic markets occur when crowd behavior prevails but there isn't a strong bias in fundamentals. These are potentially dangerous periods in which price trends are likely to persist on a short-term basis but abrupt sentiment shifts between bullish and bearish states could occur as a matter of chance.

Figure 6.4 illustrates the potential well for the situation in which the sentiment variable is above the flash point for crowd behavior, while there isn't a strong bias in fundamentals in either direction. The potential well or

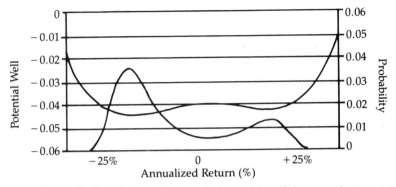

Figure 6.4. A chaotic market state with neutral fundamentals typically has strong short-term trends with little net gain over the long run. (*Reprinted with permission from* Financial Analysts Journal, *November/December 1990. © 1990 Association for Investment Management and Research, Charlottesville, VA. All rights reserved.*)

attractor has split into two low points each of which is equally likely. However the market must move one way or the other. The top of the potential barrier is not a stable point as even small news would lead to the ball (market return) making a large move toward a true stable point.

Once the ball is in either of the two low points it is likely to stay there for an extended period. For example, in the Appendix, we see that in a bistable random process, the time of first crossing (i.e., the time it takes on average to get from one side of the potential well, across the barrier in the middle) may be large. In any case, the crossing time is an exponential function of the height of the barrier. This means that any change in fundamentals during a period of crowd behavior is extremely important. The market may not react immediately to fundamentals such as change in Fed policy. However, the odds change immediately.

It is critically important to understand the difference between a change in probabilities versus an immediate change in what the market is doing. During a period of crowd behavior, once the market is in a particular state, it is more apt to stay in that state than to switch to the opposite state. However, if fundamentals are changing, the average time required for a market state change drops dramatically. Even though the market hasn't started to act any differently, but the odds are totally different.

In effect, a chaotic market is a two-state market. The extremes are more likely than the middle, but over the long run, if fundamentals are truly neutral, the expected return is not very large since big moves one way are offset by equally large moves in the opposite direction on other occasions. If there is even a slight bias in fundamentals, it can have a dramatic impact on the odds, producing more large positive returns than negative returns or vice versa.

Chaotic markets are also the most difficult periods to invest in. If you recognize that prices are trending higher in spite of weak fundamentals, you may be tempted to stay out of the market. However, in a period of crowd behavior, there is very strong pressure to join the crowd to avoid underperforming the market averages. In a period of mania, prices may rise as fast as in a fundamentally sound conherent bull market and it's difficult to take a contrary position at these times, since it may take a long time for the bubble to burst.

Manias, Panics, and Crashes

The theory of social imitation forecasts that even if fundamentals deteriorate and turn negative, there is still a significant probability of a substantial bullish trend. While this is less likely than a stable bearish trend, it could occur particularly if the market started out in a bullish state even as fundamentals are gradually deteriorating. Since prices are in a short-term stable uptrend, investors may well ignore bad news and react more to good news. This would produce a biased random walk or short-term trend with the same rate of return as in a coherent bull market. The only difference is that there is a growing probability of an abrupt change of state from bullish to bearish, accompanied by a panic and crash in share prices (i.e., anomalous volatility as the ball jumps abruptly from one side of the well to the opposite), as shown in Fig. 6.5.

When prices remain in a stable bullish state in spite of negative fundamentals, the market may be said to be in a period of mania. Historically, manias have occurred in a variety of markets, but the end result is usually the same. Prices rise well beyond any fundamental justification as a result of positive feedback among investors. However, at some point, the trend may switch abruptly from the bullish state to its mirror image, producing a panic and crash in prices.

The probability distribution shown represents a "stationary" state. The general time dependent, nonlinear problem can't be solved nicely in closed form. Rather, solutions are developed for a time independent analysis, and then linearized solutions are developed in the neighborhood of the stable states. In other words, you can think of the time dependent analysis as the usual random walk problem, except that the whole probability distribution both diffuses (widens) in time and drifts toward the most stable, stationary solution. In a chaotic market, the fat tail on the otherwise "normal" or bell-shaped probability distribution, represents big, abrupt jumps from one stable state to another.

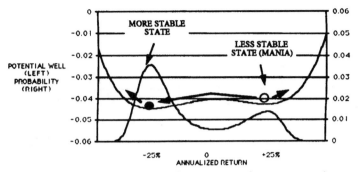

Figure 6.5. A market mania occurs when a price trend moves against the prevailing fundamental bias.

Figure 6.6 illustrates a particular scenario that could be played out in time. It begins with a random walk market and neutral fundamentals. As time goes by, there is a natural tendency for the normal distribution to widen since just by chance there is more likelihood of a greater return from the stock market if a greater period of time goes by. However, the most likely outcome is still in the neighborhood of zero, since there is no bias in fundamentals one way or the other.

If fundamentals improve, there may be a transition from random walk to crowd behavior in the market. This is characterized by the wide and flat, or near-uniform probability distribution associated with the instability that occurs during transition. Large fluctuations of the market index are likely during this transition market and you may easily get scared out of your positions especially if prices move sharply lower in spite of apparently improving fundamentals.

However, if fundamentals are positive (e.g., the Fed is cutting the discount rate, money managers have large cash reserves, and stocks are cheap) the market should stabilize in a coherent bullish trend, with the most likely return from the market is in the neighborhood of +25 percent with unusually small deviations around this rate of return. While it is in this state, prices will fluctuate as a strongly biased random walk in which good news is received enthusiastically while bad news is ignored or leads to only minor corrections.

As the business cycle ages, and fundamentals turn negative, there is a possibility of a market mania emerging. If investors continue to bid up prices in a negative fundamental environment, some unexpected event could trigger a selling panic and crash as prices switch from the less likely bullish state to the more probable bearish state.

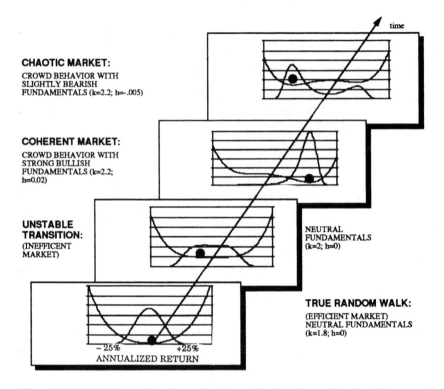

Figure 6.6. Market state transitions change the risk-reward outlook substantially and can be the basis for investment decisions.

Historical Manias

Financial history is replete with manias, panics, and crashes. Charles Mackay documented the events surrounding the events in the Netherlands which led to this classic financial bubble. The Netherlands had become a center of import for tulip bulbs from Turkey in the mid-1500s. Professional growers and wealthy purchasers were particularly intrigued with rare varieties which sold at exceptionally high prices. Prices of tulip bulbs increased steadily, to the point where owning these bulbs became a passion among the middle class as well.

By 1634, according to Mackay, "the rage among the Dutch to possess them was so great that the ordinary industry of the country was neglected, and the population, even to its lowest dregs, embarked in the tulip trade. As the mania increase, prices augmented, until, in the year 1635, many persons were known to invest a fortune of 100,000 florins in the purchase of forty roots."

In 1936, financial markets accommodated speculation in the rare tulip bulbs in various cities throughout the Netherlands. Many people were growing rich trading tulips. Everyone imagined that the demand for tulips would only grow, and they converted real property into cash to buy the bulbs. However, the fever broke and the market for tulips crashed with dire consequences for those who had speculated with their life savings. Eventually the price of tulips returned to their fundamental value, about the same as onions.

Charles Kindelberger, Professor of Economics Emeritus at MIT indicates that financial manias always tend to begin with fundamentally sound investment opportunities. The specific fundamental opportunity varies from one business cycle to the next and from one country to another. However, invariably there is some new development which becomes the object of investment, speculation, and ultimately to mania.

Manias may be fueled by the outbreak or end of war, by a new invention, by opening up of new land for exploration and colonization, or some other new factor in the economic system. Canals, railroads, and the automobile are all fundamentally important developments which have fueled speculation far beyond fundamental justifications. For example, Table 6.2 lists a number of objects of speculation compiled by Kindelberger.

Jim Rogers was one of the speculators in the gold mania of the 1970s and early 1980s. In an interview with Jack D. Schwager, in *Market Wizards*, Rogers states that: "When I see hysteria, I usually like to take a look to see if I shouldn't be going the other way." He sold gold short at $675. While that was $200 too early, the hysteria of the moment was a catalyst that tipped off the fundamental overvaluation of the market.

Rogers indicates that he has "lived through or studied hundreds, possibly thousands of bull and bear markets. In every bull market, whether it is IBM or oats, the bulls always seem to come up with reasons why it must go on, and on, and on." Rogers goes on to say, "The whole process then repeats itself on the downside."

The academic community also has a keen interest in manias. After all if the market price of an asset differs substantially from the fundamental value, it implies that the market is not efficient. Needless to say, there are divergent views as to how well asset prices correlate with "fundamental" values.

The factors that normally go into determination of fundamental value include:

1. returns received from the asset, such as dividends;

2. terminal value of the asset at the time of sale; and

3. risk-free rates of return over the period of interest.

When market prices deviate significantly from the fundamental valuation, the resulting market is said to be in a bubble or mania.

Table 6.2. Object of Speculation: Place and Time of Mania

OBJECT OF SPECULATION	TIME AND PLACE OF MANIA
British Government Debt	Amsterdam, 1763
Public Companies	South Sea Company, Compagnie d'Occident, Sword Blade Bank, Banque Generale, Bank Royale, 1720; British East India Company, 1772; Dutch East India Company, 1772, 1783.
Import Commodities	Sugar, coffee, 1799, 1857 in Hamburg; Cotton, 1836,1861 in Britain and France; Wheat in 1847.
Country Banks	England, 1750s, 1793, 1824.
Canals	1793, 1820s in Britain 1823 in France
Foreign Bonds	1825 in London; 1888 in Paris 1924 in New York
Foreign Mines	Latin American mines in Britain, 1825; German mines in Britain and France, 1850
Public Lands	United States in 1836; Argentina in 1888-1890
Railroad Shares	1836, 1847 in Britain; 1847, 1857 in France; 1857, 1873 in the United States
Private Companies Going Public	1888 in Britain 1928 in the United States
Gold	1960s, 1970s
Buildings	Hotels, condominiums, office buildings, etc

Data from Kindleberger, *Manias, Panics and Crashes*, 1978

Our nonlinear model allows for both sentiment and fundamental factors as control parameters of the market state. However, our model assumes inherently that markets are open systems in which returns can stabilize at levels well above or well below the long-term average. Assuming the long-term average represents some measure of fundamental value, short-term stable states around the long-term average can produce valuation extremes.

More specifically our model quantifies the duration of manias as being an exponential function with the mean duration being related to the fundamentals. The fundamental factors affecting a market determine the height of the potential barrier in the well. If we define a mania as the less probable state of returns in a bimodal distribution, then the duration of the state will depend on the height of the potential barrier between the two stable points.

For example, prior to the Crash of 1987, various sentiment indicators such as volume extremes had been indicating that conditions were conducive to crowd behavior. Interest rates had also been rising. Finally in September, the Fed confirmed the rising rates by raising the discount rate. From this point the market rallied over another 100 points in the Dow Industrials, reaching a short-term peak early in October. However the rally failed to carry back to earlier August highs, and the broad market had been deteriorating steadily. Valuations were at historical extremes, and a lot of people were sitting on large profits from the first nine months of the year which they wanted to protect.

As interest rates were rising in 1987, and valuation levels were approaching overvalued extremes, the fundamentals of the stock market were deteriorating. This alone did not affect the price trend of stocks immediately since the market was in a stable bullish state. However these factors affected the probabilities of a transition from the bullish state to it's mirror image. The odds of a switch within a moderate period of time was increasing exponentially. The actual events that triggered the switch are less important than the main control parameters that determine the probabilities of state transitions and large market fluctuations.

After the Crash of 1987, the Fed reversed course and flooded the market with liquidity to prevent the collapse from escalating. This again represented a slight shift in fundamentals, which during a period of crowd behavior can have a large influence on market fluctuations. However, our model doesn't provide an answer to why the market decline was as short and violent as it turned out to be.

Summary: Indexing—
Megatrend or Mania?

We observed at the outset of this book passive indexing is one of the simplest, most effective strategies for investing in chaotic markets. This approach ensures capturing all of the biggest winners in a particular universe of stocks. In fact, index investing has captured a large share of the market and itself has become a no-brainer decision. Is this still a fundamentally sound practice in a high valuation market? .

While indexing is an effective strategy as long as there is positive economic growth over the long run, it is susceptible to large fluctuations in a short-term period of mania. For example, in the Crash of 1987, index funds suffered the full blow of the decline with no downside protection other than methods such as portfolio insurance which is often cited as a reason for the crash. Stocks have once again returned to the valuation extremes not seen since prior to the Crash of 1987. However, there are some significant differences in the current environment. First, the market sentiment is not conducive to crowd behavior. Second, long-term interest rates have been declining sharply rather than rising.

However, in the current high valuation environment, the stock market is highly susceptible to a major reversal should the decline in interest rates falter. Likewise the current decline in rates is largely due to the weak economy whereas in the 1987 time frame the economy was particularly strong. A large tax increase further looms on the horizon which can further depress earnings. Hence index investing in the current environment may not be the best short-term approach. Long-term indexing should remain an elegant way to participate as long as the global economy remains in its megatrend.

Hence as with other markets, fundamentals are the real difference between megatrends and manias. Long-term investors who really aren't in the business of short-term trading need to be psychologically prepared to weather some major downside fluctuations in their index funds as a result of short-term overvaluations in periods of bullish manias. However, as long as the fundamental story of the American economy remains intact, indexing should remain an effective strategy. Global diversification in international index funds, however, would appear to be prudent to ensure participation in the global economic growth in the future.

7

Market Timing: Vindication of Technical Analysis

You know as well as I do, if something is complicated, time-consuming, stressful, causes you to lose sleep, or is in any way a nuisance, you simply will not do it. Or at least you won't do it for long. So what's the point in fooling around with some complex investment scheme. You're not going to continue with it. And if you don't continue with it, you can't make any money!

Many mutual fund companies offer a family of funds in which to invest, as well as the telephone-switching privilege for moving your money around among them. Since it is easy to invest in these mutual funds–it is only necessary to determine first, which segments are in an uptrend and are therefore profitable, and second, which segments are in a downtrend and are therefore unprofitable. All you have to do is become a trend-follower.

DICK FABIAN
Investor's Guide
(Winter, 1989)

Dick Fabian: Mechanical Market Maven

Dick Fabian is a mechanical market maven. He has created, in his own words, "the simplest plan of accumulating wealth ever devised. It takes very little time to implement and is suitable for just about everybody. That's the reason my plan is so popular—anyone can use it easily."

Fabian has a large following of individual investors who use his simple formula for timing switches between funds in families of mutual funds, simply by placing a phone call. Of course, investment managers have trouble dealing with a small army of telephone switchers on a given day, and many have taken steps to curtail switching privileges or simply stopped doing business with those who follow Fabian's advice.

Apart from the question of implementation, at issue is whether it makes sense to invest even a relatively modest amount of time and effort into a trend-following approach. After all, if the market is efficient, then even this simple mechanical approach to active management would be a waste of time. Mark Hulbert, who tracks newsletter publisher performance, has tracked Fabian's market calls over an extended period of 13 years and found that on a risk-adjusted basis, Fabian ranks number five in the performance sweepstakes as of June 30, 1993 having beaten the market with a 603 percent gain versus 558 percent for the S&P 500 market index.

What's Fabian's secret? Well it's no secret at all. He simply tracks the performance of a set of funds by means of moving averages. When a fund's value rises above a long-term moving average, he assumes that it's in an uptrend and buys. When the funds value drops below a long-term moving average, he assumes that it's in a downtrend and sells. Sound simple? That's the point. Fabian uses the magic of compound interest to keep money growing over the long run. The switches are designed to keep money in funds that are in uptrends and avoid the sectors that are not.

Clearly Fabian's strategy is based on the implicit assumption that there are underlying market trends that are persistent. He has no interest in predicting the market, explaining the market, or in any other way outsmarting the market. He uses a simple mechanical approach to investment decision making. He tracks simple moving averages and invests accordingly.

Recent academic work supports Fabian's simple strategy. Simple technical trading rules do turn out to be statistically significant both in terms of beating the buy and hold and reducing risk. The academic view that markets are efficient and that technical analysis is a waste of time or worse is now giving way to a new realization that the statistical tools on which these assertions were based did not adequately capture the nonlinear effects underlying financial market dynamics. Even simple nonlinear models can generate time series from deterministic processes that statistical analysis will think is just random noise.

While no one has discovered any simple deterministic model that can predict the market's fluctuations, there are new approaches to analyzing time series which suggest that earlier pronouncements of the death of technical analysis may well have been premature. And the discovery that simple technical trading rules reduce risk *and* improve returns directly contradicts the capital asset pricing model which maintains that above average returns are possible only with above average risk. This discovery also directly supports the coherent market hypothesis which maintains that periods of above average returns with below average risk are theoretically possible within the framework of nonlinear market dynamics.

The traditional methods of time series analysis have been augmented by *bootstrapping*. These new approaches have vindicated technical market analysis. It is exciting to witness the academics and practitioners cooperatively pursuing better techniques rather than throwing stones at each other. However, it is also early in the life cycle of this emerging new discipline and practical applications of technical analysis in other than its simplest forms may not be at hand. For example, the costs of trading are always an important factor which could readily overwhelm any benefits of an active strategy.

Time Series Analysis: A Method of Surrogate Data

In many practical problems, there is a time series of measurements and the problem is to diagnose the nature of the underlying system dynamics. James Theiler, a physicist at the Los Alamos National Laboratory, has proposed a method of *surrogate data* for detecting nonlinearity in time series. This method is based on demonstrating that simple linear models are inadequate to explain the dynamics of the system. A related approach has recently been used by William Brock and his colleagues to show that technical trading rules significantly outperform the market and do so with below average volatility. This finding supports the coherent market hypothesis which predicts the theoretical possibility of above average returns with below average risk.

With small amounts of data and a high degree of noise, the statistical significance of various indicators of chaos can be difficult to determine. Estimates of dimension and Lyapunov exponents are approximate at best and sometimes wrong if there is insufficient, noisy data. The limited amount of data has also made it difficult to assess the statistical significance of various trading systems.

Following Theiler's approach, the significance of a nonlinear indicator such as dimension, can be estimated by comparing the actual estimate with a range of results obtained for the same measure calculated on a collection of "surrogate" data sets. The surrogate data sets are randomized versions of the actual time series. Instead of putting error bars around the original estimate of the particular measure under evaluation, the error bars are established for the measure computed on the surrogate or noise series.

Statistical hypothesis testing involves two key steps. The first is to develop a *null hypothesis* which is the simple linear model that we believe to be inadequate to explain the actual dynamics of the system being evaluated. The second step is the development of a discriminating statistic which characterizes some aspect of the time series. If the discriminating statistic computed for the actual data differs significantly from the null hypothesis, then the simple linear model can be rejected.

Using this method of surrogate data, the distribution of a given statistic is evaluated by Monte Carlo simulation. A set of surrogate time series are constructed which are similar to the original time series with respect to moments such as the mean and standard deviation, but are otherwise just random noise. The discriminating statistic is computed for each of these random series to build up a mean and standard deviation (error bars) for this measure as applied to the equivalent noise process.

If the actual data produces a statistic (i.e., dimension estimate, Lyapunov exponent estimate, or some other measure) that falls within the range of the average result for noise plus or minus one or two standard deviations, then the simple random time series models can't be rejected. However, if the statistic computed for the actual time series differs substantially from that for the surrogate data, then there is evidence of some underlying nonlinear process. Theiler suggests a measure of significance, S, which he refers to as *sigmas* and is defined as

$$S = |Q_D - \mu_H| / s_H \qquad (7.1)$$

where Q_D is the statistic computed on the original time series, and μ_H and s_H are, respectively, the mean and standard deviation of the statistic computed on the surrogate data sets. If Q_D is much larger than μ_H and the difference between Q_D and μ_H is large compared to s_H, then the statistic Q_D indicates that the original series is significantly different than just random noise.

A variety of procedures are available for generating a null hypothesis. The simplest is to use a random number generator with the mean and standard deviation tuned to match the original data. It is also possible to allow for some degree of linear correlation using *auto regression* (AR), *moving average* (MA), or *combination* (ARMA) *models*. These are the tools of traditional time-series analysis.

Discriminating statistics can be indicators of chaos such as those described in Chap. 3 or any other measure of interest. The particular example of interest is the use of technical trading rules as discriminating statistics. This approach, used by Brock, Lakonishok and LeBaron, shows that simple technical rules do in fact provide statistically significant above average returns with below average risk. In effect, technical trading rules can be interpreted as measures of nonlinear dynamics in the market. At times the market may be in a true random state and such rules will not work. However, when averaged over a sufficiently long period, there are enough trending or nonlinear market periods for such rules to be significant, on average.

Before discussing the technical trading rules examined by Brock, we will review standard time series models and statistical hypothesis testing. Both linear and nonlinear models of time series have been proposed in recent years. These models can be used to construct a *null hypothesis* which is "too simple" an explanation, and which is inadequate for explaining the data. Hypothesis testing also involves computation of a discriminating statistic which is a number or indicator that is believed to be significant in capturing some important aspect of the time series. For example, technical analysts believe if the market price moves above its moving average, it signifies a positive trend. If the market's returns following such events are significantly different for the observed data than for some simple market model (e.g., random noise), then the simple model can be rejected. The technical trading rule becomes a discriminating statistic, much as a Lyanpunov exponent or dimension calculation.

For example, a simple random noise model may specify the mean and standard deviation of market returns to be the same as for the original time series, but otherwise is random. The surrogate data sets are then constructed to meet this specification and the discriminating statistic is calculated on the surrogate data to build up a distribution of the results. For example, if the market's return after a moving average break (the discriminating statistic) is significantly different for the original time series than for the random data sets, the latter can be rejected, and we can assume that the original time series involves more than just a random noise process. The market model may be more complex than simple noise. It may involve some degree of correlation between the past and future data elements. If these specifications of the time series also fail to produce the type of discriminating statistics as found in the original time series, then they too can be rejected as inadequate models of the original data.

Linear Models of Time Series

In general, a time series documents the values of some state variable of a dynamic system at different points in time. The data may be recorded and stored at discrete points in time (such as five minute intervals, hourly, daily, weekly, or monthly for financial markets) or may be recorded continuously over a period as an *electroencephalograph* (EEG) which charts the electrical activity of the brain. With time series data, the order in which measurements are recorded is of particular importance. In contrast, the order of the data in other statistical samples used to infer the characteristics of a population is statistically irrelevant.

Two assumptions are normally made in time series analysis. The first is that the series is *stationary*, (i.e., that its underlying dynamics do not vary in time and hence its statistical properties also remain constant over time). The second assumption is that the dynamics are based on a *linear* process so that the series can be decomposed into linear combinations of prior values of a random series.

These assumptions are not always valid and are being increasingly questioned and replaced with models that are nonlinear and nonstationary. However, this section will first describe the models that have been developed to characterize linear time series. These models are used as specifications for null hypothesis testing.

The simplest type of time series is generated by a white noise process. In this situation, the series is simply a sequence of independent random variables. The series will have some mean, μ, and variance, s, and the correlation between values at different times will be zero.

However, many time series are more complicated than the pure white noise process. The mean of the series may change over time and there may be correlation between the state variables at different points in time. Therefore, the goal of building a model is to explain the behavior of the mean and any correlation over time. To do this requires a model of the relationship between past, present and future values. If the model successfully explains predictable relationships in the data, the residual differences between the discriminating statistic for the actual data and the model should be normally distributed around zero.

Auto Regressive Models

One particular example of a time series model is the *auto regressive model* (AR). For example, a process may be generated by

$$q_t = aq_{t-1} + e_t \tag{7.2}$$

where e_t is white noise. This is a special case of the Markov process where the model only considers the most recent state in the time series. This approach can be generalized to include an arbitrary number, k, of prior time series data points in which case the auto regressive model of order k, AR(k) is generated by

$$q_t = \sum_{j=1}^{k} a_j q_{t-j} + e_t \qquad (7.3)$$

The coefficients, a_j can be fit by means of regression analysis to a particular time series.

Another widely used approach for time series modeling is to consider a process of the form

$$q_t = e_t + e_{t-1} \qquad (7.4)$$

where e_t is zero mean white noise. This can be generalized from a single prior time series point or moving average to a process which averages g's prior points according to

$$q_t = \sum_{j=0}^{g} b_j e_{t-j} \qquad (7.5)$$

This is the moving average of order g. It generates a smoother time series than pure white noise (when $g > 0$) due to some degree of correlation with prior data points.

Finally, a mixed model based on the MA and AR processes may be constructed in which

$$q_t = \sum_{j=1}^{p} a_j q_{t-j} + \sum_{j=0}^{g} b_j e_{t-j} \qquad (7.6)$$

This is known as a *mixed ARMA process* or ARMA (p,g) where p and g are the order of the past dependence.

In financial markets, there is a well-known effect, first pointed out by Mandelbrot, in which periods of high volatility are followed by high volatility, and periods of low volatility are followed by periods of low volatility. As a result of this, and a growing interest in currency trading, a number of time series models were developed in the 1980s that attempted to capture this effect.

Most modeling and forecasting focuses on the conditional mean. However in problems dealing with time varying variances, the modeling of conditional variances is important as well. The *auto regressive conditional heteroscedastic* (ARCH) model, developed by Engle, was the first attempt to predict volatility. Engle applied the model to inflation data in the United Kingdom and found evidence of predictable variances.

Another approach to modeling time dependent variances is based on the generalized version of ARCH (i.e., GARCH based on the work of Bollerslev). Nelson's EGARCH model introduced conditional variances that respond differently to declines versus advances; whereas ARCH and GARCH models involve a symmetric response. Brock and his colleagues examined various models of conditional variances as possible null hypotheses in their tests of technical trading rules.

Simple Technical Trading Rules

Having reviewed some of the standard time series models, we proceed now with the analysis of simple technical trading rules. In 1992, William Brock, Josef Lakonishok, and Blake LeBaron tested simple, popular trading rules, including moving averages and trading range breakouts. In the first method, buy and sell signals are generated as a short moving average crosses a long moving average; the second method generates signals as prices hit either new highs or new lows. Their results "provide strong support for the technical strategies."

Key findings are that:

1. buy signals generate higher returns than sell signals;

2. returns following sell signals are negative; and

3. returns following buy signals are less volatile than returns following sell signals.

They also demonstrate that these results are not consistent with any of four popular null hypotheses: the random walk, the AR(1), the GARCH-M, and the exponential GARCH models.

The findings of Brock and his colleagues directly contradict decades of earlier research findings by proponents of the efficient market hypothesis. "The conclusion reached by many earlier studies that found technical analysis to be useless might have been premature." This aboutface within the academic community is based in part on the use of new computationally intensive methods for analysis of time series and drawing statistical inferences. One of these techniques is *bootstrapping*, which is similar to Theiler's method of *surrogate data*. As Brock points out, the bootstrap methodology is not new, but its application to test the significance of technical trading rules is new.

The time series covered by the study is long, beginning in 1897 and extending through 1986. A large number of specific technical trading rules were included and the results of all the rules were reported to avoid the issue of data mining (i.e., reporting only those results that looked good). The results for the variable length moving average rules provided returns of 0.042 percent on a daily basis, which is about 12 percent per year. In contrast, the daily returns for the sell periods were −0.025 percent or about −7 percent per year. The standard deviation of daily returns was 0.89 percent for the buy periods and 1.34 percent for the sell periods.

The particular trading rules evaluated by Brock and his colleagues are deliberately similar to the types of rules frequently used by practitioners. Hence their findings are a vindication of technical analysis.

Trading Rules

Moving average-based trading rules used in the study were based on two moving averages of the Dow Jones Industrial Average. When the short-term average rises above the long-term average, a buy signal is generated. For example, a popular long-term moving average is the 200-day line, while a frequently used short-term average is a single day. This case can be expressed as (1-200). When the index rises above the 200-day line, a buy signal is generated; a sell is triggered when the index falls below the 200-day moving average. A band around the average (e.g., 1 percent) also can be used to reduce the number of *whiplash* signals. These types of rules lead to *variable length moving average* (VMA) signals where the holding period remains in effect as long as the short moving average remains above the long moving average less the filter band.

An alternative trading rule is to focus on the period immediately following a moving average break. For example, if the short-term moving average rises above (falls below) the long-term moving average plus the filter, it generates a buy (sell) signal which by definition lasts 10 trading days. Any other signals that occur during this period are ignored. This is the *fixed-length moving average* (FMA) signal.

Trading range breakout (TRB) rules are defined in terms of prices penetrating above (below) a resistance level, or a maximum (minimum) price over some previous period. The prior period could include any number of days, much as the moving average could include an arbitrary period. A filter can also be employed with the TRB signals.

Figure 7.1 summarizes the data characteristics for the period covered by the study. Figures 7.2, 7.3, and 7.4 present the findings for the three classes of technical trading rules. For the variable moving average rules, 10 different cases were examined, representing different moving averages and

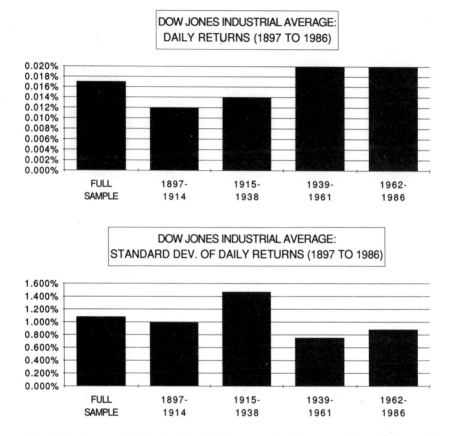

Figure 7.1. Summary statistics for daily and 10-day returns for the Dow Jones Industrial Average: (a) daily returns; (b) standard deviation of returns (*Source of data: Brock, 1992*)

cases with and without the 1-percent filter. The buy-sell differences are all positive. The *t*-tests for these differences are highly significant. The *t*-statistics for the buys (sells) are based on

$$(\mu_r - \mu)/(s/N + s/N_r)^{1/2} \tag{7.7}$$

where μ_r and N_r are the mean return and number of signals for the buys and sells, μ and N are the overall mean and number of observations. S is the variance for the entire sample. The buy-sell *t*-statistic is

$$(\mu_b - \mu_s)/(s/N_b + s/N_s)^{1/2} \tag{7.8}$$

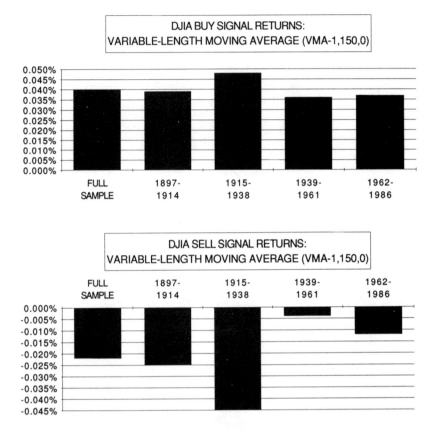

Figure 7.2. Results of variable-length moving average (VMA) trading rules applied to the Dow Jones Industrial Average: (a) "buy" signals; (b) "sell" signals (*Source of data: Brock, 1992*).

where μ_b and N_b are the mean return and number of signals for the buys and μ_s and N_s are the mean return and number of signals for the sells.

The second set of trading rules based on fixed moving averages also provides encouraging results. The 10-day average return is 0.53 percent for the buy signals. The sell signals produce an average −0.40-percent return. The least number of signals occur for the 2, 200, 0.01 rule which results in 2.8 signals per year. The most signals occur with the 1, 50, 0 rule which results in 7.6 signals per year.

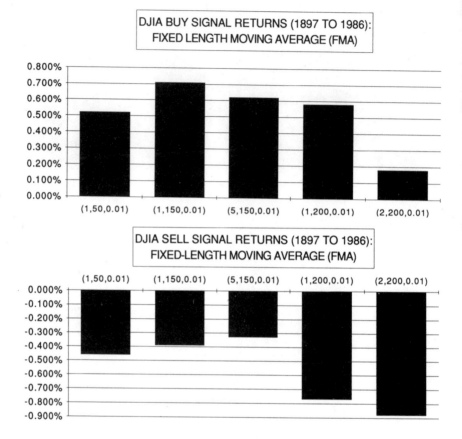

Figure 7.3. Results of fixed-length moving average (FMA) trading rules applied to the Dow Jones Industrial Average: (a) "buy" signals; (b) "sell" signals (*Source of data: Brock, 1992.*)

With trading range breakouts, the returns shown are for the 10-day holding period following a signal. The average buy signal produced a positive return of 0.63 percent while the average sell signal produced a negative return of −0.24 percent. Hence all of the technical trading rules show some significant ability to highlight periods of above average returns as well as periods of negative returns. While the rates of these returns are less than predicted by our nonlinear market model, the rules suggest that it is possible to capitalize on different market states risk-reward characteristics.

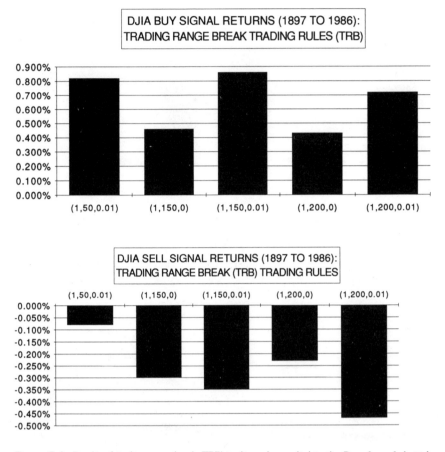

Figure 7.4. Results of trading range break (TRB) trading rules applied to the Dow Jones Industrial Average: (a) "buy" signals; (b) "sell" signals. (*Source of data: Brock, 1992.*)

Bootstrap Testing

Bootstrap testing is the process by which a set of surrogate time series is constructed to evaluate the performance of the technical trading rules on data that is generated by a particular null hypothesis model. In effect, the null model is fit to the characteristics of the actual data but is otherwise based on a random process. If the technical trading rules show the same level of performance on the null models, then it suggests that the null models in effect capture the characteristics of the Dow over the period examined.

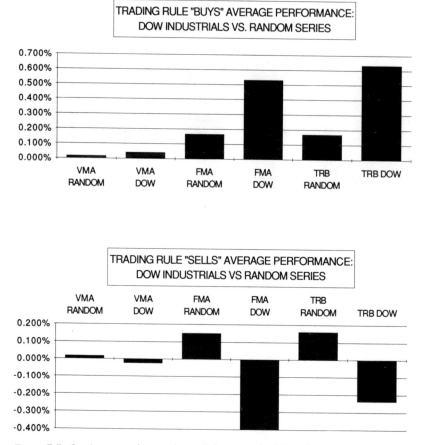

Figure 7.5. Simulation tests from random walk bootstraps for 500 replications: (a) trading rule "buy" signals; (b) trading rule "sell" signals (*Source of data: Brock, 1992*)

Brock et al. examined four null models. The first is the random walk hypothesis. As shown in Figure 7.5, none of the simulated random walks of the 500 simulated time series generated mean returns as large as obtained for the actual Dow series. Likewise, none of the mean sell returns of the simulated data were as negative as the mean returns for the actual Dow series. The bootstrapping analysis also demonstrate that "not only do the buy signals select out periods with higher conditional means, they also pick periods with lower volatilities." In contrast, sell periods, have lower returns and higher volatility. This directly contradicts the efficient market hypothesis and directly supports the coherent market hypothesis.

The other null hypothesis models used by Brock and his colleagues also failed to explain the nonlinear dependence in the original time series. While the finding that technical trading rules produce statistically significant results is very important for market practitioners, the rules evaluated by Brock and his colleagues are just a small sampling of the methods that practitioners have developed. For example, many practitioners evaluate fundamental factors behind market action. Use of both technical and fundamental factors conforms more closely with our nonlinear market model as we saw in Chap. 2. The rest of this chapter examines some additional approaches and views of practitioners with respect to the market's prospects over various time scales.

Kirkpatrick's Historical Perspectives

In his *Special Report* (September 1992), Charles Kirkpatrick offered the following appraisal for his institutional clients:

> In sum, I feel that the long rise in stock prices since 1982, generated largely by the scramble to maintain investment return rather than investment value during a secular decline in interest rates, is at its pinnacle. As has been documented from each of the financial manias over the past 300 years, the inability of historically lower interest rates to generate demand, the declining economic productivity and declining prices and wages accompanied by slowing money supply and declining real money stock, the strength in the financial stocks and the weakness of the stock market in the face of a still rising bond market, the historically high and structured optimistic opinion toward the future of the stock market, including public participation out of greed rather than reason, all point to a major secular, stock market peak.

Charles Kirkpatrick is an economic historian. He quotes the poet Bielby Porteus (1731-1808) as having said that "one who foresees calamities, suffers them twice over." Kirkpatrick adds that "one who foresees calamities that don't occur, looks comical." Having taken that risk, Kirpatrick outlines the reasons why "the danger of a very large and long stock market decline is immediately present."

Kirkpatrick argues that the economic seeds for depression and financial contraction have been sown since the early 1980s. The problem is interest rates. Declining rates are healthy in a normal business cycle. However, a secular decline (i.e., a long-term change in the direction of rates spanning more than just a typical business cycle) indicates a fundamental contraction

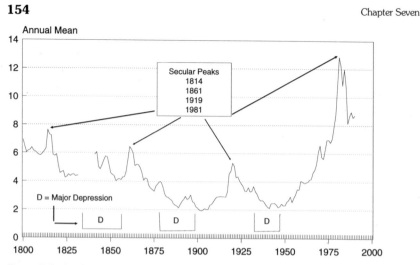

Figure 7.6. Secular peaks in interest rates have been historically followed by major economic depressions. *(Reprinted with permission. © 1992, Kirkpatrick & Company, Inc.)*

of credit demand. The last precedent for such a secular decline was in the 1920s and 1930s.

Since the early 1700s, there have been four prior periods of long term or secular declines in interest rates. Figure 7.6 illustrates the secular peaks in interest rates, which typically have also been followed by major depressions in economic activity. Since the early 1980s, each business cycle has seen lower highs and lows in interest rates as compared to the preceding cycle. This type of secular decline initially is very positive for the stock market; however, it can ultimately be very damaging.

In all of the prior secular interest-rate declines, two consequences have consistently occurred. First, periods of deflation and depression have followed the declining interest-rate trend which reflects a widespread decline in economic activity and demand for money or credit. Second, the price of financial assets tends to inflate as investors are willing to pay more for returns, without regard for the quality of the financial assets. Hence the junk bonds, the low quality stocks, and the rush for initial public offerings of new securities all reflect the need for cash to find a home. Ultimately, as the low quality of investments collides with the fundamentally weak economic environment, some unexpected event can trigger financial panic and economic depression.

Figure 7.7 illustrates four secular interest-rate peaks along with stock market performance dating back to the early 1700s. Each of these periods shows an extended (8- to 10-year) rise in stock prices and a long decline in interest rates. However, in each case the rise in stock prices was not justified

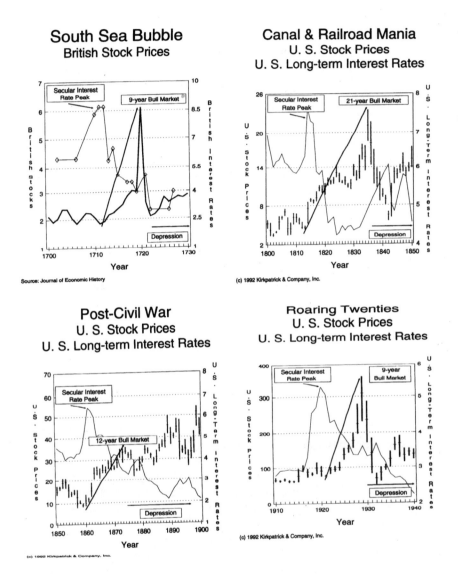

Figure 7.7. Secular peaks in interest rates have been historically followed by long-term bull markets, manias, panics, and crashes in the stock market. (*Reprinted with permission.* © *1992 Kirkpatrick & Company, Inc.*)

by economic fundamentals and led to extended market declines which often erased the entire gains of the preceding bull market.

The first mania in the early 1700s later became known as the *South Seas Bubble*. The interest rates and stock prices shown for this period are based on British markets. Inflation during this period peaked in 1711 and resulted in a nine-year bull market for stocks. However, the subsequent crash in 1720 wiped out prior gains entirely and resulted in stocks being out of favor with investors for nearly a century. Clearly the virtues of buying and holding stocks over the long run are not apparent in that period.

The 1814 secular peak in interest rates led to the *Canal Mania* which lasted for nearly two decades, illustrating the long-term relationship between secular peaks in interest rates and bull markets in financial assets. Subsequently, there were two protracted stock market declines. The first was from 1835 to 1842 during which prices fell by 76 percent. The second decline from 1853 to 1857 showed a net drop of 62 percent. The associated economic depression eventually led to the Civil War.

The third example of a secular peak in interest rates occurred in 1861 following the Civil War. Rates declined for the next 40 years with only minor counter trend moving higher. Much of this period was accompanied by one of the longest and most severe economic depressions in American history. Interestingly, the stock market did not suffer a major panic and crash as it has in the other periods of secular deflation. There were some substantial bear markets over this period; however, share prices ended the century near their highs.

Another secular peak in interest rates and inflation occurred in 1919 after World War I. This peak preceded the Great Depression of the 1930s by more than a decade. It also heralded the great bull market in stocks in the Roaring Twenties. The Crash of 1929 followed a nine-year bull market which was fueled by excessive margin borrowing and public speculation. It is still one of the most closely studied events in modern financial history.

Kirkpatrick suggests the most recent secular decline in interest rates since the early 1980s will lead to financial panic and depression. After interest rates peaked in the early 1980s, investors snapped up government-backed securities, and short-term securities to take advantage of then high yields. However, as rates continued to decline, junk bonds and other high yield instruments came into increasing vogue as institutional investors and the public both sought to maintain the high returns they had grown accustomed to. Lower quality, high risk investments were the only way to continue to capture the double digit rates of return. Stocks, the ultimate high risk investment, have now become the vehicle of choice for many who formerly shunned this risky approach.

The *Derivative Bubble* as it is called by Kirkpatrick has produced a long-term bull market in stocks from the August 1982 low point. The long-term track records of mutual funds over this bull market period are being aggressively advertised with the implication that stocks are, in fact, the best investment of all over the long run. Kirkpatrick points out two indicators that may signal that the great bull market has run its course. First, the stock market failed to rise proportionately even as interest rates continue to fall. Second, weak commodity prices, even as the economy is expanding, suggest deflation is at work.

Lower interest rates have not sparked economic demand. Housing starts are falling to new lows even though mortgage rates are in free fall. Rates are declining because of a lack of economic activity, implying that future industrial earnings will also suffer. Stocks on the other hand are rising only because of a belief that past performance and high returns will persist into the future. Investors are highly optimistic on the market's long-term prospects. Most are concerned only with the risk of a short-term correction; however that is viewed as a buying opportunity.

Indexing continues to grow in popularity and represents the current "no-brainer" decision for many pension fund managers. The total amount of under indexing was over $250 billion as of May 1992. Likewise, there are billions in liabilities associated with derivative products. A number of large firms could be at risk if the markets decline and liquidity dries up for derivative products. The futures markets were unable to deal with order imbalances in the Crash of 1987 due to the need to execute "portfolio insurance" transactions.

However, not everyone is bearish on the market's long-term prospects. One practitioner having a more upbeat forecast for the decade of the 1990s is Keith Ambachtsheer, a consultant for institutional investors.

Ambachtsheer's Eras

Keith Ambachtsheer, editor of the *Canadian Investment Review* and the *The Ambachtsheer Letter*, had these comments on our nonlinear market model shortly after its publication in *Financial Analysts Journal* (November–December 1990):

> Physicist Tonis Vaga argues persuasively that there is more to under-standing capital market returns than the normal risk premia-simple random walk behavior that standard capital markets theory assumes. Using the state transition models of both the physical and behavioral sciences as analogies, he suggests that the capital markets do, at times, truly walk randomly (i.e., rationally in psychological terms and unimo-dally with "normal" volatilities in statistical terms). But there are other times when capital markets walk chaotically (schizophrenic in psycho-logical terms and bimodally with exaggerated volatility in statistical terms).

At still other times capital markets walk coherently (strong bullish or bearish crowd behavior in psychological term and strong period-to-period return correlation with low volatility in statistical terms).

Keith Ambachtsheer applied the coherent market hypothesis to his *eras concept*, which catalogues the type of market activity we have witnessed since the late 1920s. Ambachtsheer's eras include:

1. Mostly Depression;

2. War and Controls;

3. Reconstruction and Prosperity;

4. Inflation; and

5. Invisible Hand.

Ambachsheer argues that the era of the Invisible Hand, which started in 1982 has ended and that a new era of "Degearing" has begun. "In Vaga terms, we suggest that over the last year capital markets have gone through a transition process from a state of *coherent bullishness* to a *random walk* state more consistent with capital markets theory."

The era of "Mostly Depression" began in 1928 and persisted through 1939, a period Ambachtsheer describes as one without economic or political leadership. Economic growth stagnated and prices of goods and labor declined in a widespread deflation. Stock markets were bearish to chaotic with real average returns of just 1 percent over the 11-year period. Treasury securities did better with a 3 percent rate of real return for short-term bills and a 7 percent rate of return for bonds.

In the era of "Wars and Controls," from 1940 to 1952 the economy recovered and inflation also picked up, averaging 6 percent over the period. Stocks did well and provided a 6 percent real return (above inflation). With the combination of high inflation and interest rate controls, bills and bonds suffered, providing a -5 percent real return.

A period of "Restructuring and Prosperity" followed World War II from 1953 to 1968. This period of steady economic growth and moderate inflation produced coherent bull markets for stocks which turned in a real rate of return of 11 percent over 15 years. T-bills earned only 1 percent while bonds netted nothing after inflation over the same period.

The Vietnam War ended the era of prosperity and ushered in another period of inflation from 1969 to 1981. Ambachtsheer characterizes this as a time of "troubled Presidencies, labor strife, a falling dollar, questionable monetary, fiscal, and business policies, and oil and commodity price shocks." It was also a period of falling productivity as wages and prices rise with inflation. Financial assets also did poorly over an extended period with stocks producing an inflation adjusted −3 percent, bonds returning −5 percent on a real basis and T-bills just breaking even after inflation.

The "Invisible Hand Era," from 1982 to 1990, is characterized by a return to "market rule" on a global basis. Reagan, Thatcher, and Pacific Rim counterparts all espoused the virtues of the free market. Communism's collapse further hastened the rush toward market economies in parts of the world where such thoughts, as well as actions, had been subject to severe punishment. Steady economic growth with moderate inflation brought a coherent bull market in stocks and bonds, with real returns for stocks registering a remarkable 15 percent, bonds turning in a stellar 13 percent real return, and T-bills providing a comfortable 4 percent.

The "Degearing Era" forecast by Ambachtsheer for the decade ahead predicts a period of consolidation after the excessive debt build up of the 1980s. The "Invisible Hand Era" carried with it the massive build up of debt in all sectors: Less Developed Countries (LDC); Leveraged Buy Outs (LBO); consumer debt; federal, state and local government debt; and less than conservative management of balance sheets in Japanese and U.S. financial institutions. A successful "Degearing Era" requires relatively high savings rates, positive real interest rates, moderate growth and inflation and stable exchange rates. In this environment, Ambachtsheer does not expect either coherent stock market behavior or prolonged periods of chaotic market action. His forecasts: 6 percent for stocks; 4 percent for bonds; and 2.5 percent for T-bills.

Ambachtsheer defends his positive outlook for stocks even in the current high valuation environment on three factors. The first is that the central bankers are better able to manage the economies of North America, the European Economic Community, and the Pacific Rim between the twin dangers of deflation and runaway inflation. Only two of the prior six eras were affected by such forces and caused stocks to do poorly. The second reason is that stocks are more integrated globally than ever before; they will increasingly be subject to the same disclosure and valuation standards, a development that should benefit North American markets. Furthermore, the trend to global diversification will result in portfolios being less risky and hence lower dividend premiums are acceptable. Finally, the nature of the corporate owners is changing as a result of the acquisitions of the 1980s and, increasingly, the owners of firms are also in control of their management; this is also a positive development in security valuations according to Ambachtsheer.

Kirkpatrick's historical perspectives cover a time span of nearly 300 years during which stocks have shown long-term coherence, chaos, and quieter periods of neglect. Ambachtsheer's insights span the more recent 60-year time frame which again includes decades of coherent, chaotic, and quieter periods of true random walk. However, most practitioners are concerned with much shorter periods of time such as the traditional business cycle. Again the same state transition concepts can be found across shorter as well as longer time scales, illustrating a self-similar or fractal structure in the capital markets.

The Zweig Forecast: Two Sacred Rules

Marty Zweig has two sacred and well advertised rules: Rule 1 is never to fight the interest-rate trend; Rule 2 is never to fight market "momentum." Following these rules and being careful about stock selection has enabled *The Zweig Forecast* to chalk up the number 1 risk-adjusted rating in the Hulbert performance sweepstakes over the past 13 years. His portfolio has gained 686 percent over that period, net of commission costs. Over the same period, the S&P 500 was up 558 percent and the Wilshire 5000 was up 519 percent. Significantly, Zweig's risk was only 76 percent as large as the Wilshire index. Clearly these are coherent results, having beaten the market and done so with below market risk. Worrying has its rewards.

Zweig is a graduate of the Wharton school, and like Peter Lynch, does not attribute his success as a practitioner to the theories he learned at Wharton. Zweig is known for his extensive research on market indicators which basically fall into two categories: *monetary* and *momentum*. When his composite weighted model of individual indicators in each of these categories turns positive, he increases his exposure to equities. When the indicators turn negative, he lightens up on his holdings.

While not intended as such, Zweig's two sacred rules are a practitioner's assessment and implementation of the control parameters of our nonlinear model. We have seen that two factors primarily determine the state of a financial market. The first is a technical factor related to the degree of coupling of opinions and attitudes. The second is a fundamental factor that might tend to bias or predispose market participants one way or the other. The technical factor pertains to the degree of nonlinearity and tends to magnify the impact of any fundamental bias. Hence Zweig's momentum indicators can be interpreted as measures of the degree to which groupthink is prevalent. His monetary indicators can likewise be interpreted as the fundamental bias.

Zweig's track record of beating the market over 13 years with below average risk suggests that there is more than luck involved. Our nonlinear model specifically forecasts coherent markets when the climate is conducive to crowd behavior and there is a strong fundamental bias. These are the factors that Zweig's indicators track. Hence it is reasonable to conclude that his approach is clearly consistent with the predictions of our nonlinear model which suggests that above average returns with below average risk is theoretically possible.

An area that Zweig's indicators don't explicitly address is the true random walk market. However, one of his early articles in *Barron's* (March 30, 1981) on "The Up-Down Ratio: Volume Figures Can Signal Market's Direction" points to a simple approach that can be interpreted within the framework of our nonlinear market model as an indication of transitions from a random walk period to crowd behavior in the stock market.

In his article, Zweig defines both buy and sell signals in terms of sequences of extremes greater than 9:1 on the upside and 1:9 on the downside in the New York Stock Exchange (NYSE) upside-to-downside volume ratio. A sequence of three downside extremes (without any intervening upside extremes) constitutes a sell signal. Two downside extremes followed by an upside reversal constitutes a buy signal. Either signal lasts for either a fixed period of six months or until the opposite signal cuts it short. Table 7.1 summarizes the results of both buy and sell signals as presented in Zweig's original article.

Zweig observed that the buy signals were very consistent in their results. In contrast, the sell signals, though turning in a negative net performance, were quite erratic with several large gains mixed in with the losses. Near the end of the article, Zweig added almost parenthetically that there were also periods when neither signal was in effect. At these times, the market tended to drift lower at a −9 percent annualized rate. This was a particularly intriguing observation.

If the market is an open system, transitions from periods of true random walk to crowd behavior can be signalled by extremes in the up-down volume ratio. After a period of crowd behavior has run its course, the extremes will be less likely. Hence, the "quiet periods" when both buy and sell signals have expired can be interpreted as periods of true random walk. Zweig's data showed that, at these times, the market tended to drift lower.

Hence Zweig's up-down volume extremes indicator can be used as a simple way to gauge whether the market's *collective social temperature* is above or below the flash point for crowd behavior. When crowd behavior prevails, then fundamentals (e.g., Zweig's Fed indicator) are particularly important. If the up-down volume extremes trigger a sell signal, but it isn't substantiated by a negative reading in fundamentals, then it probably makes sense to interpret the "sell" signal simply as a crowd behavior signal which more often than not is positive. However, if fundamentals are negative and the up-down ratio flashes a crowd behavior signal, then it is best to treat it as a "sell" signal.

Table 7.1. Buy and Sell Signals Based on New York Stock Exchange Upside to Downside Volume Ratio Extremes.

9-1 BUY SIGNALS: 1960 TO 1981

BUY Date	% Change Zweig Unweighted Price Index 6 Months Later*	Date if SELL Signal Ended Buy Period Before 6 Months
11/10/60	+26.3%	
06/28/62	− 1.4%	
10/29/62	+26.7%	10/19/62
06/30/65	+18.0%	
09/12/66	+23.6%	
10/12/66	+ .5%**	
06/06/67	+ 8.4%	
04/08/68	+17.1%	
05/27/70	+12.8%	
08/16/71	+ 5.3%	
01/03/74	− .1%	03/28/74
01/27/75	+23.7%	
08/28/75	+26.9%	
01/05/76	+ .9%**	
11/10/77	+12.8%	
11/01/78	− 8.3%	12/18/78
11/26/79	+ 5.2%	
03/28/80	+19.0%**	
03/12/81	?	

$10,000 =	$71,446 (in 7.5 years)
Return =	+14.1% per six months
	+30.2% per annum

*% Change is over 6 months *or* is cut off earlier if SELL signal ends bullish mode.
**When overlap signals occur within six months, the holding period on the second does not begin until six months after the prior signal, and ends six months after the second signal.

9-1 SELL SIGNALS: 1960 = 1981

SELL Date	% Change Zweig Unweighted Price Index 6 Months Later*	Date if 9-1 Signal Ended Sell Period Before 6 Months
05/23/62	−11.9%	06/28/62
10/19/62	− .1%	10/29/62
08/26/66	− .3%	09/12/66
05/04/70	−13.7%	05/27/70
08/03/71	+ 4.6%	08/16/71
11/19/73	− 4.9%	01/03/74
03/28/74	−38.3%	
08/19/75	+ .5%	08/28/75
11/11/76	+13.6%	
10/20/78	− 6.3% -	11/01/78
12/18/78	+12.3%	
03/24/80	− 2.8%	03/28/80
12/08/80	+ 5.5%	03/12/81

$10,000 =	$5,752 (in 2.3 years)
Return =	−11.6% per six months
	−21.8% per annum

*% Change is over 6 months *or* is cut off earlier if 9-to-1 Up Day ends bearish mode.

Zweig cautions against putting too much emphasis on any single indicator and has developed a composite weighted average based on a set of monetary measures and momentum measures. These are set forth in detail in his book *Winning on Wall Street* which is generally included in his set of premiums for new subscribers to his market letter.

The Elliott Wave: Self-Similar
Across Multiple Time Scales

Robert Prechter, Jr. and A. J. Frost made a long-term forecast in their *Elliott Wave Principle* published originally in 1978 and updated periodically since then. As of July 1978, the stock market was languishing after the 1975 and 1976 bull market upswings. In their original edition, they called for a major bull market which would carry the Dow Industrial average to 2860 by about 1983. This forecast was revised in 1983, to a new target of 3686. Timewise, they suggested "watching for a possible market peak is five years from 1982 or 1987." The basis of both of these forecasts was the Elliott wave concept, illustrated in Fig. 7.8.

Ralph Elliott was an accountant who made empirical observations of market fluctuations and established a set of rules that seemed to apply to his observations. These rules have collectively become known as the *Elliott*

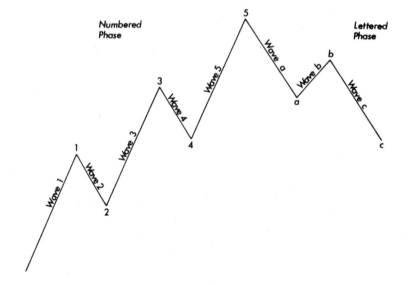

Figure 7.8. An Elliott wave pattern includes eight distinct phases, each having a unique "personality." (*Frost & Prechter, 1987.*)

wave principle which has been used by his followers to make market forecasts. Basically, what Elliott observed was that bull market waves tend to occur in sets of three. Of course, this is not news to surfers who also look for similar patterns in the breaking surf or to the superstitious who say that disasters occur in clusters of three.

The proponents of the Elliott wave seek both to make predictions by counting waves, giving them names, and keeping track of waves of different degree which correspond to market action on different time scales. Figure 7.8 illustrates the classical pattern covering both a bull market and a bear market. The bull market consists of three major advancing waves, interrupted by two smaller counter trend waves. The bear market phase consists of two large downward waves with a single smaller upward counter trend wave.

The Elliott wave further is self-similar on different time scales. Hence each major wave within the bull market phase can be decomposed into a set of five smaller waves—three up and two down. Each of these smaller waves can be further divided into similar components and so forth. Hence the Elliott wave practitioners seek to catalogue market action from the very long time frames covering centuries to the smallest of fluctuations that occur on the order of perhaps five-minute intervals. Each time scale may be of interest to investors with different objectives ranging from long-term buy and hold, intermediate trading to short-term scalping of fractional points by the professionals on the exchange floors.

The names given to waves of different degree are picturesque. The longest waves include:

1. grand supercycle;
2. supercycle; and
3. cycle.

As an example, the market's rise from the lows of the great Depression of the 1930s represents a bull market of *supercycle* degree, spanning over 50 years. Supercycle waves are labelled in Fig. 7.9 with uppercase Roman numerals in parentheses. Within this wave there are five waves of *cycle* dimension, each typically lasting five to ten years. These are labelled simply with uppercase Roman numerals. These waves can be related to Kirkpatrick's analysis of secular interest-rate peaks and Ambachtsheer's eras.

On progressively shorter time scales, the next set of waves are:

1. primary;
2. intermediate; and
3. minor.

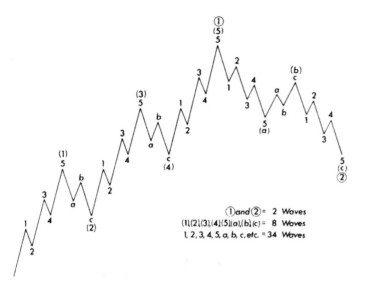

Figure 7.9. The Elliott wave principle postulates a fractal structure in the time series of financial markets *(Frost and Prechter, 1987.)*

A *primary wave* within a cycle is labelled by means of numbers within a circle, while *intermediate waves* are noted by numbers within parentheses, and *minor waves* receive just numbers.

Finally the shortest cycles are called:

1. minute;
2. minuette; and
3. sub-minuette.

Minute waves are labelled with lowercase Roman numerals. Beyond that there is no standard naming convention. Presumably there isn't time to be drawing charts and labelling them except perhaps in real-time by computer.

The long-term forecast of Frost and Prechter was based on the idea that the supercycle degree bull market from the lows of the Great Depression had not fully run its course. A fifth wave was needed to complete the pattern predicted by the Elliott wave principle. Following the fifth wave, Frost and Prechter also predicted a major bear market (i.e., the inevitable downward move following a major bull market advance). What is particularly disturbing is the idea that the size of the decline will be large and long lasting out of necessity (i.e., a bear of supercycle degree). Hence this observation is reminiscent of Kirkpatrick's warnings of a protracted bear market after the current mania (or is it a coherent bull market?) runs its course.

In this example, the major bull cycles illustrate what is known as an *impulse waves*. In contrast, the bearish cycles are known as *corrective waves*. Interestingly, Frost and Prechter observe that "Since corrective waves are generally less clearly identified and subdivided than impulse waves, which flow in the direction of the larger trend, it becomes difficult at times to fit corrective waves into recognizable patterns until they are completed and behind us." Critics of the wave principle argue that the labelling process always works best after the waves are completed. However, Frost and Prechter's forecast remains a good call of the 1980s bull market and while the timing of the supercycle bear market has clearly been premature.

One of the interesting aspects of Frost and Prechter's interpretation of the Elliott wave theory is that each wave has a "personality." We can also qualitatively relate these personality traits to our nonlinear market model. First waves are often not recognized as a new bull market. They tend to rise from the basing patterns of prior bear markets and are usually viewed by most investors as still an opportunity to sell. As a result the second (corrective) wave often erodes much of the gains made by the first wave. Within the framework of our nonlinear model, we might think of waves one and two as the "critical fluctuations" that mark the transition from a bear market base to a new bull market period.

Wave three of the Elliott wave paradigm are "wonders to behold. They are strong and broad, and the trend at this point is unmistakable." According to Frost and Prechter: "Increasingly favorable fundamentals enter the picture as confidence returns. Third waves usually generate the greatest volume and price movement and are most often the extended wave in a series. Virtually all stocks participate in third waves." Within the framework of our nonlinear model, the allusion to strong fundamentals and strong tape action suggest that third waves correspond to a coherent bull market phase.

Fourth waves tend to be complex corrections. That means that they are the corrective waves that are difficult to label until after they are over. We might draw the analogy with periods of true random walk in which there is no clear pattern. With the exhaustion of a flow of money in the preceding bullish phase, sentiment falls back below the threshold of collective thinking and action and prices also drift lower. This is a time in which many individual stocks that are laggards fall back, having been carried higher only by the general market momentum of the powerful third wave.

Fifth waves are usually less impressive than third waves. Optimism tends to run high and secondary stocks do well. The long-term nature of the bull market has been established by earlier waves and prices continue to push into new bull market high ground, even in the face of possible weakness in volume and breadth measures. In effect, the fifth waves can be periods of extended bullish market activity even in the face of deteriorating fundamentals. However, as the bull market ages and fundamentals are less positive, a chaotic market environment is more likely to emerge. Within the framework of our nonlinear model, both bullish and bearish states become nearly equally probable. Hence the fifth wave of the bull market and the first downward wave of the bear market could represent a chaotic market in which sizeable moves occur in both directions with little net progress.

The sixth wave is the first significant corrective wave of the bear market following a classic five-wave bull market. These are the "A" waves of a three wave, ABC bear market within the jargon of the Elliott wave principle. The initial bear market wave is typically viewed as "just a minor pullback prior to the next leg of advance."

The seventh wave is a "sucker rally." This is the first upward countertrend move of the bear market following a major bull market. The market may even move back to new high ground. However, breadth will not confirm the move and volume is weak. These are bull traps for those who missed the prior major bull market and are belatedly seeking gains when risk is high compared with rewards.

The third wave in the bearish sequence is usually the most devastating part of the bear market. They are third waves, except that the bias is to the downside. The rationalizations of any weaknesses in the previous waves are replaced by true fear and a high degree of liquidations. These periods would correspond to either the bearish state within a bimodal distribution of a chaotic market or possibly a full blown coherent bear market, depending on the prevailing fundamentals.

The analogy between the nonlinear market model and the Elliott wave model suggests that there are some similarities between the states forecast theoretically and the observations that have been made empirically. However, the Elliott wave model is a deterministic model of the path of the market into the future. Our nonlinear model is concerned with the probability distribution governing market action. This is a very fundamental difference.

The Elliott wave can also be recast within the framework of a nonlinear probability model. For example, another way to interpret the sequence of events in the classic eight-wave sequence is to simply observe that there are four waves higher and four waves lower. Three of the four positive waves are large; one is small. Three of the downward waves are perhaps of moderate size, and smaller than the bullish waves; one of the downward waves is quite large, perhaps of the same magnitude as the upward wave. In effect this description can be interpreted as a biased random walk. There are more large steps higher than lower.

Many of the features of the Elliott wave model are related to fractal structures. The self-similarity of the wave pattern across different time scales is essentially a characteristic of fractals. The dimensions of the Elliott wave pattern could be computed and would be somewhere between one and two. However, while it is useful to visualize the patterns generated by a biased random walk, it is not clear how useful the methods of wave counting and labelling are for prediction.

Certainly, the forecast of another bull market leg by Frost and Prechter stood out among the sceptical investment community of the early 1980s, when interest rates were very high and the back of inflation had not yet been broken. However, the timing of the ultimate peak and the subsequent bear market have not been accurate, either in the original forecast or subsequent updates in the *Elliott Wave Theorist* publication. Clearly the timing of major market moves is both a matter of chance as well as necessity.

Prechter's *Elliott Wave Theorist* market letter shows up in the number three spot over the past 13 years in the *Hulbert Financial Digest* on a risk-adjusted basis. Prechter uses the Elliott wave principle as the underlying methodology of his market letter. However, he also keeps track of investor sentiment and economic factors. These are the control parameters in our nonlinear model. Hence it appears that the wave pattern may be useful as a corroborative evidence of market action being consistent or not with the fundamentals. The tracks of the market will be quite different in coherent bull markets as opposed to random walks or chaotic markets. The wave personality characteristics described by Frost and Prechter are certainly not inconsistent with the nonlinear theoretical model of different market states. The Elliott wave can be viewed as an empirical observation of fractal structure in the market and a translation of market risk-reward profiles into chart price patterns.

Summary

The vindication of technical analysis by new research is heartening. Most practitioners believe that the market moves in trends and traders rely on this effect to make a living. However, they also know that they are dealing with a game of chance, one in which the rules can change unpredictably. For example, Mandelbrot's work suggests that the concept of a trend is itself suspect since the market may take a few large steps before settling down to a quieter fluctuation pattern.

The simple mechanical approach of Dick Fabian and other similar moving average followers, in fact, may add value. However, implementation may be difficult if too many people are following the same indicators and seek to execute position changes at the same time. Furthermore, the number of false signals may be frustrating. Even in strongly trending markets when the double bottom potential well controls market fluctuations, there is an exponential distribution in the time between crossing between one side of the well and the other. The average time depends strongly on the height of the potential barrier.

However, the evidence does support the concept that above average returns with below average risk can be achieved by following moving average breaks. This simple mechanical method would not work if the market were simply a random noise process. It does work because the interaction among investors tends to create persistent price trends. Perhaps the best approach for traders is to track indicators of major bull markets such as we described in Chap. 2 in combination with a moving average approach. This would help to capture some of the longest lasting moves and help to minimize the number of smaller, false alarm fluctuations.

Another approach for using moving averages is to identify the periods when the market is clearly out of favor with investors. At these junctures, high quality stocks may have been "taken to the woodshed" along with those that perhaps are more deserving of a strong price correction. The types of opportunities that Warren Buffet tends to invest in may be more prevalent in periods where the overall market is out of favor.

However, it should be noted that the distribution of time periods that stocks may remain out of favor also has a fat tail. Most recent bear markets have been relatively short. However, the future may bring far longer periods over which stocks fall from favor than we have witnessed in recent history. The duration of bear markets will be critically dependent on the fundamentals of the macro economy.

Interest rates are a key factor underlying bull markets. We have seen in Chap. 2 how an initial Fed easing can trigger an initial buying stampede, followed by a persistent bull market. Kirpatrick's historical observations add another dimension to the interest-rate indicator. In periods of secular (as opposed to business cycle) interest-rate declines, long-lasting bull markets often can last for a decade or more, taking on manic proportions and quite often culminating in panics and crashes. Stocks can remain out of favor for extended periods following the economic depression that occurs following secular interest-rate declines.

Keith Ambachtsheer finds that in the post-1930s environment we have gone through a number of distinct eras, each with different risk-reward characteristics. The era of the 1980s has resulted in a large build up of debt which needs to be worked off. Ambachtsheer sees this happening more through a quieter, random walk process than a crash. As a result, returns will not match the lofty levels that we enjoyed in the 1980s, but stocks will do better than fixed dollar or fixed income assets.

Zweig's timing models are far shorter in scope than either Kirpatrick's long-term views or Ambachtsheer's time horizon. Zweig use of momentum and monetary indicators is clearly consistent with our nonlinear market model and his long-term track record reinforces the idea that above average returns with below average risk are possible through active management. However, the activity level of his investment style is quite high and may not be suitable for all investors.

The Elliott wave principle bridges the gap between long-term and short-term market dynamics. The wave structure described by proponents of this approach, such as Prechter and Frost, is self-similar across all time scales. Different waves have unique "personalities" which can also be qualitatively related to the dynamics predicted by our nonlinear market model. Unlike the wave principle, our model is stochastic in nature rather than deterministic. However, the patterns generated by biased random walks may well exhibit the characteristics observed empirically as Elliott wave patterns.

Market timers look at various indicators to divine the size and direction of the next market move. Our model suggests that the duration of the market in each state is a random variable which follows an exponential distribution in which the average duration is highly sensitive to the prevailing bias in fundamentals. As long as the prospects for long-term growth remain strong, bear markets should remain short and should be considered buying opportunities. However, if fundamentals should continue to deteriorate, as Fitzpatrick suggests they will, then economic depression and poor performance could lead to an extended bear market for stocks.

Robert Farrell of Merrill Lynch has often observed that most investors hold for the long term at major market tops and become traders at major market bottoms. Our goal should be the opposite. Market timing is an important consideration in managing risk. High valuation markets can persist for long periods. However, they will not last forever. Markets tend to swing in nonlinear cycles between extremes of overvaluation and undervaluation. While these swings may not be predictable in a deterministic sense, it pays to become contrarian and to lighten up on long-term holdings when valuations are at positive extremes and to patiently wait for the bargains that inevitably occur when stocks fall out of favor.

8

Stock Selection: Earnings Momentum and Earnings Torpedoes

...the Growth Stock Outlook list boasted more than a score of companies that have rewarded Allmon with 500 percent gains or better, and half that roster were up more than 1000 percent. A few have been on the list since its debut in 1965. In little more than a decade of publishing his second service, Junior Growth Stocks, which focuses on younger companies, Allmon has compiled another stunning record, with more than 35 stocks up at least 500 percent, including a baker's dozen that have delivered 1000 percent or better gains.

JOHN C. BOLAND
Barron's, *October 18, 1982*

Charles Allmon:
Growth and Value

Charles Allmon is a value investor. He looks for values among what are traditionally considered growth stocks. Where conventional wisdom has it that you have to pay a premium for growth stocks, Allmon believes that you don't, and he has the results to back up his contention. According to the

Hulbert Financial Digest, Allmon's *Growth Stock Outlook* has the second best risk-adjusted performance record between June 1980 and June 1993. His gain of 429 percent is less than the Wilshire 5000's gain of 519 percent over the same period. However, Allmon's level of risk is remarkably only 27 percent of the Wilshire index risk.

Hulbert recommends using risk-adjusted performance ratings in the selection of an investment advisor. According to Hulbert's October 26, 1992 column in *Forbes,* "The best bets are those whose performances over at least five years rank the highest according to a measurement known as the *Sharpe ratio.* The Sharpe ratio, an element of modern portfolio theory, adjusts a portfolio's return by its volatility or variation of returns. At the time of Hulbert's analysis, Charles Allmon's *Growth Stock Outlook,* Marty Zweig's *Zweig Forecast,* Dan Sullivan's *The Chartist,* and the *Value Line Investment Survey* had attained better Sharpe ratios than the market. That's based on portfolio performance over a twelve-year period from 1980 to 1992.

More recently, Allmon has been notably bearish on the market, and while that has significantly reduced the volatility of his portfolio, it hasn't helped his performance. Allmon slipped to second place, behind *The Zweig Forecast,* but is still ahead of the *Value Line Investment Survey* and *The Chartist.* Allmon's bearishness stems from his long experience with the market, including the major bear market of 1973 and 1974 when values were defined in terms of P/E multiples typically below 10, and often half that level or less. In fact, Allmon turned bearish prior to the Crash of 1987 and in an interview in *The New York Times* on August 23, 1987 Allmon suggested that the market was due for a major correction in the 35 percent to 50 percent range and his portfolio was 80 percent in cash. He predicted the market could suffer a single-day drop of as much as 160 points.

While Allmon's short-term view remained bearish even as the market recovered after the 1987 crash, his long-term view is clearly bullish. Short term, in the post-crash environment, Allmon's expectations were that "fair value" for the Dow Industrials would be about 1700, and could fall as low as 1200 if stocks really sold off to undervalued levels. At the same time his long-term view was that the Dow could hit 5000 by the end of the century. Allmon has revised this long-term forecast up to 6000 on the Dow by the year 2000. However, short term, he remains skeptical of the market's strength.

Allmon has an impressive record of picking winning stocks and holding them for long-term appreciation. Many of the biggest winners that Peter Lynch describes at length in *One Up on Wall Street* are also part of Allmon's portfolio of growth stocks. A subscriber to the *Growth Stock Outlook* writes as follows: "...We have done very well on several stocks, but the sensational one has been The Limited. We purchased 300 shares for just over $6,000 in

July 1972. We have sold shares frequently over the years, but still own over 35,000 shares, now worth almost $1,000,000." According to Allmon:

> Our objective is to double each company's listing price in five or six years. Sometimes we do better, but let's not sound like hogs. The primary basis on which we select a company is its earning power; normally it must show a 15 percent annual growth rate compounded for four years to qualify. We look for long-range growth potential. Fast-growing companies with few shares outstanding have proved to be good capital gains vehicles for long-term investment (three–five years).

Zweig's Stock Selection Criteria

Zweig suggests that while there are a number of wrong ways to pick stocks, there is no single right way. However, he offers two broad classes of strategy. The first, a "shotgun" approach is based on screening computer data with specific criteria of interest. This approach is quick and easy. It is not based on company specific analysis. The alternative "rifle" approach is based on careful study of a small number of firms. This requires dedicated analysis and results depend on the skill of the analyst.

Zweig prefers the shotgun approach. His criteria include the following factors:

1. strong earnings growth;
2. a reasonable price to earnings ratio;
3. buying by corporate insiders; and
4. strong price action in the stock relative to the market.

This information can be easily screened by computer to highlight stocks with the best performance potential and those with the least potential. Zweig offers a service which ranks stocks by appreciation potential on a scale of 1 to 9, where stocks ranked 1 have the best prospects. Over a period between May 1976 to December 1988, the stocks ranked highest outperformed the market by a factor of more than three, while those ranked lowest appreciated less than one third of the market averages. Both of these results disregard commissions which could be substantial.

In scanning the earnings reports in the financial pages, Zweig looks for reasonable gains in both sales and earnings. Ideally earnings should show healthy progress over a reasonable period of time and stable levels of profitability. Shrinking profit margins could tip off potential future earnings problems. Another key factor is the price action of a stock when earnings come out. If the earnings fail to meet Wall Streets expectations and the stock is sold heavily, it could under perform for a significant period even after the initial impact of the earnings report.

If a stock rises on the news of a strong earnings report it may continue to do well. Strong tape action suggests that the fundamental news has come as a positive surprise to the market. The imbalance between the markets expectations and actual results can create a flow of orders from short covering and renewed interest by investors on the long side. This can often produce a persistent price trend lasting for three to six months or more. Zweig also looks for earnings stability. If a company's short-term results are erratic, the stability of long-term results becomes questionable.

The second factor Zweig considers important is the price-to-earnings (P/E) ratio. Academic studies have shown that the stocks with low P/E ratios outperform stocks with high P/E ratios. However, the average P/E of all stocks can vary widely over the long run. For example, in an environment where the P/E of the Dow Industrials or S&P 500 rises over 20, there may be many individual stocks with P/Es of 50 to 60 or even higher. On the other hand, at bear market bottoms when the P/E of the market averages can fall below 10, there may not be many stocks with P/Es over 20.

The higher the P/E ratio, the longer the stock has to maintain superior growth rates in order to justify its high price. Many stocks, in fact, do sell at high multiples and grow rapidly over extended periods. However, if earnings growth falters for any reason, stocks with high P/E ratios are extremely vulnerable to large setbacks in their stock price. As Zweig puts it "stocks with very high P/Es can on occasion do well, but from a risk-reward standpoint they're poison."

One caveat with low P/E stocks is that the market may be discounting future earnings problems. Hence stocks with unusually low P/Es require further analysis to determine if there is a fundamental problem with the balance sheet or some other major problem. Zweig usually avoids both extremes and invests in stocks with normal or slightly above average P/E ratios.

Insider trading is another important factor. Zweig suggests avoiding stocks where multiple insiders are selling, and conversely buying stocks where several insiders have been adding to holdings. In a study covering the period between 1974 and 1976, Zweig found that nearly 63 percent did better than the market averages by a factor of almost three. In contrast, only 37 percent of stocks with significant insider selling did better than the market and the average returns under performed the market by a wide margin.

Stocks with high P/E ratios and a high degree of insider selling are also dangerous. In a December 17, 1973 *Barron's* article, Zweig listed a number of glamour stocks with high P/E ratios and a high degree of insider selling.

In all cases, there were at least three insider sales and no insider purchases during the prior six months. The following year, the market had one of its worst years ever, with the Dow falling 27 percent. However, over the same period, the stocks on Zweig's high P/E insider sell list fell by an even more remarkable 41.5 percent on average.

Avoiding the big losers is a key part of Zweig's strategy for success. He suggests that eliminating the worst 10 percent of all stocks would go a long way toward above average performance. One way to avoid the losers is by tracking price action.

Zweig advises buying strength and selling weak stocks. For example, if the market has been strong, he suggests selling stocks that haven't kept up for some reason. Stocks hovering near the low end of their trading range or even those that haven't been able to break out of a trading range are not good prospects for intermediate-term gains. The rationale is that if a stock isn't doing at least as well as the market, something is wrong.

In a weak market, there are plenty of stocks on the new lows list. However, prior to a major turning point, the market may have a few false starts. Some stocks climb substantially in these rallies and hold most of their gains in subsequent declines. They begin to outperform the average stock. These issues are likely to be the leaders when the market does begin a sustained rally.

Zweig uses charts to assess trends relative to the market. A step ladder type of price action with higher highs, and higher lows is a good indication of positive performance potential. These stocks are good candidates for purchase, particularly on small five percent to ten percent pullbacks. Stocks that break out of trading ranges in an otherwise flat market are also good buying candidates.

Major economic trends can also lead to major moves in specific industries. For example, in the late 1970s, inflation was a major factor that drove gold and other natural resource stocks higher, while hurting consumers of natural resources such as the airlines, utilities, and automobile industry. Conversely, in the disinflationary environment of the 1980s, the gold and oil stocks lagged while financial services and bonds performed particularly well. Unfortunately for the average investor, identification of fundamental trends usually doesn't occur until so late in the cycle that most of the profit potential has already been discounted by the market.

Dan Sullivan: The Chartist

Dan Sullivan is a chartist. He has published a market letter by this name since 1969. Over a period of 12 years, ending on December 31, 1992, Sullivan ranked highest in total return in the *Hulbert Financial Digest*. His total return of 808 percent (19.3 percent annualized) is well ahead of the Wilshire 5000 total return of 489 percent (15.2 percent annualized). On a risk-adjusted basis, *The Chartist* ranked third.

Unlike Zweig who is a Wharton graduate and PhD in finance, Sullivan learned about investing by reading on his own. According to Peter Brimlow in *Forbes* (October 30, 1989) Sullivan was introduced to relative strength investing by Nicholas Darvas' "How I Made $2 Million in the Stock Market." Unlike Zweig, Sullivan doesn't track monetary models or economic indicators. He is as his newsletter title indicates, strictly a chartist. In this respect, like Zweig, he looks for relative strength (i.e., performance better than the market averages).

Sullivan combines his high relative strength stock selection approach with market timing. This combination has been successful in helping him achieve both performance and safety. Among his market timing indicators are the *90 percent-plus rule*. If 90 percent or more of the stocks making up the S&P 500 index are above their 10-week moving average, Sullivan expects the market trend to persist for up to a year into the future. However, his basic strategy is to be a trend follower. As long as the primary trend is up, he loads up on high relative strength stocks.

In addition to the primary trend model, Sullivan also uses shorter-term timing models as late entry points. These provide opportunities for adding to positions, but he advises holding these positions until the primary trend indicators turn negative. These risk management strategies are augmented by stop-loss thresholds. However, rather than to execute mechanical stop limits for individual issues, Sullivan begins to sell losers if the overall portfolio has dropped on the order of 10 percent to 15 percent. This avoids excessive trading due to the high degree of volatility that may occur with individual issues in the portfolio.

While Sullivan disavows the use of fundamental analysis, his market letter frequently comments on the fundamental characteristics of his portfolio stocks. Hence, while market action may be the most important factor in his stock selection style, fundamental factors also appear to at least be a consideration.

Value Line Stock Ranking System: Efficient Market Anomaly

Fisher Black observed in *Financial Analysts Journal* (September–October, 1973):

> One of the tools for active portfolio management is a ranking system for the performance of stocks. However, just as very few portfolios have been

able to pass the test of consistent performance, there are also very few ranking systems that can pass this test. The Value Line ranking system appears to be one of the few exceptions.

Fisher Black is a partner at Goldman Sachs. At the time of the quotation he was on the faculty of the University of Chicago. He was retained by Value Line to evaluate the statistical significance of the their widely followed stock ranking system. His comments, published under the title "Yes, Virginia, There Is Hope: Tests of the Value Line Ranking System," suggested that results were indeed statistically significant. This finding flew in the face of the efficient market hypothesis which was rapidly gaining acceptance at the time.

Value Line's timelines ranking system assigns high ranks to stocks with low price to earnings multiples, compared with historical levels and the overall market multiple. It also reflects favorably on stocks with upward momentum in quarterly earnings and price momentum. In effect these factors can be construed as measures of the control parameters in our nonlinear model. Price momentum is an indication that the market sentiment is above the critical threshold for collective thinking and action, while a strong fundamental bias will increase the chances of coherent positive results.

What's behind Value Line's success? There's no shortage of research on this question. In a recent article in the *Journal of Financial Economics*, John Affleck-Graves and Richard R. Mendenhall of the University of Notre Dame, suggest that the positive correlation between the Value Line ranking system and future returns is based primarily on what is known as "post-earnings announcement drift." Drift is the deterministic component of stock price fluctuations (i.e., the trend). One of the documented anomalies that contradicts the efficient market hypothesis is the "drift" in stock prices that occurs following earnings surprises.

Earnings surprise was a key element tracked by many fund managers. For example, Louis Navellier, who publishes the *MPT Review* supplements his technical stock screen with earnings surprise considerations. Affleck-Graves and Mendenhall (AGM) suggest that the Value Line ranks are due entirely to the earnings surprise factor. The tendency of stock prices to track earnings announcements was first noted by Ray Ball and Philip Brown in 1968. Other researchers have since confirmed the significance of earnings announcements and subsequent stock returns in the direction of the announcements.

The AGM study of Value Line timeliness ranks looked at the relationship between the timing of earnings announcements and changes in the Value Line ranks. They find first, that the Value Line performance and the post earnings drift are the same magnitude; they also found that when Value Line ranks changed within eight days of earnings announcements, the resulting performance differences between highest and lowest ranks was the largest. In contrast, when Value Line ranking changes occurred more than eight days after the earnings announcements, the results were quite small and statistically insignificant. Furthermore, there appears to be little predictive value in the ranking system when the earnings surprise is small.

Earnings are clearly a key factor in the Value Line ranking system. The AGM study concluded that most Value Line rank changes occur within eight days of earnings announcements. This also suggests that the predictive ability of the ranking system is greatest for issues that are furthest from equilibrium. Earnings surprise is almost by definition an indication of a market destabilizing factor. Positive earnings surprises are rewarded by a flow of money into a particular stock; negative surprises are greeted by waves of selling from disappointed investors. This flow persists for a significant period after the earnings announcement.

Another service provided by Value Line is a safety ranking. In an article in *Financial Analysts Journal* (March–April, 1988), Russell Fuller and G. Wenchi Wong examined the Value Line safety ranking system and compared it to the beta factor used in modern portfolio theory and the standard deviation of market fluctuations as alternative formulations of risk. Fuller and Wong are both academics. Russel Fuller is Professor and Chair, Department of Finance, Washington State University. G. Wenchi Wong is Assistant Professor of Finance at DePaul University. They found that the Value Line safety ranks had the highest correlation with returns, a la the capital asset pricing model. The standard deviation was second, while beta was a distant third.

The relationship between risk and reward is at the heart of the capital asset pricing model (CAPM) introduced in Chap. 4. CAPM defines risk in terms of the beta factor, a statistical variable. Specifically the beta factor of a stock is the correlation coefficient of the stock's return multiplied by the ratio of the standard deviation of the stock divided by the standard deviation of returns for the market index.

In contrast, the Value Line safety ranking system (from 1 for stocks with highest safety to five for the lowest safety) is based on two primary factors:

1. the stock price stability; and

2. the stock's financial strength.

The first factor is the ratio of a stock's standard deviation of price returns compared with the average standard deviation of all stocks tracked by Value Line. The stock's financial strength is based on fundamental variables such as debt coverage, size of the firm and accounting procedures. Hence it is based on both statistical measures as well as the types of fundamental factors that are used typically to rank a bond's safety.

Figure 8.1 summarizes the findings of Fuller and Wong's study. Over the 12-year period from 1974 to 1985, the Value Line ranking system showed the best correlation between risk and the average monthly returns. In

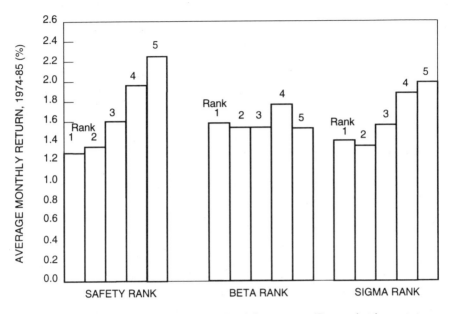

Figure 8.1. Value Line's safety ranks correlate well with future returns. *(Reprinted with permission from* Financial Analyst's Journal, March/April 1988. *© 1988 The Financial Analysts Federation, Charlottesville, VA. All rights reserved.)*

contrast, the beta factor showed virtually no correlation between risk and return. The standard deviation fell between the results of the other two systems; it showed far better results than the statistical beta factor, but not as much correlation as the Value Line ranking system.

One interpretation of Fig. 8.1 is that the Value Line safety ranks may be interpreted as a measure of the deviation of a stock from equilibrium. The "safest" stocks are those closest to equilibrium and have the lowest returns. The "riskiest" stocks are those furthest from equilibrium and, in bull markets, will produce the largest returns.

Fuller and Wong's study is just one of a series of studies in recent years that have questioned the usefulness of the traditional beta factor as a risk specification. Traditional measures of risk such as company size and balance sheet characteristics have proven effective in better quantifying the risk-reward relationship.

Characteristics of the Winners: Before They Took Off

Another well-known and widely followed approach to stock selection has been articulated by publisher William O'Neil who is the driving force behind *Investor's Business Daily*. In his popular book, *How to Make Money in Stocks*, O'Neil presents the results of his analysis of the characteristics of the biggest winners of the past, prior to their major moves. Covering the period from 1953 to 1990, O'Neil's study determined what features they shared that could be used to advantage in stock selection.

O'Neil's criteria included both fundamental and technical factors which he summarizes under the acronym, CANSLIM. Each letter of the acronym stands for one of the key properties that have helped propel stocks such as Texas Instruments, Xerox, Prime Computer, the Limited, and others on their big moves.

Current quarterly earnings are the first factor. According to O'Neil, "the profits of nearly every outstanding stock were booming." If a stock doesn't have a strong quarterly earnings increase, then it probably isn't worth bothering with since there will be other companies that are doing well. Three out of four stocks in O'Neil's study showed quarterly earnings increases of more than 70 percent before the stock began its major move. The median earnings increase was 34 percent and the mean was a whopping 90 percent.

Annual earnings growth is also important. O'Neil suggests selecting stocks with at least 15 percent to 50 percent annual growth rates over a five-year period. That's the range typically shown by the biggest winners prior to their big moves. He also advises checking the stability of earnings to avoid cyclic companies and those with erratic earnings histories. O'Neil also suggests disregard for the P/E ratio associated with the earnings; missing out on a big winner simply because the P/E is too high is as big a mistake as buying a stock simply because its P/E is low.

Often big winners took off because of something *new*. A new product or service may be the fundamental factor behind earnings acceleration. New management, distribution approach or new technology could also lead to rapid growth. Some specific examples include:

1. Polaroid's invention of the self developing camera which propelled it's stock from $65 to $355 in two years;

2. Syntex which introduced the oral contraception pill and saw its stock shoot from $100 to $550 in six months;

3. Computervision which introduced computer-aided design and manufacturing workstations and had a more than 10-fold increase in share price over three years;

4. Wang Laboratories which introduced office word processing machines and enjoyed more than a 13-fold rise over three years; and

5. Levitz furniture popularized discount furniture centers and saw its stock appreciate more than 600 percent in two years.

Supply and demand also determine the behavior of a stock. If a company is doing well as a result of some new innovation and its business has proven itself on the bottom line, then investors interested in the stock face the supply and demand associated with any market. If there is a small supply of stock and a large demand, its price will appreciate much more quickly than if there is a large supply. Hence small companies with a modest number of shares outstanding are better bets for substantial appreciation than large corporations where the impact of a new product will be diluted by a large portfolio of existing products and the impact on stock price will be damped by a large number of shares outstanding.

O'Neil urges investors to resist the desire to buy stocks that are cheap. He clearly emphasizes market *leaders* rather than laggards. Any stock not in the top 30 percent of all stocks performance wise is clearly questionable. The biggest winners averaged relative performance of 87 percent, meaning that 87 percent of the stocks were not doing as well even before these winners took off. O'Neil suggests picking stocks that have performance ranks of at least 80 percent to 90 percent and selling off the losers in a portfolio first.

Institutional interest is another key factor. Here O'Neil suggests that a stock need not have a large institutional sponsorship, but it helps to have at least three to ten institutional investors with positions in a company. Furthermore the quality of sponsorship may be important, since some institutional investors tend to be better than others at spotting potential market winners early in the game. Institutional investors include mutual funds, insurance companies, bank trust departments and corporate pension funds. On the other hand if a stock is overowned by the institutions, it could be a sign that it is late in the growth life cycle of the stock.

O'Neil adds that even if you are correct on the first six factors, but wrong on the *market's direction*, three out of four times you will lose money. He advises tracking the market averages every day, especially for those investors who may be using margin to finance a part of their investment portfolio. Among specific signs of trouble for the overall market are:

1. heavy volume without corresponding price advance;

2. failure of rallys after a downtrend has started;

3. protracted periods of declining volume; and

4. divergences in key market averages.

Other factors O'Neil notes as important include fundamentals such as Federal Reserve Board policy changes such as the hike in the discount rate in September 1987 prior to the stock market crash.

O'Neil's CANSLIM factors can be easily related to the control parameters of our nonlinear market model. The first four are *fundamental factors*; the final three are of a *technical* nature having to do with relative market performance, absolute market performance and the flow of money from potential institutional sponsors, capable of moving the stock price.

Earnings Expectations Life Cycle: The Cinderella Strategy

Earnings expectations among investors are one of the single most important factors that drives the performance of a stock. Most of the best performing investment advisers (including Zweig, Allmon, and Value Line) keep a close eye on earnings. It is a factor that reflects both the prevailing bias in a company's fundamentals as well as market sentiment.

Expectations can vary widely for individual stocks. Growth stocks with high P/E ratios represent high expectations for earnings. In contrast, value stocks with low P/E ratios represent low expectations for earnings growth. These in effect reflect *stable states* which are widely separated with respect to the premium the market is willing to pay for the stocks. However, surprises often occur and are a major factor behind market returns. In effect, the perceptions within the market on a company's prospects can be a dynamic process that can be stable for extended periods or subject to chaotic fluctuations.

A simple model of the earnings expectations life cycle has been developed by Richard Bernstein, manager of quantitative analysis at Merrill Lynch. As shown in Fig. 8.2, growth stocks in this model represent the pinnacle of the life cycle. At the point where a growth stock is widely recognized by the market, its prospects will be fully discounted and it may well be susceptible to any bad news such as an *earnings torpedo*. Earnings torpedos have been recently studied by Robert Hagin.

Bernstein's earnings expectations life cycle resembles the state space diagram of a simple pendulum. More complicated models can easily be developed resembling a Lorenz attractor in which earnings expectations may cycle around two widely separated stable points, one having a higher average earnings expectation level than the other. Normal cycles for growth stocks would revolve around the high earnings level, but major disappointments could cause expectations to jump from one stable regime to the other. Likewise value stocks may cycle around the low earnings expectation point but transition to the growth regime if the company enjoys major changes in its prospects.

Bernstein's earnings expectations model can be viewed as a clock on which the pinnacle of high growth is 12:00 midnight. He offers a method

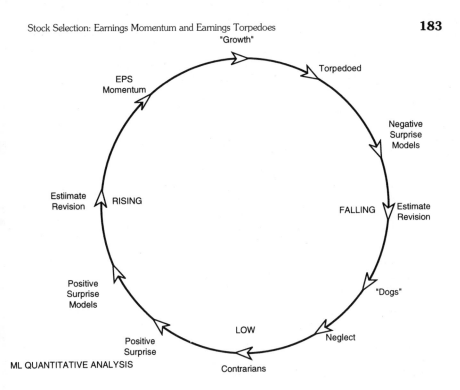

Figure 8.2. The earnings expectation life cycle has the highest expectations for growth stocks. (*Reprinted by permission. Copyright © 1991 Merrill, Lynch, Pierce, Fenner & Smith, Inc.*)

for identifying stocks whose earnings expectations are rising and moving toward the "growth" label. However, the primary motivation of his *Cinderella strategy* is to leave the party before midnight.

Bernstein has analyzed both the performance of stocks with high earnings expectations and the persistence of this performance. He suggests that it is in fact possible to identify growth stocks and that they will outperform the market. However, he cautions that the persistence will be short-lived. Growth investors should be prepared to exit these "Cinderella" stocks before the clock strikes midnight and their earnings are torpedoed.

The Cinderella strategy is based on both the level of analysts earnings forecasts and the range of the forecasts around the average. Figure 8.3 summarizes the growth estimates and the range of the estimates or degree of disagreement in the forecasts. The solid line reflects an *uncertainty frontier*. The frontier represents a boundary into which most forecasts and their associated uncertainty should fall. As the earnings forecasts increase above the average for the S&P 400, the normalization factor, the level of disagreement or uncertainty would be expected to grow.

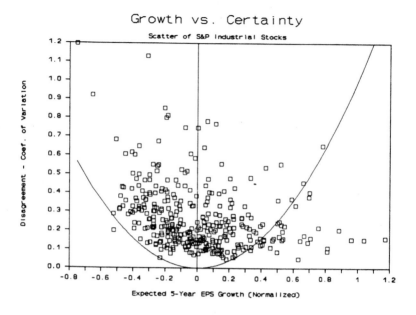

Figure 8.3. The earnings uncertainty frontier is crossed by growth stocks having a high degree of consensus among analysts. (*Reprinted by permission. Copyright © 1991 Merrill, Lynch, Pierce, Fenner & Smith, Inc.*)

The left side of the graph does show that most data falls within the uncertainty frontier. Stocks with very low earnings projections are also accompanied by a wide range of forecasts. Some analysts may expect earnings to turn around; others may project bankruptcy. However, for stocks with unusually high earnings projections, there isn't the same increase in uncertainty.

A considerable number of stocks have relatively high expected five-year growth rates and a high degree of consistency among analysts. Bernstein referred to this as *coherent earnings expectations.* These issues with a high degree of consensus among analysts are specifically the ones that Bernstein identifies as growth stocks within the context of the Cinderella strategy. Figure 8.4 summarizes the performance of the growth stocks that fall below the bottom right half of the earnings uncertainty frontier, relative to the rest of the market.

As the next step, Bernstein analyzed stocks that had newly crossed the frontier compared to those that had already been identified as growth stocks at least a year earlier. The stocks that have recently crossed the uncertainty frontier tend to do far better than those that have done so more than a year earlier. Bernstein also noted that stocks that moved back within the boundary of the uncertainty frontier (perhaps as a result of an earnings torpedo) tend to under perform the averages.

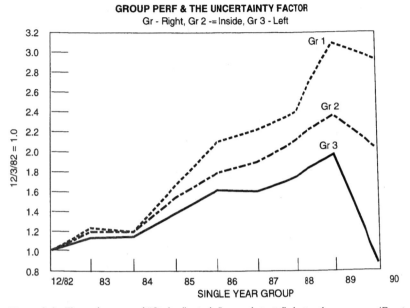

Figure 8.4. The performance of "Cinderella stocks" was substantially better than average. (*Reprinted by permission. Copyright © 1991 Merrill, Lynch, Pierce, Fenner & Smith, Inc.*)

In his report on the Cinderella strategy, Bernstein notes that his results conform to the coherent market hypothesis. The stocks outside of the earnings uncertainty frontier (i.e., those with coherent earnings expectations) had returns comparable to the volatility of returns. While this is not as large a ratio as the theoretical model predicts is possible, the Cinderella strategy does help identify issues that tend to have a higher degree of coherence than the market averages (at least for a year after initially moving across the frontier).

In a related report, Professor David F. Hawkins, an accounting consultant to Merrill Lynch, discusses the earnings quality issue and its relationship to the Cinderella strategy. He suggests that a decline in the earnings quality of a growth stock can be a strong indicator that the clock is approaching midnight and a torpedo may be approaching. While there is no strict definition of earnings quality, the approach used by Hawkins is to assess whether reported earnings are reliable indicators of future results. Low quality earnings may be misleading in this respect.

While there are numerous factors to consider in earning quality, the following are high on Hawkins' list:

1. less conservative accounting methods, such as changes in depreciation to increase current earnings;

2. accelerated shipments to customers to increase present revenue at the possible expense of future revenue;

3. reductions in controllable expenses such as research, maintenance or marketing, which could affect future revenues; and

4. slowdowns in inventory turnover.

Neural Networks: Artificial Intelligence for Portfolio Managers

Bradford Lewis is an *index killer*. His Disciplined Equity Fund has beaten the index by several percentage in each year since its inception. It enjoys a five-star rating from Morningstar, Inc., a mutual fund rating service. He has achieved above average returns with below average risks. by using *neural network technology* to screen stocks.

Gene Bylinsky, in his article in *Fortune* magazine (September 6, 1993), states:

> In Boston, Bradford Lewis, who runs Fidelity's Disciplined Equity Fund with a neural network, has consistently beaten the S&P 500—last year by 5.4 percentage points. His network usually picks little known stocks by looking for specific patterns. For example, the neural network tries to calculate how the price of a stock may be affected by changing patterns in debt level, cash flow, earnings estimates, and other variables.

Neural networks are a relatively new technology within the broad realm of *artificial intelligence* (AI). Unlike other AI technologies, such as expert systems which are based on invariant rules, a neural network is capable of learning. It is "trained" over a test period, and then turned loose on real "live" data to make predictions.

Nor is Brad Lewis alone in using this nonlinear method to support his investment decisions. Dean Barr of LBS Capital Management, Inc. in Safety Harbor, Florida has been managing over $300 million for clients. He also uses neural network technology to manage portfolio risk. LBS has beaten the S&P 500 index by 24 percent over a six-year period. Its Midcap portfolio has beaten the S&P Midcap index by an even wider margin, showing a 35.8 percent annualized return compared with 21.6 percent for the index.

Artificial intelligence is an area of growing popularity within the broad area of computer science. Its goals are to mimic the human brain's ability to reason, recognize patterns, and abstract information from data. Its potential applications on Wall Street are numerous. With traders constantly being inundated by a wide variety of information, AI technology can be used to build trading models, retrieve information intelligently, and to filter data with the goal of extracting the most relevant information to a particular task.

Among the specific technologies that are being used, expert systems and neural networks are the most popular. Other approaches that fall under the definition of AI include *case-based reasoning, genetic algorithms, fuzzy logic,* and various combinations of these approaches. With the availability of cheap computing power, techniques that required high priced, special purpose processors only a few years ago, can now be performed on 486 class personal computers. This has resulted in a resurgence of interest in AI applications in the financial markets.

The other driver behind AI technologies is the growing realization that the markets are not truly efficient. Increasingly, it is becoming evident that there is both a deterministic and random component involved in market fluctuations. Sophisticated AI techniques offer one approach to identifying and profiting from market inefficiencies.

Within the realm of AI techniques, neural networks are growing in popularity. A neural network teaches itself, rather than relying on a set of rules defined by a subject matter expert. One doesn't need to interview an expert to develop and implement a system. Rather, all that is needed theoretically is a large set of data to "train" the neural network.

Neural network technology is an emerging area of artificial intelligence with growing applications in diverse fields. Among the areas in which applications are being found are industrial process control, oil and gas exploration, marketing, and finance. Any problem that requires a complex pattern recognition approach or classification approach is a candidate for this type of solution.

Conversion of natural handwriting to machine readable characters is one example. Everyone has a slightly different handwriting. This is sometimes a valuable distinguishing feature in legal battles over hand written wills or other documents, where handwriting experts are needed to authenticate a signature. However, with computers, deviations in handwriting make automatic recognition and interpretation a difficult task. One application of automated handwriting recognition is with the U.S. Postal Service which needs to sort mail by zip code. Neural networks have had significant success in supporting this process within acceptable error limits.

Credit analysis is another area of application. With the number of business failures and personal bankruptcies on the rise, increasing concern is being placed by lenders on the analysis of the creditworthiness of customers. Banks themselves have become a problem area for the government which guarantees deposits and must worry about the risk of losses from bank failures. Likewise, accounting firms face liabilities if they fail to exercise due diligence in examining the financial condition of clients and reporting potential risks, particularly with publicly owned corporations. This is another area in which neural network technology is finding applications to look for patterns in the financial histories that are associated with a high likelihood of future insolvency.

Credit card fraud is another important application of neural network technology. Banks and other card issuers had been using expert systems based on rules defined by experts in the area to look for changing patterns in credit cards use. However the false alarm rate with expert systems has been too high; investigators spend too much time chasing down inappropriate alarms generated by the rule-based system. In contrast, neural networks have cut the number of potential fraud alarms by 90 percent, making the service far more manageable and less expensive to implement.

Numerous other examples of neural network applications are chronicled by Gene Bylinsky in *Fortune*. Among them are the military application for autonomous terrain navigation and commercial applications for waking up drivers that fall asleep at the wheel. Yet even with these promising developments in the works, the field is still in its infancy. The human brain has over 100 billion neurons. The most sophisticated applications today have only a tiny fraction of what even the simplest life forms have. Furthermore, the number of possible interconnections in artificial neural networks is much smaller than natural systems.

Neural networks superficially mimic the brain cells' approach to information processing. As shown in Fig. 8.5 a network of processors, or electronic neurons, are connected to each other by adjustable, weighted links. The net begins with a relatively large set of input data and uses algorithms to adjust the weights of each link until it "learns" to predict a desired output. After it is "trained" on a set of data it is ready to be used to make predictions in the future on a new set of input data.

In contrast, the human brain contains more than 10^{11} neurons interconnected by 10^{14} synapses. The relationship between neural network techniques and the human brain is a weak one at best. The brain is far more complex and ongoing research has long ago moved beyond neural network models. However, neural networks do offer a method for developing a nonlinear model without making many assumptions regarding the nonlinear processes underlying the market's dynamics.

In an artificial neural network there is an input layer, usually one or more hidden layers and an output layer. The input layer is used to hold the training data input. The hidden layers propagate results from the input layer to the output layer. A perceptron is the process by which an artificial neuron takes a weighted sum of inputs and computes an output based on some

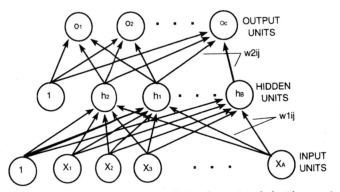

Figure 8.5. A neural network was originally thought to imitate the brain's processing functions. More recent research suggests that the brain is vastly more complex than this simple nonlinear model.

nonlinear threshold function (i.e., the weighted inputs are either enough to trigger an output or not). The training algorithm then compares the output with a desired output and readjusts the weights to attempt to bring the neural network's result closer to the desired result.

When there are hidden layers in a neural network, the intermediate results are not known. However, the weights of each hidden layer can also be varied and the final output compared to the desired output. This process is known as *back propagation training*. Hence the training process involves two passes through the network. A forward pass presents inputs to the network and computes the output. The backward pass uses error estimates to adjust the weights in the hidden layers and the errors from the hidden layer are used to adjust the weights of the input layer. After this process is completed for each layer, it constitutes one epoch of the training process.

The training process is computationally very intensive. Even small networks with relatively few links and hidden layers require many complete epochs to train the net. One solution has been to implement the process in special purpose hardware rather than software. Another approach is to use parallel processing to break the task into smaller increments and ship each piece to different computers working in parallel to speed up overall computation time required.

According to Fishman, Barr, and Loick, "Neural nets are truly black boxes. Once you have trained a neural net and are generating predictions, you still do not know why the decisions are being made, and can't find out by just looking at the net. It is not unlike attempting to capture the structure of knowledge by dissecting a human brain."

A number of neural network "shells" are commercially available. For example, Brainmaker, by California Scientific Software uses a *back propagation algorithm* to learn relationships in the input data.

Summary

The quest for above average performance without proportionately higher risk is in conflict with the efficient market hypothesis which maintains that there is no significant benefit to either technical or fundamental analysis. The only way to achieve above average returns according to classical capital market theory is to assume above average risk. Higher risks are rewarded with higher returns in the rational markets construct.

However, the classical capital market theory is coming under increasing attack even within the academic community. For example, the capital asset pricing model (CAPM) maintains that expected returns are a positive linear function of their market beta factors (the ratio of the securities return to the market's return). Furthermore, the theory maintains that the beta factor is sufficient for predicting future returns (i.e., there are no additional predictive factors). However, in recent studies, the beta factor does not show the predicted linear relationship to returns. Hence even the most basic prediction of the CAPM is in doubt. Furthermore, other variables have been found to have a significant relationship to market returns.

In 1981, Rolf W. Banz showed that there was a relationship between the market capitalization of a stock and future returns. He found that market capitalization (i.e., the price of a security times the number of shares outstanding) adds information to return prediction. Specifically, he found that small capitalization stocks returns were higher than predicted by beta alone. Likewise the average returns on high capitalization stocks are too low relative to their beta factors.

The ratio of book value to market capitalization is another factor that appears to be significant in explaining deviations from the simple beta factor model. For example, Rosenberg, Reid, and Lanstein showed in 1985 that average returns are positively related to the book value to market capitalization ratio. High earnings to price ratio stocks also tend to correlate with higher future returns according to many researchers. That's the reciprocal of the P/E ratio used by many practitioners. We have already discussed the post earnings drift factor, as a basis for Value Line's ranking success.

Within the framework of the coherent market hypothesis we would expect both technical and fundamental factors to be important in identifying coherent stocks (i.e., those that have above average reward without proportionately higher risk). Practitioners tend to focus on relative strength as a key technical factor. Zweig, Sullivan, O'Neil, and Value Line all identify relative strength as a key factor in their stock selection strategy. They also focus on earnings growth as a critical fundamental factor for stock selection. Hence the best performing practitioners do in fact track a significant number of technical and fundamental factors to identify the best future performers.

The coherent market hypothesis predicts that the relationship between risk and reward is more complicated than the linear model predicted by the CAPM theory. It does not offer specific indicators or implementation strategies. Academic work is now confirming that there is more to market risk and reward than the simple linear model of classical capital market theory and practitioners have identified specific strategies that have performed well over extended periods.

Hence we conclude that both technical and fundamental analysis can add value to those who wish to implement an active management approach. Perhaps the simplest technical screen is that which has been successfully used by Louis Navellier and James Collins where they consider both the relative strength and the volatility of a stock. Stocks having the highest ratio of relative strength with the least volatility qualify for their "buy" lists. However, at that point, fundamentals and absolute risk levels determine which candidate stocks are suitable for meeting particular investment objectives.

On the fundamental side, size and value clearly are the variables that Charles Allmon focuses on. Earnings, earnings growth, earnings quality, and earnings stability are all important fundamental factors. However, William O'Neil's insights are perhaps most important: new developments tend to drive major market moves and new developments will have the greatest impact on companies with the smallest market capitalization. The large capitalization stocks are closest to equilibrium. Small capitalization stocks are furthest from equilibrium.

If a relatively small company successfully innovates and gains a competitive advantage in the market, it will see a flow of new revenues and profits. This flow will show up on the bottom line and lead to a flow of investors interested in establishing a position and adding to a position as the growth continues. Both the underlying business of the company and the behavior of the stock in the financial market represent "open" systems behavior. The performance of the business is limited only by the ultimate size of the market. Small companies in large markets have tremendous growth opportunity. Likewise their stocks can appreciate by orders of magnitude over relatively short periods of time. These are situations that are far from equilibrium. Capturing them can substantially add to portfolio returns; missing them can lock in under performance.

9

Option Strategies: Hedging in Chaotic Markets

On that fateful day of October 19, 1987, the Dow plunged 22.6 percent. Using my time tested indicators and strategies, I had taken certain fail-safe steps before the crash…. As a result, our portfolio gained 9 percent on Black Monday.

If I were a genius–and there aren't any in this business–I would have sold everything right before the break, bought even more puts, held them all right up to the bottom day and made zillions. But that's not reality. Reality is cutting risk to the bone when the indicators weaken, hoping that you can make a few bucks when conditions are good, and praying that you'll survive crashes, plagues and earthquakes long enough so that someday you'll see the pleasant light of another bull market and have some money left to play with.

MARTIN ZWEIG,
Winning on Wall Street

Zweig: Worrying Has Its Rewards

Zweig's worrying paid off handsomely during the Crash of 1987. Zweig had been worrying throughout 1987 about the market's excessive valuation levels. Prior to the crash, he compared the market's vulnerabilities to the 1929, 1946 and 1962 periods. The latter two periods both had violent selloffs in the wake of a discount rate hike by the Federal Reserve in periods of unusually high market valuations.

The October 9, 1987 issue of *The Zweig Forecast* clearly stated that market risk was the highest since the bear market of 1981. As a result Zweig advised his readers to put 1 percent of their portfolios into November put options. Puts give their owner the right to sell a certain number of shares at a certain defined price within a fixed period. The specific puts Zweig recommended were 8 percent out of the money, so even if the market had dropped, but not by any more than 8 percent, the puts would have expired worthless. Furthermore, had the market not dropped before November, the puts would have also expired.

This was only the second time in 16 years that Zweig had adopted a hedging strategy using puts, and the second time in the two-year period prior to the crash. The events of October bore out the wisdom of the insurance policy. The puts which were purchased at a price of $2\frac{3}{8}$ in September, began to soar in price as the market declined. Zweig unloaded them in five increments, beginning on October 15, at prices between $9\frac{1}{4}$, $19\frac{1}{4}$, 54, $86\frac{1}{2}$, and, on October 20, he dumped the last of the puts at a remarkable price of 130. These transactions added a 20.8 percent gain to the portfolio, less a 9 percent loss on stocks, prior to their hitting stop-loss limits. His net gain was 9 percent on the day of the crash.

Zweig's use of put options represents a dramatic example of the potential benefits of hedging in chaotic markets. His approach was not based on any formal valuation models. It was more a special situation in which Zweig felt that the risk-reward outlook for the market had changed clearly enough to warrant aggressive action to protect his position. Clearly, when markets are far from equilibrium, and volatility becomes hard to quantify, the value of options can change even more dramatically than the underlying securities. The classical option valuation models are based on the premise of rational markets and equilibrium pricing. The Crash of 1987 was an example of an anomalous fluctuation in a chaotic market far from equilibrium. At these times the standard option valuation models can clearly be misleading and possibly dangerous because the theoretical probability distributions neglect the fat tails found on the empirical distributions.

Someone who had shorted the same options Zweig had purchased, perhaps on the basis of a standard option valuation model would have been in deep trouble. The financial earthquake of Black Monday illustrates the fact that events which are theoretically next to impossible within the context of classical equilibrium models, are far more likely in the complex world we live in. Hence there is a need for option valuation models that can provide an estimate of both the "normal" valuation levels, and a more realistic estimate of the potential risk or reward associated with abnormal fluctuations.

Option valuation in coherent and chaotic markets can take advantage of the standard baseline model as a starting point. Most of the time, the market's fluctuations are nearly normally distributed, and the valuation models that are based on this assumption provide good results. However, in coherent markets, there will be a strong drift which, though negligible on a short-term basis, will compound into an important factor when the option contract's life is relatively long. In chaotic markets, there may be a significant probability of a state transition from one stable state to it's mirror image; hence the valuation of an option would depend on the probability of a state transition within the lifetime of the contract.

Zweig's assessment of a significant change in market risk, in part, was based on quantitative indicators and perhaps in part on a subjective judgment that chances of a large fluctuation were substantially higher than normal. His indicators were clearly bearish, but not at a bearish extreme. What was equally important, most market participants remained bullish in spite of the negative bias in the quantitative indicators. Even though the indicators were not highly negative, the difference between the market's highly bullish expectations and the reality portrayed by the indicators was very large. Given the combination of a climate conducive to crowd behavior and a significant change in fundamentals, conditions were ripe for a reversal of expectations and the associated volatility.

In a chaotic market (i.e., when there is a bimodal probability distribution governing price fluctuations), there is an exponential distribution that governs the time required for transitions between the two stable states. As discussed further in the Appendix, the exponential factor depends on the height of the potential barrier, which in our nonlinear model depends on fundamentals. When the fundamentals change significantly, the odds of a transition between the two extremes of the bimodal distribution grow exponentially. This is the case that existed prior to the Crash of 1987, though conventional option valuation models are not capable of dealing with these types of anomalous events.

Our goal here is to review the baseline option valuation theory and to look for ways to enhance it to more effectively hedge in chaotic markets. Since our nonlinear model includes random walk as a special case, the standard option valuation models are a good starting point. However, the unique aspects of coherent and chaotic markets suggest that a nonlinear model is ultimately required. Development of a general nonlinear option model remains an area for further research.

Derivative Products and
Program Trading

Derivative products (i.e., the options and futures markets) have become the basis for a wide range of hedging tactics. Arbitrage, program trading, and portfolio insurance are all examples of the widespread use of derivative securities to manage risk. Using such techniques, the large institutional investors have the ability to change their risk exposure significantly at moderate cost.

Arbitrage is a tactic for taking advantage of small price differences in similar markets at different locations. With high-speed telecommunications, any price difference between markets can be quickly detected and exploited. For example, index arbitrage may involve the S&P 500 index futures traded on the Chicago Board of Trade and the underlying value of the index as traded on the New York Stock Exchange. If the differences between these two markets grow too large, there may be an opportunity for arbitrage profits between these essentially similar markets.

Program trading is related to the execution of arbitrage transactions. For example if the S&P 500 futures market in Chicago is selling at a discount relative to the cash market in New York, short-term profits can be generated by purchase of the undervalued futures contracts and simultaneous sale of the equivalent stocks. This is a game that can be profitable for the large institutions who deal in large volume and negotiate the smallest of commissions. Hence it has become a source of bitterness for traditional investors who see large price fluctuations in stocks as a result of events in the futures markets.

Portfolio insurance is based on the creation of a "synthetic" put option. This is usually done in the futures markets by means of selling short futures contracts against an equivalent stock portfolio to hedge against downside losses. For example, an institution with a large index portfolio may want to offset market risk by insuring all or part of the portfolio. The purveyor of insurance then implements a "dynamic" hedge where more and more futures are sold short as the index declines in value. A basic assumption in portfolio insurance is that there will be someone willing to buy the futures contracts, at a fair price. Events during the Crash of 1987 demonstrated first that there may not always be buyers when there is a need to sell, and second, when buyers step up they may not pay what would be considered a fair price.

Aggressive shorting of futures by portfolio insurers in a declining market can further accelerate the decline. The short sales can eliminate the premium at which futures usually trade, and even drive them to a discount. This creates profitable arbitrage opportunities where the futures purchaser sells the underlying securities short. A cycle of forced selling can ensue, since the portfolio insurers must sell futures into the declining market to execute the strategy they are committed to.

While portfolio insurance is implemented in the futures market, the net effect is to sell stocks into a declining market. This was one of the factors that accelerated the decline on October 19, 1987. The amount of dynamic hedging had grown so large that the market specialists simply couldn't handle the volume of sales.

Hence there are two types of players in the derivatives markets. One group tends to drive the markets out of equilibrium. They are forced to implement a strategy regardless of the price and value factors in order to manage the overall market exposure of the portfolios they are insuring. The other group tends to detect deviations from equilibrium and profit by helping the markets regain equilibrium prices and values.

The amount of activity related to the derivatives market has become staggering. Figure 9.1 shows the total volume of transactions on the New York Stock Exchange as well as the associated options and futures markets. This relatively new development is viewed with concern by some market observers, including Charles Kirkpatrick who views derivatives as major financial vulnerability in the current secular stock market peak.

Classical Option Valuation:
The Black-Scholes Baseline

Fair values of option contracts depend on a variety of factors. The most important is volatility. It is easy enough to compute what a put or call option would be worth at the time of expiration if the underlying security moves by a particular amount above or below the strike price. However, computing the probability of market moves of a given magnitude over a given period of time is more difficult.

Regardless of the specific assumptions made about the probability distribution governing market returns, the goal of any option valuation model is to assess the fair value of an option contract. The user of the model can then compare the actual market price to determine if the market is too high or too low relative to "fair value." Presumably the sale of options when they are overpriced and repurchase when they are under priced can lead to profitable results.

A variety of option valuation models have been proposed over the years. The best known is the *Black-Scholes model*, published in the *Journal of Political Economy* in May–June, 1973. Fisher Black and Myron Scholes based their model of fair value on the concept of a neutral hedge. This assumes that it is possible to set up a perfectly hedged position (e.g., long

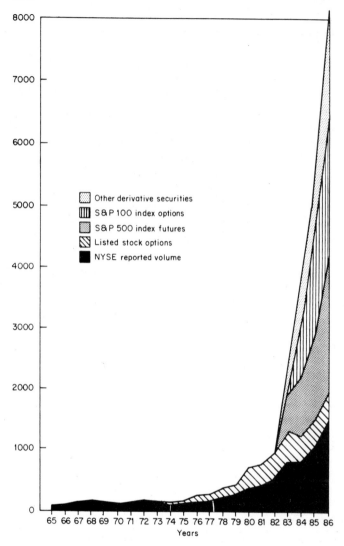

Figure 9.1. Derivative products have become a major and somewhat controversial factor in the financial markets. *(Source: Gastineau, The Options Manual. Reprinted by permission. Copyright 1988, McGraw-Hill, Inc. All rights reserved.)*

position on a stock and short position on calls) such that any increase (or decrease) in the stock value is offset by a decrease (increase) in the corresponding option price. The relative amount of stock and number of options contracts at which this occurs is known as the *hedge ratio.*

By adjusting the hedge ratio, the Black-Scholes model assumes that market risk can be eliminated for a stock portfolio. Since the perfectly hedged position is essentially risk free, assuming the options are fairly valued, the hedged position should earn the same rate of return as the prevailing Treasury bill rate. This premise is essentially based on the concepts of modern portfolio theory and the capital asset pricing model. The Black-Scholes model linked options to other securities and the capital market theory. As such it represents the baseline or classical financial valuation model.

Basic parameters and assumptions for the Black-Scholes model are summarized in Table 9.1. Inherent in this model is the assumption that the logarithm of price changes in the underlying security is normally distributed. This is a good starting point. However, empirically it has been found that there are substantial deviations between actual securities price fluctuations and the log normal distribution.

Fat-Tailed Distributions: Critical Market States

One active area of research has been the attempt to extend the Black-Scholes option valuation model to other underlying probability distributions. For example, Fig. 9.2 illustrates typical empirical distributions overlaid on the log normal distribution. This illustrates a tendency for clustering of data around small price changes to a far greater extent than expected from the log normal distribution. The second differences is in the fat tail characteristic of empirical distributions.

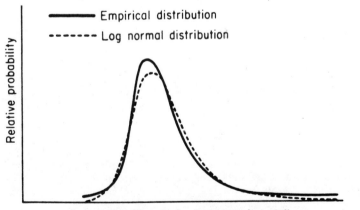

Figure 9.2. Empirical data actually deviates from a log normal price change distribution as a result fo nonlinear effects, which can have a significant influence on fair option pricing. *(Source: Gastineau, The Options Manual. Reprinted by permission. Copyright 1988, McGraw-Hill, Inc. All rights reserved.)*

Table 9.1. The Black-Scholes Option Model

$$V_c = P_s N\ (d_1) - Se^{r(t-t^*)}\ N(d_2)$$

$$d_1 = \frac{\ln\ (P_s\ /\ S) + (r + \tfrac{1}{2}v^2)(t^* - t)}{v\sqrt{(t^* - t)}}$$

$$d_2 = \frac{\ln\ (P_s\ /\ S) + (r - \tfrac{1}{2}v^2)(t^* - t)}{\cdot v\sqrt{(t^* - t)}}$$

where V_c = fair value of option

P_s = stock price

S = striking or exercise price

$N(d)$ = cumulative normal density function

r = "risk-free" interest rate

t = current date

t^* = maturity date of option or warrant

v^2 = variance rate of return on stock

e = base of natural logarithms = 2.71828

$\ln$ = natural logarithm

Key Assumptions of the Black-Scholes Model

1. The short-term interest rate is known and is constant through time.
2. The stock price follows a random walk in continuous time with a variance rate proportional to the square of the stock price.
3. The distribution of possible stock prices at the end of any finite interval is lognormal.
4. The variance rate of return on the stock is constant.
5. The stock pays no dividends and makes no other distributions.
6. The option can only be exercised at maturity.
7. There are no commissions or other transaction costs in buying or selling the stock or the option.
8. It is possible to borrow any fraction of the price of a security to buy it or to hold it, at the short-term interest rate.
9. A seller who does not own a security (a short seller) will simply accept the price of the security from the buyer and will agree to settle with the buyer on some future date by paying him an amount equal to the price of the security on that date. While this short sale is outstanding, the short seller will have the use of, or interest on, the proceeds of the sale.
10. The tax rate, if any, is identical for all transactions and all market participants.

SOURCE: Fischer Black and Myron Scholes, The Pricing of Options and Corporate Liabilities, *The Journal of Political Economy*, May–June 1973, pp. 637–654. Copyright © 1973 by the University of Chicago. All rights reserved.

With respect to option valuation, the fat tails imply that out of the money options are worth substantially more than expected from the log normal distribution function. The tail of the log normal distribution suggests that there is a vanishingly low probability of a large price change. The empirical distribution says that actual market experience demonstrates otherwise. There is a much larger likelihood of seeing very large price changes.

In effect the investor is caught in a dilemma first identified by Benoit Mandelbrot. The volatility of capital markets is difficult to quantify. If the nonlinear effects are taken into account, the second moment of the price change probability distribution essentially becomes undefined (i.e., it doesn't converge to any particular limit). Some periods will have far higher volatility than others depending on if they include an anomalous event (i.e., a large price change that falls somewhere on the tail region of the distribution).

The empirical distribution may be viewed as an "average" of the market's action in the different states predicted by our nonlinear market model. If no attempt is made to predict which state the market is in and all price changes are averaged together, then the result is the empirical distribution. It can be used to value options based on an approach proposed by Gary Gastineau and Albert Madansky. Gastineu is currently with the Swiss Bank Corporation, while Madansky is a professor at the University of Chicago.

According to Madansky, "A number of years ago, Gary Gastineau and I got together (as most tinkerers do) in my garage, trying to develop an options analysis system." Gastineau and Madansky looked specifically at the distribution associated with optionable stocks. They examined four years worth of daily data for 40 optionable stocks and fit a probability distribution. They found the empirical distribution to be significantly different from the log normal distribution and as a result went on to develop an option valuation model based on use of empirical rather than theoretical distributions. Subsequently, Gastineau and Madansky expanded the number of stocks used to build up the empirical distribution from 40 to 389 optionable stocks. However the empirical distribution was largely unaffected by this larger sample.

Figure 9.3 outlines the *Gastineau-Madansky option valuation model.* Table 9.2 summarizes the differences in prices between the Black-Scholes and Gastineau-Madansky models. It shows that substantial differences occur with out of the money options, where Black-Scholes systematically under prices such options, though when the stock price and option striking price are the same, the two models produce very nearly the same result.

$$V_c = a_1 e^{a_2 r(t-t*)} \int_{a_3 S/P_S}^{x} a_4(ZP_S - S)dQ\,[Z;\,(t*-t);\,a_5]$$

$a_1 \ldots a_5$ = adjustment factors designed to reflect commission charges, dividends, interest rates, taxes, and other variables. Each adjustment factor in this formulation may incorporate part or all of the adjustment for more than one variable. The adjustment factors are frequently complex functions in their own right

r = basic interest rate

t = current date

t^* = maturity date of option or warrant

$\int_{a_3 S/P_s}^{x}$ = integral over interval from $\dfrac{a_3 S}{P_s}$ to x

x = infinity

S = striking or exercise price

P_s = stock price

Z = random variable return per dollar invested in common stock

$dQ[Z;(t^*-t);\,a_5]$ = an empirical probability density function of Z over a time period of length t^*-t

e = base of natural logarithms = 2.71828

Key Assumptions of the Gastineau-Madansky Model

1. The interest rates at which an investor can borrow and lend money are known and constant through time.

2. Stock price fluctuations conform to the efficient markets model which states that the stock price at any moment reflects all information available to the market participants. The variance is proportional to the square of the stock price.

3. The distribution of possible stock prices at the end of any finite interval confors to an empirical probability function.

4. The variance of the stock price distribution is the same for each period.

5. The effect of dividends and other distributions is reflected in the adjustment factors.

6. The option can be exercised at any time prior to expiration.

7. Commission and other options transaction costs are reflected in the adjustment factors.

8. Investors are subject to standard margin requirements and borrow at a higher rate than they lend..

9. The short seller can, thorugh option conversion, effectively have the use of the proceeds of a short sale, provided exchange-listed put options are available.

10. The tax rate, if any, is the actual rate paid by each market participant. The tax rate is symmetric in that the tax credit for a loss is computed at the same rate as they tax payment on a gain. Tax rates may differ on each of three types of income: (a) ordinary income, (b) short-term capital gains, (c) long-term capital gains.

Figure 9.3. The Gastineau-Madansky option valuation model is based on empirical price change frequency distributions. (*Source: Gastineau, The Options Manual. Reprinted by permission. Copyright 1988, McGraw-Hill, Inc. All rights reserved.*)

Table 9.2. Differences in Black-Scholes versus Gastineau-Madansky

Assumptions:

Daily stock price variance (log)	0.632×10^{-3}
Interest rate	10% per annum
Remaining life of option	3 months
Exercise price	$40
Dividends, commission, and taxes	No adjustment

Stock price (1)	Gastineau-Madansky option value (2)	Black-Scholes option value* (3)	Ratio (col. 2 ÷ col. 3) (4)
$28	$ 0.22	$ 0.13	1.69
32	0.70	0.60	1.17
36	1.76	1.72	1.02
40	3.72	3.67	1.01
44	6.59	6.38	1.03
48	10.12	9.66	1.05
52	13.99	13.29	1.05

*From Fischer Black, "Fact and Fantasy in the Use of Options," *Financial Analysts Journal,* July–August 1975, pp. 36–72.

Call Option Purchases in Coherent Bull Markets

Do option buyers or writers make money? This important question has been at the heart of a long standing controversy. Here we suggest that it depends on the market state. In a coherent bull market, buyers of call options have the best odds of making money, provided that they hold on for a significant period of time.

The general time dependent solution to our nonlinear market model is not tractable in closed form. However, approximate solutions are possible based on a linearized analysis around the stationary states. For example, in a coherent bull market there is essentially one stable state, far from equilibrium. The time dependent model in this situation involves a bell-shaped, normal distribution in which there is a strong drift as well as the usual time dependent diffusion in the probability distribution. This situation is illustrated in Fig. 9.4.

On a short-term basis, the drift is small compared to the volatility associated with the distribution. Hence the pricing of options with short expiration periods would not be expected to deviate significantly from the prediction of the baseline Black-Scholes model. However, if the option lifetime is relatively long, then the effects of the drift would become significant and significantly affect the value of the option.

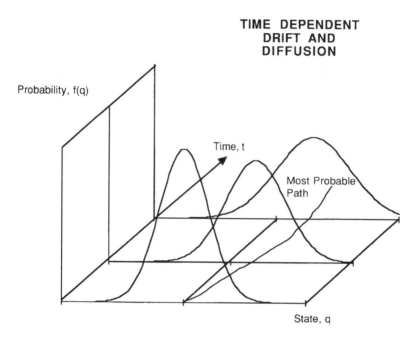

**TIME DEPENDENT
DRIFT AND
DIFFUSION**

Probability, f(q)

Time, t

Most Probable
Path

State, q

Figure 9.4. In a coherent bull market, a persistent drift, as well as diffusion of prices, can be a significant valuation factor for long life-time option contracts.

Furthermore, the initial state of the market is important. If prices have been in a negative state prior to a change in fundamentals (i.e., initial Fed easing) there is a possibility of anomalous volatility in the early stages of a bull market. For example, if a new bull market is signaled by extremes in the up-down volume ratio as described in Chap. 7, there may be further large price change events on the upside. This would be the mirror image of the situation that Zweig describes prior to the Crash of 1987. A change in fundamentals from negative to even slightly positive when investor senti-ment is highly negative could provide a special situation for the call option buyer, just as the pre-Crash of 1987 situation was a special situation for the put option buyer.

In general, the question of whether it makes sense to buy options or to write them has been examined by Robert Merton, Myron Scholes, and Matthew Gladstein (MSG) in the *Journal of Business* (April 1978). They simulated the performance of portfolios using a variety of strategies based on call options, common stocks, and commercial paper over a 12½-year period ending in December 1975. Their results in Fig. 9.5 show that the options buyers would have enjoyed the best performance based on a strategy

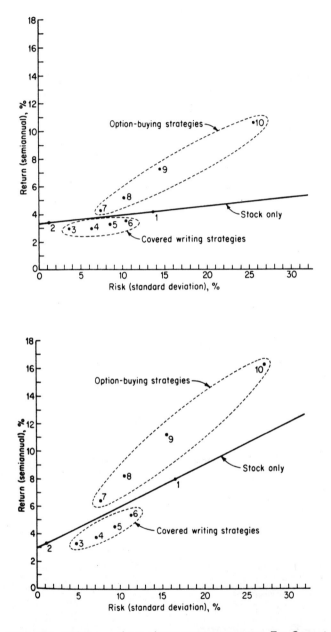

Figure 9.5. Performance of option buyers versus option writers. *Top:* Comparison of the Merton-Scholes-Gladstein simulation results—Dow Jones sample. *Bottom:* Comparison of the Merton-Scholes-Gladstein simulation results—136-stock sample. *(Source: Gastineau, The Options Manual. Reprinted by permission. Copyright 1988, McGraw-Hill, Inc. All rights reserved.)*

of holding 90 percent commercial paper and 10 percent call options with a fixed six-month holding period. Tables 9.3 and 9.4 provide a description of the performance of each portfolio examined in the study.

The MSG study looked at both the Dow Jones stock sample and a second sample of 136 optionable stocks. The results for each portfolio are similar, showing that call option buyers should have enjoyed results better than holders of the equivalent stock portfolio. In contrast, option writers would have fared more poorly than the equivalent stock portfolio. The period covered was not a particularly strong one overall for stocks. However, there was considerable volatility and large market fluctuations that would have benefited options buyers at least over certain periods of time.

A number of criticisms have been leveled at the MSG study. Gastineau suggests that the option valuations may have been undervalued by amounts ranging from 20 percent for the 136 stock portfolio to 28 percent for the Dow Jones portfolio. Among the sources of undervaluation are that the Black-Scholes model used to simulate the option portfolio tends to systematically under price options by about 1 to 2 percent. This would adversely affect the returns received by option writers and would inflate the number of calls the option buyers would be able to purchase.

A second possible source of underpricing comes from the use of the commercial paper rate as the risk-free rate of return in constructing neutral hedge positions. A higher rate is generally considered more appropriate and could account for another two percent or so of under valuation.

Table 9.3. Comparison of the Merton-Scholes-Gladstein Simulation Results—Dow Jones Sample

Strategy	Semiannual return (return), %	Standard deviation (risk), %
1. Dow Jones stock portfolio	4.1	13.7
2. Commercial paper	3.3	1.1
Simulated covered call writing (D-J stock sample):		
3. Exercise price = 0.9 × stock price	2.9	3.7
4. Exercise price = 1.0 × stock price	2.9	6.2
5. Exercise price = 1.1 × stock price	3.2	8.6
6. Exercise price = 1.2 × stock price	3.5	10.4
Simulated 90% commercial paper–10% call purchase (D-J stock sample):		
7. Exercise price = 0.9 × stock price	4.2	7.3
8. Exercise price = 1.0 × stock price	5.1	10.1
9. Exercise price = 1.1 × stock price	7.2	14.6
10. Exercise price = 1.2 × stock price	10.6	25.7

SOURCE: Gastineau, *The Options Manual*. Reprinted by permission. Copyright 1988, McGraw-Hill, Inc. All rights reserved.

Table 9.4. Comparison of the Merton-Scholes-Gladstein Simulation
Results—136-Stock Sample

Strategy	Semiannual return (return), %	Standard deviation (risk), %
1. 136-stock portfolio	7.9	16.6
2. Commercial paper	3.3	1.1
Simulated covered call writing (136-stock sample):		
3. Exercise price = 0.9 × stock price	3.3	4.9
4. Exercise price = 1.0 × stock price	3.7	7.1
5. Exercise price = 1.1 × stock price	4.5	9.3
6. Exercise price = 1.2 × stock price	5.3	11.2
Simulated 90% commercial paper–10% call purchase (136-stock sample):		
7. Exercise price = 0.9 × stock price	6.3	7.8
8. Exercise price = 1.0 × stock price	8.2	10.6
9. Exercise price = 1.1 × stock price	11.1	15.7
10. Exercise price = 1.2 × stock price	16.2	27.2

SOURCE: Gastineau, *The Options Manual.* Reprinted by permission. Copyright 1988, McGraw-Hill, Inc. All rights reserved.

A third source of undervaluation of calls may have been the method used to measure stock price volatility. The prior six-month variance of daily logarithmic stock price changes was used in the valuation of options. However, for the period of the study there was a secular increase in market volatility, which meant that the option valuation would have been too low on average. Finally, suggests that low risk stocks were overweighted in the MSG portfolios.

In addition to the above factors, Gastineau also suggests that the arbitrary six-month holding period is not a rational investment management strategy for options. "Avoiding all changes in investment policy for a fixed time interval might make sense if a portfolio consisted entirely of common stocks. However, few economists, psychologists, or even ordinary investors would consider this a rational investment policy when options are involved." In effect Gastineau suggests that if the market rises, portfolios that initially started with 90 percent cash and 10 percent in options could suddenly find themselves with far higher exposures to stocks as a result of the options having appreciated. Under these conditions, they would be under strong pressure to take some profits and to reduce their overall portfolio risk.

Merton, Scholes, and Gladstein themselves offer the following observation regarding their study:

The relative risk characteristics of the strategies described by the simulations are representative of the strategies. The specific levels of the returns generated, however, are strongly dependent on the actual experience of the underlying stocks during the simulation period. To avoid the creation of new myths about option strategies, the reader is warned not to infer from our findings that any one of these strategies is superior to the others for all investors. Indeed, if options and their underlying stocks are correctly priced, then there is no single best strategy for all investors.

Having duly noted all of the issues raised by critics of the study and disclaimers by the authors themselves, we now suggest that another factor affecting the outcome has to do with coherent markets during the period of the study. In a coherent market, the risk-reward ratio shifts substantially in favor of the bulls, provided that the underlying assets are held for a long enough period. The MSG study has a six-month holding period for each of the 25 portfolios constructed over the 12½ years of the study. The option valuation models would have undervalued calls substantially during coherent bull markets if the probability distribution associated with a coherent bull market had been used as the correct option pricing probability distribution.

Option writers are in effect giving away their stocks and underperforming substantially in a coherent bull market. The persistent bias or underlying trend in a coherent bull market can become the dominant pricing factor over a period as long as six months. If the option writer uses either the log normal distribution or the empirical distribution which averages price changes over all states, then the option value would be dramatically understated and the writer would be severely under compensated in a coherent bull market where risks are relatively low and returns are relatively high.

Over the period of the MSG study, there were 10 coherent bull markets, based on the six-month signals presented in Chap. 7 which covered nearly 40 percent of the period of the study. Returns for the Zweig Unweighted Price Index for these periods were: −1.4 percent, 26.7 percent, 18.0 percent, 23.6 percent, 0.5 percent, 8.4 percent, 17.1 percent, 12.8 percent, 5.3 percent, −0.1 percent. Five of these periods provided double digit returns over six months for a broad-based market average. A leveraged option strategy over such periods would benefit not only from the characteristic volatility of the market but from the correlation of returns over an extended period. A persistent bias though hardly noticeable in daily price changes would compound into a major move over a six-month period.

Hence it appears the long holding periods in the MSG study capture the coherent returns when they occur, substantially increasing the portfolio value. In the remaining periods, options may expire worthless, but with 90 percent of the portfolio in cash at the beginning of every new six-month period, the negative effects of the trendless markets or downward biased markets would be limited. The net performance of the option buying strategy over the period shown appears quite attractive provided the option buyer holds positions and disregards the high volatility associated with the options as they appreciate.

As the authors warn, the results of the MSG study may not reproduce in future periods. We would suggest the performance of the call buying strategy would depend on the prevalence of coherent bull markets relative to bearish or random walk markets. However, by tracking the parameters that control market states, a conservative option purchase strategy (options positions offset by 90 percent cash reserves) timed with indicators of coherent bull markets could be an attractive approach that provides significant appreciation potential with a well defined level of risk.

Summary: Option Strategies for Chaotic Markets

Another situation where fair option values could deviate significantly from the prediction of the baseline Black-Scholes model and the empirical Gastineu-Madansky model is the chaotic market. As in the coherent market state, the short-term behavior of the market in a chaotic state can usually be adequately represented by the log normal distribution. However, in the longer term, there will be a significant drift toward one of two stable states or, in other words, there will be price trends that must be considered over longer holding periods. The main difference between chaotic and coherent markets lies in the probability of a state transition and anomalous short-term volatility.

For example, Zweig's experience prior to the Crash of 1987 illustrates the potential impact of anomalous short-term volatility. While this is an extreme case, similar events can be expected more frequently on a smaller scale. In these situations, option valuation must reflect both the baseline valuation model and an additional consideration of the probability of a state transition within the lifetime of the option.

State transitions were found to depend on the height of the potential barrier separating the two states within our nonlinear market model. This situation does not exist in the linear case where there is only one stable point. However, in a chaotic market, the probability of a state transition depends explicitly on the height of the barrier between the states and the magnitude of the random fluctuations. If fluctuations are small relative to the height of the barrier, the chances of a crossing or state transition are small. The barrier height itself depends on prevailing fundamentals, and if fundamentals change, the chances of a state transition increase accordingly.

Zweig observed that the fundamentals had clearly turned negative prior to the Crash of 1987. They were not extremely negative. However even a small negative bias in a chaotic market is enough to substantially increase the odds of a state transition from a bullish to bearish state. This situation doesn't occur that often. Zweig had only purchased calls twice in the 16 years of publishing his letter. This again reflects that an analysis of the risk-reward outlook within the framework of our nonlinear model can be used to advantage.

While it may be possible to construct detailed quantitative models of option values based on state transition probabilities which are functions of control parameters, our goal here is simply to set forth the concepts that appear to be applicable. Our conclusion is that the Black-Scholes model is a good baseline tool and that "second generation" models such as the Gastineau-Madansky model offer refinements that reflect the "fat-tail" effects that occur in the complex world beyond simple random walks. Beyond that, it pays to recognize the potential for state transitions. A coherent market can provide significant opportunities for those prepared to hold options long enough to take advantage of persistent price trends. The most dramatic hedging opportunities such as demonstrated by Zweig, require both luck and a real belief in market indicators that determine the prevailing risk-reward outlook.

10
Conclusions: A Role for Active Management

Bagging the Tenbaggers

Peter Lynch, manager of one of the most successful mutual funds, expresses a deep faith that there will be a significant number of big winners (or tenbaggers, as he calls them) over the next five to ten years. His view is supported by the work of theoreticians such as Benoit Mandelbrot, who, in the early 1960s, suggested that the markets follow stable Paretian distributions. These distributions may be viewed as a generalization of the normal or Gaussian distribution. They imply the existence of far more large price changes than expected from pure Gaussian noise alone. While this is normally taken to mean short-term price fluctuations, the distribution also ensures more tenbaggers over the long run than expected from a normal distribution.

Physicist Per Bak and his colleagues have shown that the stable Paretian distribution characterizes the behavior of a wide variety of complex systems in critical states. These states occur when the elements of the system, coupled together and acting collectively, produce more large fluctuations than would be expected if the elements behaved independently.

For example, the size of avalanches in a sand pile follows a power law distribution. This is analogous to the frequency of earthquakes of various size on the Richter scale. While large earthquakes may occur far more frequently than would be expected by chance, the power law distribution characteristic does not allow prediction of where or when the next large earthquake will hit. The active manager has the same problem in picking the big winners within a given universe of stocks. In contrast, passive indexing will include all the big winners within a given universe, and hence is a tough benchmark to beat.

The factors that control market return distributions are of particular importance to active managers seeking to beat passive indexing. Our nonlinear market model offers a simple explanation of nonlinear market dynamics and suggests that both technical and fundamental factors control market risk and reward. It suggests that the stocks furthest from static equilibrium offer the best risk-reward relationships when fundamentals are positive.

The Origins of Bull Markets

Practitioners have discovered the conditions leading to the safest, most rewarding markets. Marty Zweig, publisher of *The Zweig Forecast* and manager of a large mutual fund family, has analyzed the performance of numerous technical and fundamental indicators. Based on this work, he has come up with a double-barrel buy signal which has caught all of the largest bull markets in recent market history. The signal is based on both a technical and a fundamental indicator and can be interpreted as evidence of coherent markets, consistent with the prediction of our nonlinear market model.

Is this the ultimate exercise in data mining? Anyone can construct an indicator with the aid of hindsight and show remarkable performance. There certainly isn't enough forward experience with this long-term indicator to be sure. Zweig's double-barrel buy signal occurs when the 10-day advance-decline ratio averages more than 2:1 and the Fed has begun to ease interest rates. These factors can be interpreted as measures of the two key control parameters in our nonlinear model. We can interpret these indicators as evidence that the market is far from equilibrium and that there is a positive fundamental bias.

Systems far from equilibrium have become an area of intense research in recent years. This stems in part from the discovery of the laser and the properties of the transition from ordinary random light to coherent laser light. One of the remarkable features of the laser transition is that it exhibits properties similar to the transitions that occur with systems that are in thermal equilibrium. For example, a bar of iron may exist in either an ordered (magnetic) state or disordered (nonmagnetic) state. The transition from one state to the other depends on a critical transition threshold in the temperature of the material.

Our nonlinear market model includes a critical state at the transition between random walk and crowd behavior. This critical state may not be reached in all financial markets. In the capital markets there must be enough of a flow of money to create a state transition. If there isn't enough investor interest in a market, it will remain at equilibrium in a true random walk state. However, if there is enough money flow, then the risk-reward characteristics may change dramatically, as evidenced by the emergence of powerful, coherent bull markets and volatile chaotic markets.

Coherent bull markets are characterized by an inversion in the risk-reward ratio. Historically, stocks have provided a 10 percent total return with more than a 20 percent standard deviation in returns or risk. However, our nonlinear market model predicts that when crowd behavior prevails and fundamentals are clearly positive, then the market should provide more than a 25 percent annualized rate of return, while risk drops to approximately 10 percent. Intuitively, we would expect markets to be more volatile and risky when they are far from equilibrium and dominated by crowd behavior. Far less obvious is the prediction, that crowd behavior also produces the safest most rewarding investment opportunities.

No Need to Predict Market Path

Doyne Farmer is one of the best known chaos theorists who has been retained by financial firms to develop short-term nonlinear prediction models. While Farmer's work is proprietary, related academic work shows little evidence of low-dimensional chaos in the financial markets. This implies that deterministic model development may be difficult at best. Fortunately prediction need not be limited to deterministic methods.

Deterministic chaos produces uncertainty at an exponential rate. There is a close relationship between deterministic chaos and random processes. Simple deterministic algorithms have been shown to produce time series which by all appearances are random. An analytic methodology exists for diagnostic testing of time series for chaos. If chaos exists, a nonlinear model may predict the future path of the system far more accurately than a linear model for short periods into the future. This could offer important benefits for short-term traders and market makers and a number of researchers besides Doyne Farmer are building nonlinear models and testing their effectiveness for short-term market prediction.

It is still too early to draw far-reaching conclusions on the effectiveness of deterministic forecasting in the capital markets. Some success has been achieved with interest rate forecasting by Dr. Maurice Larrain. However, the quest for nonlinear models need not be limited to deterministic prediction. Our nonlinear market model involves both a low-dimensional chaotic attractor, the double well potential, and the element of chance. Within this framework, short-term market dynamics follow a random walk on a nonlinear dance floor. The double-well attractor creates a biased random walk which may either lead to stable megatrends or unstable manias, panics, and crashes. The shape of the attractor depends on the combination of sentiment and fundamentals. In turn, the probability distribution governing market fluctuations depends on the shape of the deterministic attractor.

Our view is that capital market forecasting needs to be of a stochastic rather than deterministic nature. The most successful traders deal in probabilities even with short-term strategies. They expect to lose a certain number of bets, whether they be hourly, daily, or longer. However, they expect to have more winners than losers, make more money on winners than they lose on bad bets, or both. In contrast, traders who expect to always be right, not admit making mistakes, and stay with losing positions don't last in the business.

Portfolios at the Edge of Chaos

Louis Navellier and Jim Collins, formerly partners, have similar strategies. They screen stocks on the basis of high excess returns with low volatility. These are some of the methods associated with modern portfolio theory (MPT). However, unlike standard MPT, the time frame over which they measure risk and reward is far less than the comparable academic analysis is often performed. In effect, they use excess return as an indicator rather than a long-term invariant characteristic of a stock. Their results show that this can be a highly effective method, at least in strong bull market periods.

Modern portfolio theory doesn't recognize bull and bear markets. The market is always assumed to be governed by a normal distribution function in which returns are merely the appropriate compensation for a given level of risk. In our nonlinear market model, we expect that under the right conditions, there will be transitions from true random walk to biased random walks in which the bias or trend is stable. Hence the market will spend significant amounts of time in trending states (i.e., bull markets or bear markets) as well as quieter periods of true random walk. Our model is stochastic in nature, but accounts for trends, manias, panics, and crashes as well as short-term random fluctuations.

The stochastic approach to chaos theory appears more relevant to the financial markets where there is strong evidence of nonlinearity, but little evidence of deterministic predictability. In our model, short-term price fluctuations nearly always follow a random walk, but when crowd behavior prevails, the long-term drift will tend toward either a positive or negative stable state (i.e., either bull markets or bear markets).

Bull and bear market states are of paramount importance to practitioners. Yet the classical capital asset pricing model recognizes only a single average rate of return for the market over the long run. The linear capital market line which relates risk with reward is presumed to be the most likely outcome in a normally distributed random process. However, actual data shows capital market lines that tend to cluster well above or well below the long-term average.

While the amount of data relating risk and reward in the financial markets is limited and not enough to draw definitive conclusions, an alternative interpretation of the capital market line is possible. In chaotic markets, when a bimodal distribution is predicted for market stabilities, the risk-reward relationship can be represented by two capital market lines. One corresponds to risk-reward characteristics associated with bull markets; the other, with a negative slope, corresponds to risk and reward in bear markets.

Advisors, such as Louis Navellier in *MPT Review* and James Collins in *OTC Insight*, appear to be perched at the edge of chaos. Their portfolios are comprised of issues that are on the positive bull market line of our chaotic market asset pricing model. The stocks in these portfolios all have enjoyed above average returns for a given level of risk.

Our nonlinear model suggests that the success of this approach depends on the persistence of the bullish state. This depends exponentially on the height of the potential barrier separating the bullish and bearish market states. As long as fundamentals are strong, picking stocks on the basis of high excess returns with low volatility is consistent with the characteristics of coherent bull markets. However, during periods of weak fundamentals, trend persistence is apt to be far shorter and the relative strength strategy may produce far more transactions with fewer big winners.

In periods of true random walk, a single capital market line is the most appropriate model of the risk-reward relationship. However, if random walks are normally associated with periods in which there isn't a strong flow of money in the markets, then these periods may accompany weak markets in which the capital market line has a flat or even negative slope.

Megatrend or Mania: Fundamentally Different

John Naisbitt expresses a very positive attitude in his best-selling books, *Megatrends*, and *Megatrends 2000*. He views the expanding global economy as one of the most important megatrends. This has important implications for investors. However, in the financial markets we are often concerned about manias as well as stable long-term trends.

There have been numerous examples throughout recent financial history of financial assets having been bid up to price levels that seem absurd. Land, tulip bulbs, gold, as well as stocks and other financial instruments have from time to time been the subject of intense speculation. Within the framework of our nonlinear model, these situations represent the markets locked in stable states of growth as a result of the coupling of opinions and attitudes among market participants.

As long as the fundamentals are sound, such states far from equilibrium represent stable, profitable, coherent bull markets. Manias occur if fundamentals change but the market sentiment remains in the original state. The mania may last for an extended period. Our nonlinear model suggests that trends in a bimodal potential well depend exponentially on the height of the barrier in the well. Fundamentals determine this height when market conditions are conducive to crowd behavior. However, even though the height of the barrier may change, affecting the odds of a state transition, the market's reaction need not be immediate.

For example, the Crash of 1987 was preceded by a period of crowd behavior and positive sentiment, with market averages typically up more than 25 percent in the first half of the year. At the same time, interest rates had started to rise, a negative fundamental development. The market remained in a positive trend even after the Fed hiked the discount rate in September of 1987. However, this action changed the odds of a state transition, and even though the fundamentals were not strongly negative, the risk of a state transition (i.e., bullish sentiment switching abruptly to the mirror image) had increased dramatically.

While manias, panics, and crashes are a key risk associated with crowd behavior, stable, long-term megatrends are far more important. If Naisbitt is correct about a booming global economy, stocks will remain a good investment over the long run. However, periods of short-term overvaluation could be corrected by bear markets in the future that follow a financial Richter scale in terms of intensity and duration.

Both Warren Buffet and Charles Allmon look for the values that emerge when the market turns negative and stocks with solid fundamentals are sold off to excess. These situations may not emerge that often. On the other hand as Buffet's results suggest, you don't need that many of them to do well over the long run.

Befriending the Trend

Dick Fabian has done well with the simplest possible active strategy. It involves no prediction. It involves no fundamental analysis. Rather it's based on a simple trend following strategy based on moving averages.

Simple technical trading rules offer one approach to improving returns and cutting risk. The significance of moving average penetration has been confirmed by means of new statistical testing methods based on the use of technical trading rules as discriminating statistics and use of surrogate data to establish the statistical significance of the results. This vindicates the methods of many practitioners who use these technical indicators.

However, more sophisticated timing systems make use of fundamental as well as technical indicators. For example, *The Zweig Forecast* tracks both technical and fundamental indicators to assess the prevailing risk-reward outlook. Zweig weights his portfolio according to the overall level of market risk.

The Elliott wave principle maintains that market trends come in sets of three. Actually there are eight waves in a complete cycle, three big upside waves, followed by two downside waves in the corrective phase. The three upside waves are interrupted by two downside corrections and the two downside waves are interrupted by an upside bear market rally. The wave principle further maintains that the waves on any particular time scale can be further decomposed into a self-similar set on a shorter time scale. Hence the analysis seeks to catalogue waves and infer what the most probable future scenario might be.

If nothing else, the Elliott wave principle illustrates what a biased random walk looks like typically as a financial time series. The different waves within the Elliott wave context may also be related to the different market states predicted by our nonlinear model. Currently, one of the leading practitioners of the Elliott wave principle, Robert Prechter Jr., sees a very bearish long-term outlook, with long-term waves apparently all building to major peaks which he expects to be followed by major bear markets. Prechter sees the market as reflecting social conditions and unlike the positive view of booming global economy presented by Naisbitt, Prechter's views are just the opposite, more in line with Fitzpatrick's assessment of a secular contraction and depression in economic activity.

Our own view is that the global economy will continue to grow far into the future. However, it will be subject to the same nonlinear forces and market cycles that individual economies have been subject to. There will be periods of expansion and contraction with a net positive bias. Global bear markets will follow a power law distribution in which we can expect to see many short, minor periods of contraction and occasional big, large lasting economic setbacks—the economic equivalent of a magnitude 7 or 8 earthquake on the financial Richter scale.

The purpose of market timing is not to say that we can predict when the next bear market will hit, how large it will be or how long it will last. Rather, market timing is simply the recognition that there will be more big downside moves in the economy and capital markets than would be expected from a purely Gaussian noise process. It is an attempt to manage the risk associated with such periods. Our nonlinear model suggests that the size and duration of bear markets will also depend on the fundamental bias in an exponential fashion. Raising cash reserves or switching to less risky stocks are a prudent approach to risk management when the market is far from equilibrium as a result of negative fundamentals.

Earnings and Stock Selection

Many active managers view their job as simply stock selection rather than market timing. The strategy of being fully invested works well in bull markets, especially long-term bull markets. In this situation, the key is to pick stocks that offer the best return for a given level of risk.

Our nonlinear market model suggests that stock selection should be based on both fundamental as well as technical factors. Successful investors do just that. Relative strength is a frequently used technical factor. Earnings momentum or surprise is used as a fundamental benchmark. These factors suggest that a stock is far from equilibrium. For example, the Value Line ranking system appears to be most effective in reclassifying stocks after earnings announcements. This is known as *post-earnings drift*. Value Line stock performance also tend to correlate well with the inverse of safety ranks.

Stocks that are deemed most risky on the basis of fundamental factors as well as the size of market fluctuations tend to provide higher returns. It may also be safe to assume that the markets for smaller companies tend to on average be further from equilibrium. Hence, the Value Line safety ranks may also be a measure of how close a stock is to the critical transition threshold.

Richard Bernstein has shown that stocks outside the earnings estimate frontier tend to do better than average. These are issues for which analysts predict well above average earnings and for which there is a high degree of consensus among the analysts. Coherent earnings expectations are the hallmark of growth stocks. Valuations may be unusually high for growth stocks at times because of excessive belief in the inevitability of earnings growth. If these expectations are not met, an earnings torpedo (i.e., unexpectedly weak earnings report) can sink the growth stock in dramatic fashion.

Stocks perched on the bull market line have the furthest to fall in our two-state chaotic capital asset pricing model. While the bull market line is stable, it will be subject to the same exponential distribution of state transition times in which the mean transition time is determined by fundamentals. If the stock appreciates to excessive valuation levels relative to earnings growth, it will become susceptible to a bullish to bearish state transition even if earnings are strong but slightly less than consensus expectations.

One way to identify potential pending earnings torpedoes is to look at the quality of earnings. Significant accounting method changes, accelerated shipments to customers to increase present earnings at the expense of the future, and reductions in future investment by cuts in research, or advertising are all potential bad signs. Hence a look behind the numbers is important for active managers.

Options: Insurance or Smart Investing?

Options can be an effective insurance policy when implemented in special situations as done so effectively by Zweig prior to the Crash of 1987. They may also be the basis for a more aggressive strategy to invest with well-defined downside risk. The latter underlies the simulated portfolios in the study by Merton, Scholes, and Gladstein in which they found that option buyers who keep 90 percent of their portfolios in cash and invest 10 percent in call options tend to outperform option writers and straight stock portfolios.

These controversial results suggest that the market is not efficient, or, at least, that option pricing is not efficient for long-term options. The simulated option purchase portfolios had capital market lines well above the comparable lines for the stock portfolios. In effect, the option buyers are doing better than the writers. Classical option valuation models do not consider the effects of drifts or trends in the underlying security price. In coherent bull markets, this can be a dominating factor over six months, the period for which option portfolios were held. Hence in coherent bull markets, the options can generate large returns over short periods. The rest of the time, options may lose, but the overall portfolio losses are small since only 10 percent is at risk over any six-month period.

Risk-Reward Principle at Risk

The risk-reward principle maintains that above average returns are only possible with above average risk. This is not the case with successful practitioners and our nonlinear model offers an explanation. Risk is more complicated than expected from the simple normal distribution. This fact was brought out by Mandelbrot who offered an alternative distribution.

Our nonlinear model further identifies the risk-reward characteristics of major market states and the parameters that control state transitions. Within the framework of this model, the critical state at which the stable Paretian distribution occurs is only one possibility. However, this state may also be viewed as a long-term average for market fluctuations. The coherent state helps explain the success of practitioners who rely on a relative strength approach. The chaotic state helps explain the source of bearish manias that produce the golden buying opportunities that investors such as Warren Buffet are adept at spotting.

Our own experience has been best with passive indexing. Indexing is sometimes viewed as settling for mediocrity. We see it as an elegant method for capturing all the big winners within a given universe of stocks. One of the pioneers of indexing is the Vanguard Group. They offer a selection of index funds including small cap issues, and international index funds as well as the traditional S&P 500 index. Any index fund will include all the stocks furthest from equilibrium within a given domain and, therefore, is a tough benchmark for the active manager to beat. However, it isn't impossible to beat the market and those who have done so appear to have more behind their success than blind luck.

There is a role for active managers. When fundamentals are positive, active managers must seek out the stocks furthest from equilibrium. These may include stocks in stable bullish states perched uncomfortably on the edge of chaos as Navellier and Collins recommend. They may also include stocks with fundamentally sound businesses that have lapsed into temporary bearish market manias. This contrarian approach has been used effectively by savy investors such as Warren Buffet, Peter Lynch, and Charles Allmon who look for stocks being sold at bargain prices by investors who focus on short-term negatives while ignoring long-term potential. In either event, a portfolio of stocks closest to equilibrium and fair pricing is least likely to beat the market while those issues with solid fundamentals, but far from equilibrium are apt to provide the best returns.

Mathematics of Polarization of Opinion in Social Groups

W. V. Smith of IBM's Watson Research Laboratory noted that "The phase transitions and cooperative phenomena observed in solid state science are analogous to phenomena observed in the management of scientific research and in other organized human activities." For example, in the 1950s the computer industry had an intense interest in ferromagnetic phenomena, motivated by the usefulness of such materials as memory elements for computers. Recording a binary 1 or 0 in early computers was achieved by switching the polarization of a magnetic material between two stable states.

The magnetic material at the core of the early computer's memory exhibits an interesting and useful macroscopic property. The behavior of a ferromagnet is a carefully studied problem in statistical physics, both from a microscopic viewpoint and a macroscopic level. At the microscopic level, the interactions of individual molecules among themselves and with their external environment determine whether or not there will be useful state transitions that can be effectively harnessed to store information. Given these state transitions in a particular material, the microscopic details of the effect become unimportant with respect to the macroscopic processes of information storage and retrieval.

In effect, there are independent domains of activity within a magnetic material. On a microscopic level, there is a degree of coupling among individual molecules, each acting as a tiny magnet and interacting with neighboring magnets, external magnetic forces and at the same time being bombarded by random thermal forces. However, on a macroscopic level, all of this busy behavior reduces to an underworld of activity that averages out to simply a one or a zero in the computer's memory. Are the molecules lined up one way or the opposite way?

Of course, every so often the underworld of random fluctuations raises its ugly head and causes an unexpected spontaneous flip in the magnetic field from one orientation to the opposite. This, in turn, causes a bit error in memory which could have anywhere from a minor nuisance effect to a catastrophic effect on the operation of the system. It could show up as an unexpected error in a bill, or it could cause the entire system to malfunction and stop operating unless error detection and correction methods are used to eradicate the problem at the expense of additional bits of information needed to perform such functions.

Researchers at facilities such as the IBM Watson Laboratories include some of the world's leading solid state scientists. Their mission is to investigate the ultimate limitations of the computation and information storage processes. These scientists include Rolf Landauer who in 1962 was the first to describe the fluctuations in bistable computer circuits in terms of state transitions. So it is not surprising that these pioneers of information theory also noticed the similarities between complex physical and chemical processes and the behavior or social groups, particularly in a research environment. However, they were not alone.

A detailed statistical model of polarization phenomena in society was developed in 1971 by Wolfgang Weidlich, a physicist at the University of Stuttgart in Germany. Weidlich started with the Ising model of the ferromagnetic phase transition and reinterpreted the basic parameters to describe the polarization of opinions and other cooperative behavior of individuals in social groups.

In a magnet, the macroscopic order parameter may be defined as the number of molecules pointing one way minus those pointing the opposite way. If nearly equal numbers are pointing in each direction, then the order parameter is a small number (0 if exactly the same number point in each direction). Likewise in a social group, a political opinion poll may be defined as the order parameter. If equal numbers are for and against a candidate, there isn't much order or net preference one way or the other.

Under the right conditions the molecules in a bar of iron may be highly polarized (nearly all pointing the same way) leading to a high degree of order. Similarly in a social group, one candidate may win by a landslide over another if voters become highly polarized over a particular political issue.

The Ising model was also used to describe social behavior by American physicists, Don Callen and Earl Shapero in their "Theory of Social Imitation" which suggested that a wide array of biological and social groups showed characteristic transitions between disordered, structureless states and more ordered or structured states. Among their numerous examples were fish aligned in schools, birds flying in flocks, and people conforming to the dictates of fads and fashions.

Examples of Social Imitation

Callen and Shapero described a number of fascinating examples of ordered, collective, social behavior including fireflies flashing in unison, the rhythms of human heart cells, and physics professors driving Volkswagen beetles while the rest of society preferred larger more expensive cars. The following quotes are from their *Physics Today* article:

> In the Spring, one sees thousands upon thousands of young minnows in the creeks off the Chesapeake Bay along the Maryland shore, all swimming in the same direction. Sometimes the whole school suddenly rotates to a new direction, faster than the eye can follow. Is there a leader? How does the wave propagate? Are there critical fluctuations in the spin reorientation? Sometimes one sees a closed ring of fish slowly rotating. We have seen figure eights maintain themselves.
>
> Ducks in a field, suddenly flushed, rise up a few feet, flap about, and then fly off all in the same direction. A cloud of flying midges hovers in the still air, stationary. In the next instant they are three feet away, off to one side. The whole tenuous cloud has moved together. How have they done it? Is there a leader among the midges? Can thousands follow one midge, as they dart among each other in the cloud? Or are they somehow acting collectively?
>
> What makes the heart beat and give it its rhythm? How is the frequency and phase maintained throughout the whole heart muscle? The beginning of an answer is found in the behavior of individual isolated mammalian heart cells in vitro. They beat. When first separated from one another, leader cells—about one percent of the total—beat, each at its own frequency. As the cells settle to the bottom they send out filaments to each other, and the more cells that come in contact, the more that beat. When all cells are interconnected, they all beat, but no longer at different frequencies. They beat at a single frequency and phase; a nascent heart.
>
> People imitate. In the preface to his *Memoirs of Extraordinary Popular Delusions and the Madness of Crowds*, Charles Mackay wrote: "Men, it has well been said, think in herds; it will be seen that they go mad in herds, while they recover their senses slowly, and one by one."

The theory of polarization in magnetic materials can also be used to describe the behavior of a group of n individuals, where N^+ have one opinion on an issue and N^- have the opposite opinion. The other variables include: k, the degree of coupling of opinions among people within a group; h, an external preference or bias causing a preference for one opinion over the other; and q, the order parameter which is a measure of the net polarization of opinion in the group [i.e., $q = (N^+ - N^-/2n)$]; and w, the rate at which individuals on average may change their mind and switch from one opinion to the opposite.

There are fundamental differences between molecules in a bar of iron and people in a social group. For example, in a magnet, conservation of energy is a constraint which doesn't exist for opinions in a social group. While the analogy between social groups and physical systems can't be taken too literally, the model illustrates the concept of state transitions in social groups. When the variable, k, exceeds a critical threshold, the theory predicts that there will be a transition from a state of net macroscopic disorder (q fluctuating around zero) to a state of order (q fluctuating around either of two large values or stable points far from zero).

In a magnet, the ordered state is defined by the orientation of molecules. Most molecules point in a preferred direction and generate a large magnetic force field that tends to keep them aligned that way long after the original aligning force is gone. In a social group the ordered state reflects agreement on a particular issue. Furthermore, a political opinion within a social group may tend to persist for a long time when the individuals within the group become strongly polarized for or against a particular political view.

In a magnet, there is a critical temperature at which transitions from disorder to order will occur. Temperature reflects the intensity of random thermal forces which tend to break down any alignment or order within the magnetic material. When the temperature falls below a critical threshold, the material becomes susceptible to magnetization. Likewise, in a social group the analogy with the Ising Model suggests that there will be a critical "social temperature" or flash point for crowd behavior. When a group becomes susceptible to crowd behavior, as with a magnet, even slight external biasing forces can have a large, long-lasting impact on the polarization of opinions within the group. Group think may or may not be rational; but once established, you can count on it to persist.

As Callen and Shapero suggest: "Fish aligned in schools, fireflies flashing in unison, and even humans following the dictates of fashion are examples of ordered systems to which we can apply ferromagnet theory." Figure A.1 illustrates a bar of iron or other magnetic material. It is made up of an enormous number of individual molecules, each of which can be thought of as a miniature magnet. Each molecule has a "spin" which points either up or down. Assuming that there are a total

MAGNETIC MATERIAL

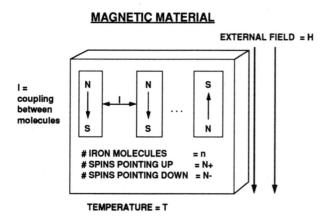

Figure A.1. Molecules in a magnetic material interact with their neighbors and external field.

of n molecules in the bar, then N^+ of these have spins pointing up while N^- have spins pointing down.

In order to understand the magnet, it is also necessary to introduce the parameters: I, a measure of the coupling of magnetic forces between individual neighboring molecules; H, an external magnetic field which also influences the direction in which individual molecules point; and T, the temperature of the material which is a measure of the amount of random thermal noise that buffets individual molecules and may cause them to flip their orientation from pointing up to pointing down or vice versa.

The mathematical expression for the probability of finding N^+ molecules pointing up and N^- pointing down at any given time, t is as follows:

$$f(N^+, N^-, t) = \text{probability of } N^+ \text{ spins up and} \atop N^- \text{ spins down at time, } t. \tag{A.1}$$

To evaluate this probability function, it is necessary to first evaluate the transition probabilities:

$$P^{-+}(N^+, N^-) = \text{probability of transition} \atop \text{from } N^+, N^- \text{ to } N^+ + 1, N^- - 1 \tag{A.2}$$

and

$$P^{+-}(N^+, N^-) = \text{probability of transition} \atop \text{from } N^+, N^- \text{ to } N^+ - 1, N^- + 1) \tag{A.3}$$

These transition probabilities define the likelihood of a single molecule flipping its orientation from a spin pointing down to spin pointing up and vice versa.

Master Equation: Derivation of the Fokker-Planck Equation

One of the most basic principles of physics is the continuity equation. This basically expresses the idea that the rate of change in any population is equal to gains minus losses in the population. In mathematical terms for the magnet which has a population of N^+ molecules with spins pointing up and N^- molecules with spins pointing down.

Gains into the state (N^+, N^-) may come from neighboring states. A state with one more molecule pointing up and one less pointing down has a certain probability for a spin to flip from up to down and, therefore, go into the state (N^+, N^-). Likewise a state with one less molecule pointing up and one more pointing down has a probability of a molecule flipping from down to up and going into the state (N^+, N^-). However, the state (N^+, N^-) is also depleted at the rate at which spins flip from down to up and go into the $(N^+ + 1, N^- - 1)$ state and vice versa.

The continuity equation is like balancing a check book. Money is deposited at one rate and paid out at a second rate. If the latter is greater than the former, the account will be depleted in time. If more money flows in than out, a nice reservoir of cash will be accumulated in time.

When the discrete variables shown below are replaced by continuous variables, the continuity equation may be expressed as follows:

$$\partial/\partial t\, f(q, t) = \text{gains} - \text{losses}$$
$$= \{w^{+-}(q) + w^{-+}(q)\}f(q, t) + w^{+-}(q + \Delta q) \qquad (A.4)$$
$$f(q + \Delta q, t) - w^{-+}(q - \Delta q)f(q - \Delta q, t)$$

where $q = (N^+ - N^-)/2n$, $\Delta q = 1/n$, $w^{+-} = N^+ p^{+-} = n(1/2 + q)p^{+-}(q)$, and $w^{-+} = N^- p^{-+} = n(1/2 - q)p^{-+}(q)$.

A Taylor expansion of this finite difference equation then leads immediately to the Fokker-Planck equation governing the probability distribution for finding the system in any particular state, q, as follows:

$$\partial/\partial t\, f(q, t) = -\partial/\partial q\{K(q)f(q, t) + 1/2\, \partial^2/\partial q^2\{Q(q)f(q, t)\} \qquad (A.5)$$

where $K(q) = \Delta q\{w^{-+}(q) - w^{+-}(q)\}$ and $Q(q) = \Delta q2\{w^{+-}(q) + w^{-+}(q)\}$.

Transition Probabilities

The Fokker-Planck equation can be solved in closed form for a special stationary case (i.e., when $\partial/\partial t = 0$. In this situation, a solution can be found as follows:

$$f(q) = c^1 Q^{-1}(q) \exp\left\{ 2 \int_{-\frac{1}{2}}^{q} [K(y)/Q(y)]dy \right\} \tag{A.6}$$

where

$$c^{-1} = \int_{-\frac{1}{2}}^{+\frac{1}{2}} Q^{-1}(q) \exp\left\{ 2 \int [K(y)/Q(y)]\, dy \right\} dq \tag{A.7}$$

This is the general solution. So far no assumptions have been made about spin flipping probabilities.

In a bar of iron, there is coupling between the spins of adjacent molecules. If for any reason more molecules are pointing one way than the other, this will tend to influence neighboring molecules to also point in the same direction. Any external magnetic field would provide a bias favoring alignment in one direction rather than the opposite. Furthermore, the random thermal forces characterized by the temperature of the material tends to decrease the coupling among molecules and with external fields. All of these competing factors influence the transition probabilities of molecular spins in a bar of iron, and are *quantitatively* expressed as:

$$w\pm(q) = r \exp[-(Iq + H)/k_b T] \\ = r \exp[-(kq + h)] \tag{A.8}$$

and

$$w\pm(q) = r \exp[+(Iq + H)/k_b T] \\ = r \exp[+(kq + h)] \tag{A.9}$$

where r is a rate of molecular spin flips; I is the magnetic coupling between molecules; H is the external magnetic field; k_b is Boltzmann's constant; T is the temperature; $k = I/k_b T$; and $h = H/k_b T$.

With these assumptions, the *drift coefficient, K(q)*, and the *diffusion coefficient, Q(q)* become

$$K(q) = r \{\sin h(kq + h) - 2q \cosh(kq + h)\} \tag{A.10}$$

and

$$Q(q) = (r/n) \{\cos h(kq + h) - 2q \sinh(kq + h)\} \tag{A.11}$$

This is the Ising Model of ferromagnetism which can also be reinterpreted as a model of polarization in social groups and which we have adopted as our nonlinear market model, and presented previously in Chap. 1.

Stability of Continuous Markov Processes

In Chap. 3, we examined the conditions under which a deterministic process would be stable or become unstable. The same issue is applicable to random processes. In this case the characterizing functions $K(q,t)$, $Q(q,t)$ determine whether or not the process will be stable.

It is convenient to define a *potential function* by

$$\varphi(q) = -\int_2^q K(y)/Q(y)\, dy \qquad (A.12)$$

where the characteristic functions $K(q)$ and $Q(q)$ do not explicitly depend on time. A stationary Markov state density function, $f_s(q)$ can then be expressed as

$$f_s(q) = [2c/Q(q)]\exp[-\emptyset(q)] \qquad (A.13)$$

The potential function is analogous to the potential energy function of classical mechanics. The potential function slopes upward or downward at a point, q, depending on whether $K(q)$ is positive or negative. If a process is in state, q, at time, t, it will be more likely to move to the right if $K(q) > 0$ and $\emptyset$ is sloping downward or to the left if $K(q) < 0$ and $\emptyset$ is sloping upward. The steeper the slope, the greater the probability bias. Hence a continuous Markov process has a tendency to move toward the nearest local minimum of the potential function. Therefore, these are the stable states or the most probable regions in which the Markov process will be found.

The stable states are separated by a *barrier function*

$$B(q) = C^{-1}\exp[\emptyset(q)] \qquad (A.14)$$

The barrier function is of particular importance in computing the average time required for a state transition to occur between the stable states.

The problem of transition times between stable states is known as the *first exit time problem*. The mean stable state transition times for a bistable process are given by Gillespie (1992) as

$$T(q_1 \to q_2) = \int_{q_1}^{q_2} dq B(q) \int_{-\infty}^{q} dy f_s(y) \qquad (A.15)$$

and

$$T(q_2 \to q_1) = \int_{q_1}^{q_2} dq B(q) \int_{q}^{-\infty} dy f_s(y) \qquad (A.16)$$

This can be approximated as

$$T(q_i \to q_f) \approx [\int_{q_b} dqB(q)][\int_{q_i} dqf_s(q)] \qquad \text{(A.17)}$$

Hence the average time for a spontaneous transition is approximately equal to the product of the area under the barrier $B(q)$ and the area under the initial stable state probability distribution.

If the slope of the distribution, $f(q)$ near a peak is approximately Gaussian, and the diffusion coefficient is a constant, Q, the mean transition time from stable state, q_i, to stable state, q_f, is approximately

$$T(q_i \to q_f) \approx 2\pi |1/[K'(q_i)K'(q_b)]|^{\frac{1}{2}} \exp[2/Q | \int_{q_i}^{q_b} K(q)\, dq |]$$

$$\text{(A.18)}$$

Note that the size of fluctuations is of particular importance in transition times. If Q approaches zero, the average transition time approaches infinity at an exponential rate.

The standard deviation of first exit time estimates is typically as large as the norm. Hence the uncertainty of the approximation is small relative to the uncertainty of the process itself.

Figure A.2 illustrates the duration of buy and sell signals for a 4-percent trading rule anlayzed by Martin Zweig (1991). A buy is triggered if the market index rises by 4 percent or more from a recent low; a sell is triggered when the market falls by 4 percent or more from a recent high. Zweig tabulated the magnitude and duration of each of these signals over a period from 1966 to 1988. The average duration of buy signals was 97 days with a standard deviation of 85 days; sell signals lasted an average of 67 days with a standard deviation of 45 days. Buy signal results are more or less consistent

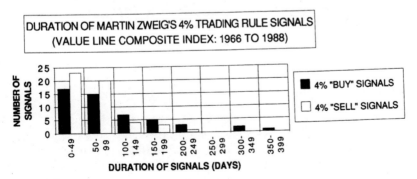

Figure A.2.

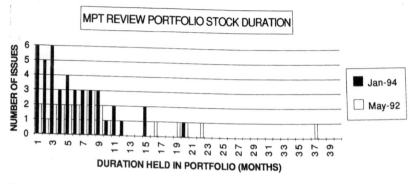

Figure A.3.

with an exponential distribution in which the standard deviation is equal to the mean of the distribution.

Figure A.3 summarizes the duration of stocks in the *MPT Review* model portfolio. The largest of the model portfolios was used in order to obtain the most data. The results for the May 1992 portfolio show an average holding period of 9 months with an 8-month standard deviation. This period covered a strong bull market. Results for January 1994 show a significantly reduced holding period of about 6 months with a 4-month standard deviation. This reduction in the duration of portfolio holdings suggests a change in climate from the strong positive coherent bull market (signaled by Zweig's indicator in February 1991) to a true random walk market in which "trends" would tend to disappear.

The bistable or chaotic market state, including coherent markets, are expected theoretically to exhibit an exponential duration of trends. The height of the potential barrier is a key factor determining the duration of trends. In effect, the greater the degree of polarization, the longer trends would persist. However, the market may also be at the edge of chaos where the barrier between states disappears. This is the region where power law distributions govern the size and duration of market fluctuations.

Fat-Tailed Distributions

Benoit Mandelbrot, one of the legendary figures of mathematics, coined the term fractals, which is frequently used to describe nonlinear systems. Less well known is Mandelbrot's work related to the behavior of prices in speculative markets. In 1963, he observed that Louis Bachelier's random walk model of security and commodity market fluctuations was an important "path-breaking contribution." However he felt it did not account for the empirical evidence which showed that price distributions were too sharply peaked, with too many outliers to be part of a normal distribution process. Mandelbrot proposed a radical new approach based on *stable Paretian distribution functions.*

In physics, there is an important principle that is used to test new ideas and models. It is known as the correspondence principle. If a new theory does not correspond to established baseline theory where the latter has proven effective, then the new theory is suspect. For example, Einstein's theory of special relativity shocked the world with fantastic predictions when the relative velocity between objects approaches the speed of light. However, the beauty of Einstein's theory lies in its correspondence with classical Newtonian physics as a special limiting situation (i.e., at speeds far less than the speed of light). Likewise quantum mechanics introduces radically new ideas on the atomic scale, but corresponds to Newtonian mechanics at large spatial dimensions.

Stable Paretian probability laws also introduce radically different concepts into our understanding of market behavior. These distributions have infinite or undefined variance, something that has made the concept hard to accept within the financial community. These distributions are not commonly used since they are not as well behaved as the normal or Gaussian distributions. The stable Paretian distribution typically has a tighter main lobe and fatter tails or outliers than a Gaussian distribution. Its shape is determined by a number of parameters, including an index of *peakedness*, a, that varies from 0 (excluded) to 2 (included), and an *index of skewness*, b, which varies between −1 and +1.

The normal or Gaussian distribution corresponds to the special case where $a = 2$. The Cauchy distribution corresponds to $(a = 1; b = 0)$. These distributions are special cases of the stable Paretian. In effect, Mandelbrot's proposal amounts to a generalization of Bachelier's random walk model. Hence Mandelbrot's proposal satisfies the correspondence principle of physics; the Gaussian is a limiting case of the stable Paretian.

The most important feature of the random walk model is the scaling of the standard deviation over time. If the price changes are taken over a single day the standard deviation is $s(1)$. However if the differencing interval is T days, then the standard deviation will be $s(t) = T^{1/2}s(1)$. The corresponding prediction of Mandelbrot's model is more difficult to formulate since the standard deviation is undefined. However, an alternative approach can be based on the expected range defined as

$$E[U + (T) - U^- (T)] = T^{1/a}E [U^+ (1) - U - (1)] \qquad (A.19)$$

where U^+ is the quantity which is exceeded by one sixth of the data and U^- is the quantity which is larger than one sixth of the data. If $a = 2$, corresponding to the Gaussian distribution, the scaling is as expected for the random walk. However, the other extreme, when $a = 1$, the Cauchy distribution involves a scaling proportional to T.

The Gaussian or normal distribution and the Cauchy distribution are both special cases of the stable Paretian distribution. Both of these cases can be defined in terms of closed form mathematical expressions. Except for these special situations, there are no closed form mathematical expressions for the stable Paretian for other parameter values. However, numerical analysis by computer, performed by Mandelbrot, is shown in Fig. A.4.

As seen in the doubly logarithmic graph, in the Gaussian case the probability of large events drops very quickly to extremely small values. However, if the parameter a deviates even slightly from $a = 2$, there is a substantial shift in the slope of the probability density function. Large values of "outliers" become much more likely. As a is varied further from the Gausssian limit the density function takes on a near-linear asymptotic behavior on the log, log graph. Large values become far more probable, by many orders of magnitude. than they are for the normal distribution.

Imagine that the x axis in Fig. A.4 represents the return from a stock over a given period of time (perhaps the five to ten years that Peter Lynch suggests as a reasonable time frame for expecting a significant number of tenbaggers). Assume the logarithmic scale shown is related to the size of the move a single stock, where the origin represents no change in price and each increment represents the logarithm of the price appreciation. If the Gaussian distribution law governs returns, then the chances of getting even a five-fold return are very small. Out of a 1000 stock universe, you might only find a few. Chances of finding even a single tenbagger are virtually nil.

In contrast, if $a < 2$ the chances of finding big winners goes up dramatically. If $a = 1.95$ you would expect to find seven or eight big winners in a pool of 1000 stocks. If $a = 1.5$ you might expect to see 40 or 50 tenbaggers in a portfolio of 1000 stocks. Practitioners such as Peter Lynch expect to see a healthy number of big winners over a five- to ten-year period. They do not express this view mathematically in terms of graphs, but their instincts amount to an endorsement in a qualitative sense that markets tend to follow Pareto-Levy distributions and aren't just a simple Gaussian noise or random walk process.

Mandelbrot offers no explanation of why markets follow the power law distributions of Pareto-Levy. However he did show that empirical cotton price data tended to follow a stable Paretian distribution roughly equivalent to the case governed by $a = 1.7$, $b = 0$. As seen in Fig. A.4, this situation is far from a normal distribution, with far more large price changes than expected purely from a random process. Mandelbrot also observed that "a closer examination suggests that the positive tails contain systematically fewer data than the negative tails," suggesting that b actually takes a small negative value.

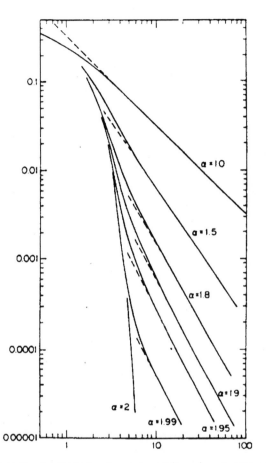

Figure A.4. The stable Paretian distribution characterizes nonlinear dynamic systems that evolve to the crtical state between linear and nonlinear domains. In the financial markets this occurs in markets far from equilibrium and implies that large returns are more likely than predicted by the normal distribution over the same time interval. (*Source: B. Mandelbrot, "The Variation of Certain Speculative Prices,"* Journal of Business, *October 1963. Reprinted with permission.* © *1963 University of Chicago Press. All rights reserved.*)

Mandelbrot points out a variety of problems that exist with analysis of stable Paretian processes. These are the result of infinite second moments. For example the method of least squares forecasting fails when the squares of sample deviations are infinite. Likewise spectral analysis techniques are of questionable value. *Second-order random processes* such as the evaluation of covariances all encounter the problem of infinite variances. Likewise the concept of a trend or drift in the data becomes more difficult to define since much of the price change over a long period of time may be the result of a few periods of very large movement.

While stable Paretian distributions can make life miserable for the Wall Street "quant," it supports the gut feelings of practitioners such as Peter Lynch. Where the random walk model suggests that big market movers should be few and far between, Mandelbrot's more general statistical model suggests that they may be tens or hundreds of times more likely than would be expected from just random "noise" processes.

The good news of the stable Paretian is that there will be more big winners for sure than would be expected from a Gaussian noise type of market. The bad news is that it is still a random distribution and picking the winners isn't made any easier by knowledge of the distribution. For example, in a similar physical problem, the distribution of the frequency of large and small earthquakes follows a similar type of law. However, knowing that doesn't make it any easier to predict where the next earthquake will occur or how large it will be.

While Mandelbrot offered no mechanism that would generate a stable Paretian distribution, more recently, physicist Per Bak and his associates have proposed nonlinear models that lead to stable Paretian distributions. Under the banner of self-organized critical systems, Bak has proposed that a wide variety of systems in the physical sciences, and elsewhere appear to evolve to critical states where they follow power law distributions. The fluctuations found in financial markets are just one example of where this occurs.

Our nonlinear market model also exhibits the unstable transition state at which the stable Paretian type of distribution occurs. Furthermore our model identifies explicitly the control parameters which govern the state transitions and associated probability distributions for each state. Hence our model generalizes Mandelbrot's approach further. The critical state with stable Paretian characteristics and fat-tailed distributions is only one particular market state. Other states are possible with risk-reward characteristics that are equally important to the active manager.

Bibliography

Chapter 1

Brock, W., Lakonishok, J., and LeBaron, B.,"Simple Technical Trading Rules and the Stochastic Properties of Stock Returns," *The Journal of Finance*, Vol. XLVII, No. 5, December 1992.

Brock, W., Hsieh, D. A., and LeBaron, B. D., *Nonlinear Dynamics, Chaos, and Instability: Statistical Theory and Economic Evidence*, The MIT Press, Cambridge, Massachussetts 1991.

Callen, E., and Shapero, D., "A Theory of Social Imitation," *Physics Today*, July 1974.

Larrain, M., "Empirical Tests of Chaotic Behavior in a Nonlinear Interest Rate Model," *The Financial Analysts Journal*, Sep/Oct 1991.

Laing, J., "Efficient Chaos Or, Things They Never Taught in Business School," *Barron's*, July 29, 1991, p.12.

Lewin, R., *Complexity, Life at the Edge of Chaos*, Macmillan, New York 1992.

Lynch, P., *One Up on Wall Street*, Simon and Schuster, New York 1989.

Naisbitt, J., *Megatrends*, Warner Books, New York 1982.

Naisbitt, J., and Aburdene, P., *Megatrends 2000*, Avon Books, New York 1990.

Peters, E., *Chaos and Order in the Capital Markets*, John Wiley & Sons, New York, 1991.

Prigogine, I., and Nicolis, G., *Exploring Complexity*, W.H. Freeman and Company, New York, 1989.

Schwager, Jack D., *Market Wizards*, New York Institute of Finance, New York, 1989.

Vaga, T., "Stock Market Fluctuations," *Physics Today*, Letters, February 1979.

Vaga, T., "The Coherent Market Hypothesis," *Financial Analysts Journal*, Nov/Dec 1990.

Waldrop, M. M., *Complexity, The Emerging Science at the Edge of Order and Chaos*, Simon and Schuster, New York, 1992.

Weidlich, W., "The Statistical Description of Polarization Phenomena in Society," *British Journal of Mathematical and Statistical Psychology*, 24, 1971.

Weidlich, W., and Haag, *Concepts and Models of a Quantitative Sociology*, Springer-Verlag, New York, 1983.

Chapter 2

Anderson, Philip W., Arrow, Kenneth J., and Pines, David, *The Economy as a Complex Evolving System*, Addison-Wesley Publishing, New York, 1988.

Haken, H., *Synergetics*, Springer-Verlag, New York, 1978.

Nicolis, E. and Prigogine, I., 1989, *Exploring Complexity*, W. H. Freeman and Company, Inc., New York, 1978.

Bak, Per, and Tang, Chao, "Earthquakes as a Self-Organized Critical Phenomenon," *Journal of Geophysical Research*, Vol. 94, B11, November 1989.

Bak, Per, and Chen, Kan, "Self-Organized Criticality," *Scientific American*, January 1991.

Bak, Per, Chen, Kan, Scheinkman, Jose, and Woodford, Michael, "Aggregate Fluctuations From Independent Sectoral Shocks: Self-Organized Criticality in a Model of Production and Inventory Dynamics," National Bureau of Economic Research, Working Paper No. 4241 1992.

Barnsley, M., *Fractals Everywhere*, Academic Press, San Diego, California, 1988.

Brock, W., Lakonishok, J., and LeBaron, B., "Simple Technical Trading Rules and the Stochastic Properties of Stock Returns," *The Journal of Finance*, Vol. XLVII, No. 5, December 1992.

Degiorgio, V., "The Laser Instability," *Physics Today*, October 1976.

Gardner, M., "The Fantastic Combinations of John Conway's New Solitaire Game of Life," *Scientific American*, 236, pp. 120-123, 1970.

Haken, Hermann, "Cooperative Phenomena in Systems Far From Thermal Equilibrium and in Non- physical Systems," *Reviews of Modern Physics*, January 1975.

Haken, Hermann, *Synergetics*, Springer-Verlag, New York, 1978.

Hulbert, Mark, "Out of the Ivory Tower," *Forbes*, May 28, 1990.

Langton, Christopher, G., Taylor, Charles, Farmer, J. Doyne, and Rasmussen, Steen, *Artificial Life II*, Addison-Wesley Publishing, New York, 1992.

Lynch, Peter, *One Up on Wall Street*, Simon and Schuster, New York, 1989.

Mandelbrot, Benoit, The Variation of Certain Speculative Prices, *Journal of Business*, Chicago, Illinois, 1963.

Mandelbrot, Benoit, *The Fractal Geometry of Nature*, W. H. Freeman and Co., New York, 1983.

Moon, Francis, C., Chaotic and Fractal Dynamics, John Wiley & Sons, Inc., New York, 1992.

Peitgen, Heinz-Otto, Jurgens, Hartmut, and Saupe, Ditmar, *Chaos and Fractals*, Springer-Verlag, New York, 1992.

Waldrop, M. Mitchell, *Complexity*, Simon and Shuster, New York, 1992.

Wolf, A., Swift, J.B., Swinney, H.L., and Vastano, J.A., "Determining Lyapunov Exponents From a Time Series," *Physica*, 16D, July, 1985.

Wolfram, S., "Computer Software in Science and Mathematics," *Scientific American*, September, 1984.

Zweig, Martin, "The Fed and the Tape," *Barron's*, February 4, 1985.

Zweig, Martin, "It's a Bull Market!" *Barron's*, February 11, 1991.

Chapter 3

Eckman, J. P., and Ruelle, D., Ergodic Theory of Chaos and Strange Attractors, *Reviews of Modern Physics*, 57, pp. 617-656, 1985.

Farmer, J.D., and Sidorowich, J.J., "Predicting Chaotic Time Series," *Physical Review Letters*, 59(8) pp. 845-848, 1987.

Farmer, J.D., "Chaotic Attractors of an Infinite-Dimensional Dynamic System," *Physica*, 4D, pp. 366-393, 1982.

Farmer, J.D., and Sidorowich, J.J., "Exploiting Chaos to Predict the Future and Reduce Noise," *Evolution, Learning and Cognition*, ed. Y.C. Lee, World Scientific Press, 1988.

Frost, A.J., and Prechter, R., *Elliott Wave Principle*, New Classics Library, Gainesville, Georgia, 1978.

Gleick, James, Chaos: *Making a New Science*, Viking Penguin, Inc., New York, 1987.

Grassberger, P., and Proccacia, I., "Characterization of Strange Attractors" *Phys. Rev. Lett.*, 50, pp. 346-349, 1983

Jubak, Jim, "Can Chaos Beat the Market? Connecting the Dots," *Worth*, March, 1993.

Larrain, Maurice, "Empirical Tests of Chaotic Behavior in a Nonlinear Interest Rate Model," *Financial Analysts Journal*, October, 1991.

LeBaron, B., "Empirical Evidence for Nonlinearities and Chaos in Economic Time Series: A Summary of Recent Results," University of Wisconsin, Social Systems Research Institute, 9117, 1991.

Moon, F. C., and Li, G. X., "The Fractal Dimension of the Two Well Potential Strange Attractor," *Physica* 17D, pp. 99-108, 1985.

Peters, E., "Fractal Structure in the Capital Markets," *Financial Analysts Journal*, July-August, 1989.

Wolf, A. J., Swift, J., Swinney, H., and Vastano, J., "Determining Liapunov Exponents from a Time Series," *Physica* 16D, pp. 285-317, 1985.

Chapter 4

Alexander, Sidney S., "Price Movements in Speculative Markets: Trends or Random Walks," *Industrial Management Review*, 2, 2, May, 1961.

Black, Fisher, Jensen, Michael C., and Scholes, Myron, "The Capital Asset Pricing Model: Some Empirical Tests," in *Studies in the Theory of Capital Markets*, by Michael C. Jensen, ed., Praeger Publishers, Inc., New York.

Callen, E., and Shapero, D., "A Theory of Social Imitation," *Physics Today*, July, 1974.

Fama, Eugene F., "The Behavior of Stock Market Prices," *Journal of Business*, Vol. 38, No. 1, January, 1965.

Fisher, L., and Lorie, J. H., "Rates of Return on Investments in Common Stocks," *Journal of Business*, Vol. 37, No. 1, January, 1964.

Gillespie, Daniel, T., *Markov Processes, An Introduction for Physical Scientists*, Academic Press, Inc., San Diego, California, 1992.

Hagin, Robert, *Modern Portfolio Theory*, Dow Jones-Irwin, Homewood, Illinois, 1979.

Haken, H., "Cooperative Phenomena is Systems Far From Thermal Equilibrium and in Non-Physical Systems," *Reviews of Modern Physics*, January, 1975.

Houthakker, Hendrik, S., "Systematic and Random Elements in Short Term Price Movements," *American Economic Review*, Vol. 51, No. 2, May, 1961.

Markowitz, Harry, "Portfolio Selection," *Journal of Finance*, Vol. 7, No. 1, March

Mandelbrot, B. "The Variation of Certain Speculative Prices," *Journal of Business*, October, pp. 394-419, 1963.

Risken, H., *The Fokker-Planck Equation*, Springer-Verlag, New York, 1989.

Sharpe, William F., and Alexander, Gordon J., *Investments*, Prentice-Hall, Inc., Englewood Cliffs, New Jersey, 1990.

Weidlich, W., and Haag, G., *Concepts and Models of a Quantitative Sociology*, New York, 1983.

Chapter 5

Callen, E., and Shapero, D., "A Theory of Social Imitation," *Physics Today*, July, 1974.

Callen, E., Sculley, M., and Shapero, D., "Imitation Theory—The Study of Cooperative Social Phenomena," *Collective Phenomena and the Application of Physics to Other Fields of Science*, edited by Chigier, N., and Stern, E., Brain Research Publications, Fayetteville, New York, 1975.

Kilpatrick, Andrew, *Warren Buffet, The Good Guy of Wall Street*, Donald I. Fine, Inc., New York, 1992.

Haken, H., "Cooperative Phenomena in Systems Far From Equilibrium and in Nonphysical Systems," *Review of Modern Physics*, January, 1975.

Haken, H., *Synergetics*, Springer-Verlag, New York, 1978.

Rosser, Jr., J. Barkley, *From Catastrophe to Chaos: A General Theory of Economic Discontinuities*, Kluwer Academic Publishers, Boston, Massachusetts, 1991.

Smith, W. V., "Research Management," *Science*, Vol. 167, February, 1970.

Thom, Rene, *Structural Stability and Morphogenesis*, Benjamin, Reading, Pennsylvania, 1972.

Weidlich, W., "The Statistical Description of Polarization Phenomena in Society," *British Journal of Mathematical and Statistical Psychology*, 24, 1971.

Weidlich, W., and Haag, G., *Concepts and Models of a Quantitative Sociology*, Springer-Verlag, New York, 1983.

Zeeman, E. Christopher, *Catastrophe Theory: Selected Papers*, 1972–1977, Addison-Wesley, Reading, Pennsylvavia, 1977.

Chapter 6

Callen, E., and Shapero, D., "A Theory of Social Imitation," *Physics Today*, July, 1974.

Landauer, Rolf, "Stability in the Dissipative Steady State," *Physics Today*, November, 1978.

Naisbitt, John, *Megatrends*, Warner Books, New York, 1982.

Naisbitt, John, and Aburdene, Patricia, *Megatrends 2000*, Avon Books, New York, 1990.

Peters, Edgar, *Chaos and Order in the Capital Markets*, John Wiley & Sons, Inc., New York, 1991.

Schwager, Jack, D., *Market Wizards*, New York Institute of Finance, New York, 1989.

Vaga, Tonis, "Stock Market Fluctuations," *Physics Today*, Letters, February, 1979.

Weidlich, Wolfgang, "A Statistical Description of Polarization Phenomena in Society," *British Journal of Mathematical and Statistical Psychology*, 24, 1971.

Chapter 7

Bollerslev, T., "Generalised Autoregressive Conditional Heteroscedasticity," *J. Econ.*, 31, 1986.

Brock, William, Lakonishok, J., and LeBaron, B., "Simple Technical Trading Rules and the Stochastic Properties of Stock Returns," *The Journal of Finance*, XLVII, No. 5, December, 1992.

Engle, R. F., "Autoregressive Conditional Heteroscedasticity with Estimates of the Variance of United Kingdom Inflation," *Econometrica*, 50, 1982.

Granger, C. W. J., and Newbold, P., *Forecasting Economic Time Series*, Academic Press, Inc., San Diego, California, 1986.

Mandelbrot, B. "The Variation of Certain Speculative Prices," *Journal of Business*, October, pp. 394- 419, 1963.

Mendel, Jerry, M., "Tutorial on Higher-Order Statistics (Spectra) in Signal Processing and System Theory: Theoretical Results and Some Applications," *Proceedings of the IEEE*, Vol. 79, No. 3, March 1991.

Nelson, D.,"Conditional Heteroskedasticity in Asset Returns," *Econometrica*, 59, 1991.

Priestly, M. B., *Nonlinear and Nonstationary Time Series Analysis*, Academic Press, New York, 1988.

Theiler, James, Bryan Galdrikian, Andre Longtin, Stephen Eubank, and J. Doyne Farmer, "Using Surrogate Data to Detect Nonlinearity in Time Series," in *Nonlinear Modeling and Forecasting*, ed. Martin Casdagli and Stephen Eubank, Addison-Wesley, Redwood City, California, 1992.

Tong, H. and Lim, K. S., Threshold Autoregression, Limit Cycles and Cyclical Data, *J. R. Stat. Soc.*, B42, 1980.

Tong, H., *Nonlinear Time Series: A Dynamical Systems Approach*, Oxford Science Publications, New York, 1990.

Chapter 8

Afleck-Graves, and Richard R. Mendenhall, The Relation between the Value Line Enigma and Post- Earnings-Announcement Drift, *Journal of Financial Economics* 31, pp. 75-96, 1992.

Ball, Ray, and Philip Brown, "An Empirical Evaluation of Accounting Income Numbers," *Journal of Accounting Research*, 6, pp. 159-178, 1968.

Banz, Rolf W., "The Relationship Between Return and Market Value of Common Stocks," *Journal of Financial Economics* 9, pp. 3-18, 1981.

Black, Fisher, "Yes Virginia, There is Hope: Tests of the Value Line Ranking System," *Financial Analysts Journal*, September-October, 1973.

Bylinsky, Gene, "Computers That Learn By Doing," *Fortune*, September 6, 1993.

Egan, Jack, "Artificially Intelligent Investing," *U. S. News & World Report*, March 15, 1993.

Fishman, Mark B., Dean S. Barr, and Walter, J. Loick, "Using Neural Nets in Market Analysis," *Technical Analysis of Stocks and Commodities*, 1991.

Fuller, Russell J., and Wong, G. Wenchi, "Traditional versus Theoretical Risk Measures," *Financial Analysts Journal*, March-April, 1988.

Hulbert, Mark, "Sharpe shooters," *Forbes*, October 26

Rosenberg, Barr, Reid, Kenneth, and Lanstein, Ronald, "Persuasive Evidence of Market Inefficiency," *Journal of Portfolio Management*, 11 Spring), pp. 9-17, 1985.

Schmerken, Ivy, "Wiser Systems Deliver on AI's Promise," *Wall Street and Technology*, December, 1992.

Zweig, Martin, *Winning on Wall Street*, Warner Books, New York, 1990.

Chapter 9

Black, Fisher, "Fact and Fantasy in the Use of Options," *Financial Analysts Journal*, July-August, 1975.

Gastineau, Gary, *The Options Manual*, McGraw-Hill, Inc., New York, 1988.

Merton, Robert C., Myron S. Scholes, and Mathew L. Gladstein, "A Simulation of the Returns and Risk of Alternative Option Portfolio Investment Strategies," *Journal of Business*, April, 1978.

Zweig, Martin, *Winning on Wall Street*, Warner Books, New York, 1990.

Appendix

Bak, Per, and Tang, Chao, "Earthquakes as a Self-Organized Critical Phenomenon," *Journal of Geophysical Research*, Vol. 94, B11, November, 1989.

Bak, Per, and Chen, Kan, "Self-Organized Criticality," *Scientific American*, January, 1991.

Bak, Per, Chen, Kan, Scheinkman, Jose, and Woodford, Michael, "Aggregate Fluctuations From Independent Sectoral Shocks: Self-Organized Criticality in a Model of Production and Inventory Dynamics," National Bureau of Economic Research, Working Paper No. 4241, 1992.

Callen, E., and Shapero, D., "A Theory of Social Imitation," *Physics Today*, July, 1974.

Callen, E., Sculley, M., and Shapero, D., "Imitation Theory–The Study of Cooperative Social Phenomena," *Collective Phenomena and the Application of Physics to Other Fields of Science*, edited by Chigier, N., and Stern, E., Brain Research Publications, Fayetteville, New York, 1975.

Gillespie, Daniel, T., *Markov Processes, An Introduction for Physical Scientists*, Academic Press, Inc., San Diego, California, 1992.

Haken, H., *Synergetics*, Springer-Verlag, New York, 1978.

Landauer, Rolf, "Stability in the Dissipative Steady State," *Physics Today*, November, 1978.

Mandelbrot, Benoit. "The Variation of Certain Speculative Prices," *Journal of Business*, October, pp. 394–419, 1963.

Mandelbrot, Benoit, *The Fractal Geometry of Nature*, W. H. Freeman and Co., New York, 1983.

Risken, H., *The Fokker-Planck Equation*, Springer-Verlag, New York, 1989.

Smith, W. V., "Research Management," *Science*, Vol. 167, February, 1970.

Weidlich, W., "The Statistical Description of Polarization Phenomena in Society," *British Journal of Mathematical and Statistical Psychology*, 24, 1971.

Weidlich, W., and Haag, G., *Concepts and Models of a Quantitative Sociology*, Springer-Verlag, New York, 1983.

Index

About the Author

Tonis Vaga first proposed that the stock market is a nonlinear "open" system in *Physic Today* in 1979. He is the author of an award-winning hypothesis on "coherent" markets that *Investing* magazine hailed as an "Innovation of the Year." He has lectured on the "Coherent Market Hypothesis" for the Society of Quantitative Analysts, New York Society of Security Analysts, Boston Society of Security Analysts, and the Society of Industrial and Applied Mathematics. Currently Mr. Vaga is a senior associate in the Advanced Technology Group of Booz-Allen & Hamilton. He is a member of the Institute for Electrical and Electronic Engineers, American Physical Society, and the Society of Quantitative Analysts.